The Fiction OF Kiran Desai

The Fiction
OF
Kiran Desai

FOCUS ON

The Inheritance of Loss

Winner of Booker Prize

Edited by

Tapan K. Ghosh

Prestige

an international publishing house

Published by
Prestige Books
3/28, East Patel Nagar
New Delhi 110 008
Ph. 9818755529
email: prestigebooks@gmail.com
website: asiabookclub.com

Associate Office
60/29-45 Parramatta Road,
Concord, NSW 2137
Australia

ISBN: 81-7851-054-8

Printed at Chaman Offset Press, New Delhi 110 002

Contents

Preface 7

Kiran Desai: Life and Works 9

***The Inheritance of Loss*: A Critical Evaluation** 19

***The Inheritance of Loss*:**
A Critical Analysis of the Text 80

Critical Perspectives

Kiran Desai's *Hullabaloo in the Guava Orchard*
as a Satirical Novel
Shubha Tiwari 217

Kiran Desai's *The Inheritance of Loss*:
The Story of a Diverse Diaspora Called India
Prasanta Bhattacharyya 222

Identity Virus and the Antidote:
Reading *The Inheritance of Loss*
Sisir Kumar Chatterjee 240

Kiran Desai's *The Inheritance of Loss:*
Looking beyond the Wide Waste
Sarita Veerangana 276

The Singularity of New Indian Fiction
Aude Ferrand 286

Preface

Daughter of an eminent Indian English author Anita Desai, Kiran Desai has carved out a name for herself as a novelist by writing just two books. Published to a great international acclaim, her second novel, *The Inheritance of Loss*, won the prestigious Man Booker award in 2006 by eclipsing the works of five other short-listed authors. It has been described as 'a globalized novel for a globalized world' and it deals with several contemporary issues like migration and exile, the lingering effects of colonialism and struggles with modernity, the search for a better way of living and the price it exacts, globalization and the discontent it breeds, subnational movement of a disgruntled ethnic group and the resultant violence that unsettles an established order of life. This multi-layered novel that tells parallel stories set in India and America is written in a riveting prose that shimmers with uncompromising honesty and astonishing humanity.

The present book, divided into two sections, is an attempt at examining this outstanding novel from critical perspectives. It begins with a brief overview of Kiran Desai's life and works and a general introduction to the text of *The Inheritance of Loss*. This is followed by exploratory essays by eminent scholars that throw critical light on the author and the text.

I am indebted to Dr. R.K. Dhawan, University of Delhi, who advised me to work on the present project. My wife, Sipra, has extended great support to complete the work. To her, as to the scholars who have contributed well-researched articles to this book, I shall remain always grateful.

Kiran Desai: Life and Works

Winner of the Booker Prize 2006, Kiran Desai was born in India in 1971. When she was growing up, she briefly went to school in St. Joseph's Convent of Kalimpong where her aunt was a doctor, and her family had a house named, after a snow mountain, Chomomo. She lived in Delhi until she was 14, then spent a year in England, before her family moved to the U.S.A. Kiran completed her schooling in Massachusetts before attending Bennington College in Vermont. After graduation she joined a writing programme called Hollins in Virginia where she started writing *Hullabaloo in the Guava Orchard*. Then she went to Columbia University to study creative writing but took two years off to finish her debut novel.

Kiran's father is Ashwin Desai and her mother is the renowned Indian English author, Anita Desai, who has won five different awards and written fourteen novels, three of which have been shortlisted for the Booker Prize (*Clear Light of Day*, 1980; *In Custody*, 1984; and *Fasting, Feasting*, 1999). Anita, who now teaches writing at M.I.T, has long lived in America but she was born in a hill station north of Delhi in 1937. Kiran's maternal grandmother was German but she left the country before World War II and never returned. Her grandfather was a refugee from Bangladesh. (They spoke German at home and Hindi to their friends.) Her paternal grandparents came from Gujarat, and her grandfather—like the judge Jemubhai in her novel—was educated in England. Although Kiran has not lived in India since she was fourteen, she returns to the family home in Delhi every year.

Anita's works examine the themes of foreignness and division which stem from observing her own mother who experienced identical situation in wartime Germany, a country she left for good. These are the themes which Kiran has inherited. The plot of *The Inheri-*

tance of Loss narrates the parallel stories of a Gujarati family in the foothills of the north-eastern Himalayas and of undocumented immigrants in the New York. And Kiran has described her own sense of alienation from America even though it is her permanent home now. A member of the Indian diaspora, Kiran's love for India is unlimited. She has said that she will celebrate the winning of Booker award in India than anywhere else.

Born and brought up in a multi-cultural atmosphere, Kiran is a voracious reader who reads all different kinds of books. But her favourite authors are Ichiguru, Marquez, and R.K. Narayan. As she herself admits, "I like Ichiguru's work a lot and Kenzaburo Oe, Gabriel Garcia Marquez, Narayan. One of my favourite books is *Pedro Paramo* by Juan Rulfo, which I read over and over again. I also read a lot of poetry."[1]

Kiran is very close to her mother who supports, and greatly influences, her writing. In reply to a question: 'Was your mother a direct influence on your writing?,' she has said: "I'm sure she did have a big influence, because all my life I've grown up hearing her talk about writing and literature and books. It was wonderful to have her around when I was writing . . . . to talk to her through this whole process. She was wonderful through the whole thing. It's a big risk to take, spending years of your life doing something that you're not sure how it's going to turn out, and she was very good through that whole time, not providing critical support as much as emotional support. A very motherly role really."[2]

Her father is also an ardent admirer of Kiran's writing. It was Ashwin Desai who had first predicted her Booker win in January 2006. About him, she has said in an interview: "I am asked why I never mention my father. It's because everyone asks about my mother. . . . I see my father every year and I stay in his house while in Delhi. He is my closest link to India and what it means to me."[3] She is also on very intimate terms with her two brothers and her sister.

Kiran Desai first came to literary attention in 1997, in the *New Yorker* and in *The Vintage Book of Indian Writing*, an anthology of fifty years of Indian writing edited by Salman Rushdie and Elizabeth West. Kiran's 'Strange Happenings in the Guava Orchard' was the closing piece. In 1998, *Hullabaloo in the Guava Orchard*, which had taken four years to write, was published to unanimous acclaim in over twenty-two countries. The novel announced the advent of a refreshingly new voice and was praised by Salman Rushdie himself as a 'highly original book . . . a Calvinoesque fable . . . and [a] welcome proof that India's encounter with the English language, far from proving abortive, continues to give birth to new children, endowed with lavish gifts.'[4]

The novel, which has won the Betty Trask Award, is set in a small town named Shahkot in the foothills of the Indian Himalayas. It tells the story of a black sheep son, Sampath Chawla who, after losing his job at the post-office following a scandal, climbs into a guava tree in search of a life of freedom, peace and contemplation and refuses to come down. Unexpectedly he becomes a sort of petty guru, Monkey Baba, telling people's secrets and uttering philosophical profundities. The news of the holy man perched on a guava tree and surrounded by a band of langurs spreads far and wide; inquisitive visitors including businessmen and pilgrims begin to arrive. Sampath's father starts scheming about the ways to charge pilgrims for the chance to ask a question to him. The bank account of the Chawla family begins to swell until the monkeys, who have developed an unquenchable thirst for liquor, raise an unprecedented hullabaloo in the hermitage and destroy the peace of the orchard and the town. Written with rich humour and an eye for the fantastic, *Hullabaloo* extends all preconceived notions of sane and insane, holy and profane with its quirky characters and amusing location. The regaling tale, with its rich themes and motifs, grips the readers' undivided attention until they, too, begin to laugh and learn alternately with its strange but all-too-human characters.

The story, cast in the form of a fable and told with understanding and tenderness, took off from a real-life incident. As Kiran has admitted in an interview: "I'd read a story in *The Times of India* and heard about a character from many people, a man who was a very famous hermit in India and who really did climb up a tree, who lived in a tree for many, many years, until he died. . . . So I began to wonder what it was about someone like this who would do something as extreme as to spend his life in a tree. So it really started with that character, and then the story built up around it."[5]

About this debut novel, which evinces the novelist's maturity of vision, deep understanding of her country and its tradition, and her rare gift of story-telling, Kiran says, "I think my first book was filled with all that I loved most about India and knew I was in the inevitable process of losing. It was also very much a book that came from the happiness of realizing how much I loved to write."[6]

While *Hullabaloo* is a brassy and somewhat whimsical novel, *The Inheritance of Loss* is a dark and ambitious glimpse at globalization and its discontents. It was published by Penguin India in early 2006 and it won that year's Man Booker Prize for providing 'a distinctive original voice and audacious imagination'[7] to the world of modern literature. Kiran became, at the age of 35, the youngest ever woman writer to win the prestigious British award, eclipsing the works of five other short-listed authors. It created a hullabaloo in the literary orchard and brought its author a £ 50,000 cheque and worldwide recognition. The fact that Kiran Desai could finally make it to the short-list of six from the long-list of 112 books was itself a wonder. The bookmakers had initially dismissed her as the 7/1 outsider. But the novel made a triumphant comeback as the judges' panel—that included poet and novelist Simon Armitage, novelist Candia McWilliam, critic Anthony Quinn and actress Piono Shaw—held a different opinion. After a session that lasted about two hours, the panel unanimously chose Desai's novel over five other short-listed books including the bookmakers' favourite, Sarah Water's *The Night Watch*. Ms Hermione Lee, chairperson of the Judges and Goldsmiths' Professor of English Literature at Oxford, said about *The Inheritance of Loss*: "This is a magnificent novel of humane breadth and wisdom, comic tenderness and political astuteness."[8]

Remembering the elder Desai, the noted Indian English novelist, she enthused: "I think her mother would be proud. It is clear to those of us who have read Anita Desai that Kiran Desai has learned from her mother's work. Both write not just about India but about Indian communities in the world."[9]

Highlighting Kiran's originality and the strength of her novel, Prof. Lee added: "The remarkable thing about Kiran Desai is that she is aware of her Anglo-Indian inheritance . . . but she does something pioneering. She seems to jump on from those traditions and create something which is absolutely her own. The book is movingly strong in its humanity, and I think that in the end is why it won.[10]

Despite the parental prediction, Kiran was not prepared for the surprise. Accepting the award at a ceremony held at the Guildhall, London, on 11th October, 2006, Kiran said, "I didn't expect to win. I don't have a speech. My mother told me I must wear a sari . . . a family heirloom, but it's completely transparent."[11] After thanking her publisher, editor and agent, she added: "I'm Indian and so I'm going to thank my parents."[12] Of her mother Anita Desai (69), to whom *The Inheritance of Loss* is dedicated, she said: "I owe a debt so profound and so great that this book feels as much hers as it does mine. It was written in her company and in her wisdom and kindness in cold winters in her house. . . . One minute is not enough to convey it."[13]

The Inheritance of Loss is set partly in India and partly in the U.S.A. Kiran Desai described it as a book that "tries to capture what it means to live between East and West and what it means to be an immigrant."[14] The book also explores, at a deeper level, the consequences of the introduction of a western element into a non-western country, which happened during the British colonial period in India, and is happening again with India's improved relationship with America from the last decade of the 20th century. Her third aim is to examine what happens when a person from a poor and undeveloped country migrates to a rich and developed one: "How does the imbalance between these two worlds change a person's thinking and feeling? How do these changes manifest themselves in a personal sphere, a political sphere, over time?"[15]

These are, however, not new themes but old ones which continue to be relevant in today's fast-changing globalized world, where the past informs the present and the present unveils the past.

The Inheritance of Loss is, to a large extent, a story of migration and lives being made over. In page after page, one finds the stories of Indian village life and of her people's attempts to grapple with modernity side by side with the stories of illegal immigrants in a modern centre of globalized economy and politics like New York. The question of migration has always bothered Kiran Desai. As she admits in an interview: "It is something that has been going on forever. I did not realize it at first. There are so many interlinked patterns that it becomes important to examine it. It is quite a pertinent issue. Politicians are still talking of taking non-westerners to western countries, people from poor countries to rich ones. It has a darker side. There is a reverse journey happening too, like in my grandfather's time, when they went abroad to study and then returned."[16]

Both Kiran and her mother write about the Indian experience of migration. There is a common thread because the mother and the daughter have gone through the same experience. As Kiran says, "There is a parallel thread. . . . My mother is half German and her father was from Bangladesh. I didn't see the connection until much later, especially with her *Fasting, Feasting*. So, there are connections and parallels, the process of leaving India together."[17]

The novel, which took eight years to complete, draws on Kiran Desai's own experience of leaving India. While talking of the characters in *The Inheritance of Loss* and of her own life, she remarks: "The characters of my story are entirely fictional, but these journeys [of her grandparents] as well as my own provided insight into what it means to travel between East and West and this is what I wanted to capture. The fact that I live this particular life is no accident. It was my inheritance."[18]

Even though Kiran Desai's imagination is enriched by a delectable but judicious mix of the Eastern and the Western elements, India and Indians remain at the core of her novel. The book moves back and forth from Kalimpong to Manhattan, like the author herself, and tells parallel stories of insurgency and immigration. But rediscovering her Indianness was essential to her success. Kiran, who still holds an Indian passport and feels more and more Indian, sees everything through the lens of her Indianness. She tells Laura Barton: "I see everything through the lens of being Indian. It's not something that has gone away—it's something that has become stronger. As I've got older, I have realized that I can't really write without that perspective."[19]

While she was writing about the immigrant experience in New York, she realized that she would have to return to India. She came back and wrote the Kalimpong bits in Kalimpong, staying in a wild and beautiful house which had been lent to her for the time. This explains why her description of both Kalimpong and Darjeeling come across as something authentic. The same is true about the political information provided in the novel. As she says: "The political information is accurate to my knowledge and based on my memories and the stories of everyone. Also, the details are accurate. Gobbo the town thief with a relative in the police, the two old cobras in the house, the pair of Afghan princesses, a Swiss priest who ran a cheese making enterprise, I remember him with great affection."[20]

Although the story unfolds against the background of Gorkhaland movement that rocked West Bengal for several years and irrevocably altered the political map of the Darjeeling hills, the book does not take any sides. It is equally critical about the barbarity of the state police and the inhuman violence perpetrated by the insurgents. The novel is more about the effect this movement had on the people of Kalimpong, how they reacted to it and how it changed the settled pattern of their lives than about its reasons and justification. It is about the victims and the survivors.

Kiran Desai's India is largely an imagined country. After all she had left her homeland as a school girl in her early teens. But, as a character in her novel puts it, 'What was a country but the idea of it? She thought of India as a concept, a hope, or a desire.'[21] The country continues to inform and influence her literary imagination long after she has left its shores. She chose to write about the 1980s because that was the India that was most familiar to her, the place where she had lived until she was 14. But she is aware of the fact that the country she knew has changed so much that she finds herself at a disadvantage and feels that the subject really belongs to Indian writers living in India. As she says: "And then, of course, I find myself at a disadvantage because India has changed, moved on. I go every year, yet it belongs to Indian author living in India. The subject belongs to him. So the only way I could put this book together was to go back to the India of the 1980s, when I left."[22]

Kiran's Booker win and her representation of India in her novel have raised a kind of anxiety in India about her Indianness. Questions have been raised whether she writes like an outsider and whether her success is a triumph for the diasporic writer at the expense of the local Indian kind. Nilanjana S. Roy has reported[23] the complaint, among a section of non-resident Indians about Kiran's depiction of India in *The Inheritance of Loss*, a complaint which she terms, "the *Pather Panchali* complaint," in memory of those who excoriated Satyajit Roy for making films about the 'wrong' India. These nationalist Indians argue why, when India—as an important role-player in the process of economic globalization—shines so brightly with a nearly 10% growth rate, should Kiran write a derogatory passage like the following from the perspective of an impoverished Indian cook's son, who struggles to survive as an illegal and ill-paid immigrant worker in New York's basement restaurants:

> From other kitchens, he was learning what the world thought of Indians:
>
> In Tanzania, if they could, they would throw them out like they did in Uganda.
> In Madagascar, if they could, they would throw them out.
> In Nigeria, if they could, they would throw them out.
> In Fiji, if they could, they would throw them out.
> In China, they hate them.
> In Hong Kong.
> In Germany.
> In Italy.
> In Japan.
> In Guam.
> In Singapore.
> Burma.
> South Africa.
> They don't like them.
> In Guadeloupe—they love us there?
> No. (77)

In Kiran's India, people are afflicted by incurable poverty and privation. Their minds are filled with anguish and anger that result from non-fulfilment of their basic needs and that lead them to resort to terrorist violence. On the other hand, there are people who want to leave the country because of poverty, mal-development and lack of opportunities. But many of them find it difficult to be happy and successful in the West.

The cook's son, Biju, is a representative of these Indians who live miserably both at home and abroad and whom happiness eludes forever. To people like Biju, who are enraptured by the West and blinded by the glare of American affluence, India is a backward space, an underdeveloped and uncivilized country. The backwardness of India which breeds discontent and violence, the cringing habit of her people and their willingness 'to undergo any kind of humiliation to get into the States' (184)—all these are, her detractors believe, facets of a myth which diasporic writers like Kiran Desai, with their eyes on the Western readers, seek to perpetrate. They seem to forget conveniently, or—to be more precise—try to ignore, the 'other' India which exists outside this marketable myth. The story of the 'other,' self-reliant, and self-respecting India is not received cordially in the West, because the sale value of that story is minimal. To write in English is to write for the non-Indians, to write for their satisfaction, to sustain and reinforce their beliefs, to translate India and Indianness, according to their predilections. Kiran's novel bears ample testimony to this unavoidable literary phenomenon.

But to read Kiran Desai, who has been brought up in two worlds, through the lens of nationalism is to ignore what Salman Rushdie has termed 'the cultural cross-pollination'[24] that has contributed to the making of an author like her. To approach her novel with a blinkered attitude is to miss her essential humanity, her genial *spirit*, her humour as well as the sharp dissections of globalization and unrelenting exposures of economic inequality, the profound understanding with which she depicts the figure of the immigrant or the outsider, and, above all, the subtle crafting of her lucid and lyrical prose.

The Inheritance of Loss may register 'the multicultural reverberations of the new millennium,'[25] it may have innumerable worlds residing in its basements ("above the restaurant was French, but below in the kitchen it was Mexican and Indian") but India resides at its centre. One finds in the novel a diasporic India where past and present live in uneasy juxtaposition, where lives are being pulled and pushed into varied corners, in a world where migration is the unavoidable law of life. It is, in brief, a novel which, according to its author, is concerned with "the enormous anxiety of being a foreigner."[26]

NOTES

1. file: //H: /Kiran Desai \Bold Type Interview with Kiran Desai.htm
2. *Ibid.*
3. *India Today*. October 30, 2006
4. 'Damme, This is the Oriental Scene for You!,' *Step across This Line* (London, Jonathan Cape, 2002). P173
5. Bold Type Interview with Kiran Desai.htm
6. *Ibid.*
7. Qtd. Pamela Philipose in 'And the Booker goes to Kiran Desai,' *The Indian Express*, 15.10.2006,
8. *The Telegraph*, 12.10.06
9. *Ibid.*
10. *Ibid.*
11. *The Statesman*, 12.10.06.
12. *Ibid.*
13. *Ibid.*
14. 'Human warmth is such an innate part of India,' file: //G: /kd/'Human warmth is such an innate part of India'/.htm
15. *Ibid.*
16. *India Today*, October 30, 2006
17. *Ibid.*
18. file: //H: /Kiran Desai/Kiran Desai—A biography of Kiran Desai.htm
19. 'A Passage from India,' *The Guardian*, October 12, 2006.
20. 'Human warmth is such an innate part of India.'
21. *The Inheritance of Loss* (New Delhi: Penguin, India, 2006), p. 236.
22. 'A Passage from India'
23. *Hindustan Times,* October 16, 2006.
24. 'Influence,' *Step across This Line*, P.76
25. John Sutherland, qtd. Amit Ray in 'Inheritance of the Lost Booker,' *The Telegraph,* 12.10.2006
26. Qtd. Pamela Philipose, *The Indian Express*, 15.10.2006

The Inheritance of Loss: A Critical Evaluation

Set partly in India and partly in the USA, *The Inheritance of Loss* explores with uncommon intimacy and insight some of the very pertinent issues of today's globalized world. It deals with, on the one hand, the quest for individual identity and the struggle for self-determination of an ethnic group that results from postcolonial despair and sense of deprivation and that uproots a settled order of life and leads to displacement, exile and loss. On the other hand, it explores the irresistible desire for modernity leading to migration, the discontents of globalization, multiculturalism, economic inequality, the pain of exile and the anxiety of being a foreigner.

Briskly paced, the novel, which consists of 53 chapters, ricochets between the two worlds—the third and the first, between an Indian hill station in the north-eastern Himalayas and the grim underbelly of New York and tells two parallel stories. The Indian part deals with the story of a makeshift family comprising an irascible and retired judge, his young granddaughter, his old and loyal cook and his pet dog, and a small coterie of Anglophiles in the wake of a political ferment that shakes them out of genteel retirement and challenges their old way of life. It delineates the historical relationships between peoples from different cultures and socio-economic backgrounds and tells, with infinite tenderness and infallible wisdom, interconnected stories of love, longing, betrayal and loss—of the collapse of human beings' faith in one another and its reclamation.

The American section narrates the story of Biju, the son of the judge's cook, who struggles to survive as an illegal immigrant worker in New York, moving from one ill-paid job to another and trying to stay a step ahead of the INS, and is compelled to experience the anxiety of being a foreigner as well as the unfairness of a world in which "one side travels to be a servant, and the other side travels to be treated like a king" (269). The two strands of the narrative are linked by the cook, Panna Lal. What connects these apparently dissimilar characters is a shared historical background and an identical experience of powerlessness, humiliation and loss. Some common historical factors like colonialism and the century-old economic and cultural subjugation of the third world by the affluent West have shaped these characters and their destiny. "Certain moves made long ago," Desai writes in the novel, "had produced all of them" (199).

Set in mid-1980s' India, on the cusp of the GNLF (Gorkha National Liberation Front) movement for an independent state, the novel brings together many contemporary issues like the lingering effect of discredited colonialism, postcolonial despair leading to self-assertion of ethnic groups and consequent violence, struggles for cultural identity and with forces of modernity, the unfairness of economic globalization and migration from the third world to the first. It is a layered story in which personal and political histories are inextricably linked.

The Inheritance of Loss draws on Kiran's own experience of leaving India. The novel is certainly not an autobiography of Kiran Desai or an autobiographical novel, but it seems to provide a fictionalised version of her own journey from East to West. Kiran was born in India where she spent the first fourteen years of her life before migrating to England and then to America for higher education. In this book she takes a literary route to revisit her past and her ancestral history in Gujarat (the place from where her father and paternal grandfather came) and Kalimpong (the home of her own aunt). This search for personal and familial roots is inextricably linked up with many larger issues of India's colonial and postcolonial history, which also includes the history of a thriving Indian diaspora and its amazing story of continuous displacement, migration and return.

The narrative begins in the Darjeeling hills of West Bengal. In a decayed and crumbling estate in Kalimpong, situated at the foothills of the north-eastern Himalayas, 'where India blur[s] into Bhutan and Sikkim' (9), Jemubhai Popatlal Patel—a retired and reclusive judge—lives with his teenage granddaughter named Sai, his aged and chatty cook, Panna Lal, and his purebred dog named Mutt. The

Cambridge-educated judge, who is withdrawn from the niceties of social interaction but clinging to the fraying inheritance of colonial high office, seeks comfort and peace in the unfamiliar. A shadow of his once imposing self, Jemubhai retreats from society to live in this large and sprawling bungalow, named Cho Oyu, which was built years ago by a Scotsman pursuing the dream of romance in the Himalayas. The site was chosen for a magnificent view of the Kanchenjunga 'that could raise the human heart to spiritual heights' (12). But the judge was not interested in either the agricultural or the spiritual possibilities of the land. When first introduced to this isolated but spacious mansion by the departing Scotsman, Jemubhai 'had felt he was entering a sensibility rather than a house' (28). He was so impressed by the house that he gave up his job and began to live here like a foreigner: 'The judge could live here, in this shell, this skull, with the solace of being a foreigner in his own country, for this time he would not learn the language. He never went back to court." (29)

Cho Oyu is as far away from the real world as the embittered judge could get. Owing to neglect and apathy, its once beautiful floors are rotted; mice run about freely, termites slow-mill the furnitures into dust, and extreme cold permeate everything. The old man, who still powders his dark brown face white, and likes scones for tea, is not blind to the decay that surrounds him; he, in fact, embraces it. He is looked after by his old, underpaid but devoted cook, Panna Lal, who originally hailed from a village in Uttar Pradesh. The cook has been working with the judge since he was fourteen but he is treated by him like a menial. The only creature the judge truly loves is his pet dog, a purebred and cute-looking redsetter with an elegant snout, who lives with him like an 'adoring spouse' (33). He spends his time within the confines of his house, playing chess against himself and regurgitating the memories of his past. But the outside world intrudes with the arrival of Sai, his young granddaughter—a girl he never even knew existed. Sai had come to Cho Oyu some years ago, orphaned and expelled from her convent at the other end of the Himalayas, when her cosmonaut parents died of a bus accident in the Soviet Union. Sai instinctively dislikes her grandfather who, with his shrivelled figure, looks more like a reptile than a human in her eyes:

"There was more than a hint of reptile in the slope of his face, the wide hairless forehead, the introverted nose, the introverted chin, his lack of movement, his lack of lips, his fixed gaze. Like other elderly people, he seemed not to have travelled forward in time but far back." (33)

A relationship between the two builds up throughout the narrative. Sai is watched over by the judge's cook who loves her very much, but his thoughts are mostly with his own son, Biju, an illegal immigrant in New York who hop-scotches from one restaurant job to another, trying to dodge the immigration authorities and desperately seeking a green card. But the very fact of having his son in America enhances the cook's status among his own people in the town.

Lonely and introspective, Sai waits in the half shadows of the house, hungrily reading the old issues of *National Geographic*, longing to get out and see the world: "Books were making her restless. She was beginning to read faster, more, until she was inside the narrative and the narrative inside her." (68)

In Cho Oyu, time does not move forward, and the habits of her grandfather seem to curtail her spirit. Young and sensitive, Sai is the moral centre of the novel. She lattices to life on the hillside and sees what others have neglected or learned to ignore: the ineffable poverty and deprivation of the people in the hills as well as the indestructible beauty and wealth of nature.

The arrival of the orphaned granddaughter upsets the balance of the judge's life. It opens the floodgate of memories, compelling him to think 'of his own journeys, of his own arrivals and departures, from places far in his past' (35). The revisitation of the past is not, however, a pleasant experience for him: "When he thought of his past, he began, mysteriously, to itch. Every bit of him filled with a burning sensation. It roiled within until he could barely stand it" (56).

The story of the judge's life prior to his arrival in Kalimpong is narrated bit by bit throughout the novel. Jemubhai had been born in 1919 to a family of peasants in Piphit, a seemingly ageless and sleeping Gujarati town, near Baroda. It had been slowly transformed into a thriving business centre under the impact of colonial rule. Jemu's father had a modest business of supplying false witnesses to appear in the court of law. He trained the poor scoundrels to tell lies before the judge and thus subvert justice: "He was proud of his ability to influence and corrupt the path of justice, exchange right for wrong or wrong for right; he felt no guilt." (57) The business succeeded so much that when his first and only son, Jemu, became old enough to go to school, he decided to give him English education. Jemu, an exceptionally talented child, was sent to a mission school.

From his early student life, Jemu developed a profound respect for the English and all they stood for. It was here—in this mission school—that he rose to the promise of his gender. Jemu was the first son of the Patel lineage whose intelligence seemed 'modern in its alacrity' (58), and his parents deprived their daughters to ensure that he received the best of everything in the family, from love to food. He was the chosen son of the family and much was sacrificed for his success. When he matriculated at the top of his class, the father's ambition began to soar. He ignored the principal's suggestion that Jemu should sit for the local pleaders' examination, because he had other plans for his son: "The father walked out thinking, well, if he could do that, he could do more. He could be the judge himself." (59) The intensity of the father's fantastic dream touched the son so much that 'it took form, began to exert palpable pressure' (59). They aimed for the I.C.S. Examination. Jemu attended Bishop's College on a scholarship and then left for Cambridge.

Thus, Jemubhai was the first boy of their community who studied his way out of the pettiness of family circumstances in Gujarat and went to an English university. His father borrowed money from rapacious money-lenders at an excessive rate of interest to meet the expenses. Since that was not enough, the family began to search for a bride with lucrative dowry bids. Jemu married, at the age of twenty, the beautiful daughter of a rich businessman, Bomanbhai Patel. It was a marriage of convenience and thus destined to fail. Jemu married Bela (her name was changed to Nimi Patel by his family after marriage) for the money he required for his passage to England. If he succeeded in the I.C.S. Examination, Nimi would be, her calculating father thought, the wife of one of the most powerful men in the country. He left for England within a month of his marriage, even before he could know the girl well, and the only happy memory of his married life was a ride together on his father's Hercules bicycle down a village slope when 'their hearts were left behind for an instant, levitating amid green leaves, blue sky' (92).

Jemu sailed for Liverpool from Bombay on S S Strathnaver with a trunk that contained, among other things, a sweater knit by his mother, a new Oxford English Dictionary, and a decorated coconut to be tossed into the sea waves to bring luck to his journey. He was seen off on the dock by his father. It was British India and the time was 1939, only eight years before Independence. Even before he left the country, the would-be judge felt ashamed of his parents, his culture and tradition: "Jemubhai looked at his father, a barely educated man venturing where he should not be, and the love in Jemubhai's heart mingled with pity, the pity with shame. His father felt his own hand rise and cover his mouth: he had failed his son." (37) So ashamed did he feel that he did not throw the coconut into the sea and he refused to cry. He would never again experience love for any human being 'that wasn't adulterated by another, contradictory emotion' (37)

It is interesting to note that the Anglophile future judge was stunned by his encounter with the West. It was a time when people of colour were not particularly liked in England. He was ridiculed by the White people for his accent, colour and smell. As a student, isolated in racist England, Jemu experienced a remarkable change in his personality: "He worked twelve hours at a stretch, late into the night, and in thus withdrawing, he failed to make a courageous gesture outward at a crucial moment and found, instead, that his pusillanimity and his loneliness had found fertile soil. He retreated into a solitude that grew in weight day by day. The solitude became a habit, the habit became the man, and it crushed him into a shadow." (39)

Under the unbearable pressure of solitude, his mind began to warp. He became a stranger to himself and forgot to laugh. For five long years, he did not make a single friend and see anything of the English countryside. He took refuge in the library, dreading the ridicule of young girls who giggled at his curry smell. Nobody would speak to him at all and he seemed to have found 'his heart and mind turned into blunt aching things' (39). Unable to cope with the conflict of identities, he became consumed by self-loathing. The prejudice and rejection he experienced in England fuelled in his soul a shame and a dislike for his heritage, his culture and the colour of his skin. In the end, Jemu 'barely felt human at all' and he leaped when touched on the arm as if from an unbearable intimacy (40). He passed the ICS examination by securing the lowest qualifying marks and being placed at the bottom of a supplementary list of successful candidates.

It was during the period of probation in London (where he met his only friend—Bose) that Jemubhai underwent the final transformation by becoming what originally he was not and by rooting out everything native from his personality: "He envied the English. He loathed Indians. He worked at being English with the passion of hatred" (119). But this ill-conceived attempt to emulate the colonial masters and despise the native people backfired. Because, "for what he would become, he would be despised by absolutely everyone, English and Indians, both." (119) He felt ill-at-ease in the company of the English and among his own people. He developed a crushing sense of defeat, inferiority and acquiescence towards the British and a hatred and apathy for the native Indians. This explains why he did not protest when he was taunted and jeered at by a group of British boys or, in another incident of racist violence, he ran away cowardly when an Indian boy, whom he did not know, was mercilessly kicked and beaten and pissed on by a crowd of jeering red-faced men behind a pub (209). Thus, the conscious and prolonged endeavour to be like the masters led to a sense of inferiority and cultural uprootedness and left him bereft of vitality, merit and dignity, which were his racial inheritance. The encounter with England left him only a mimic man, whose allegiance was firmly directed to the colonial authorities and culture, and a mere shadow of his native self.

The judge is described by the narrator as one of 'those ridiculous Indians who couldn't rid themselves of what they had broken their souls to learn' (205) and whose Anglophilia resulted in self-hatred and hatred for their own people and culture. On his return to India, Jemu found himself despising his relatives and his apparently unsophisticated Indian wife. In fact, he had forgotten that he had a wife back home. She had become irrelevant to him like everything else in his past. So thoroughly Anglicised he had become that he could not like his beautiful wife whom he had once found desirable: "He did not like his wife's face, searched for his hatred, found beauty, dismissed it . . . An Indian girl could never be as beautiful as an English one." (168)

It was no wonder, therefore, that Jemu would feel embittered by the childish stealth of his fancy powder puff by Nimi, which he regarded as a violation of his newly acquired idea of privacy. It gave rise to an inexplicable hatred in his mind: '"You filth!" he shouted and, from between her sad breasts, pulled forth, like a ridiculous flower, or else a bursting ruined heart—*His dandy puff.*' (168) He chased her down and, in blind fury, raped her: "Ghoulishly sugared in sweet candy pigment, he clamped down on her, tussled her to the floor, and . . . in a dense frustration of lust and fury . . . he stuffed his way ungracefully into her." (169) His civilized mask was dropped and he resorted to this 'gutter act' (170), again and again to 'teach her the same lessons of loneliness and shame he had learned himself' (170). He did not speak to her or look in her direction in public. This hatred, cruelty and indifference in his dealing with Nimi slowly destroyed her personality and turned her into a living corpse.

When he was posted in the district of Bonda in Uttar Pradesh, Jemu took Nimi along with him. He rented a bungalow and hired a female companion, Miss Enid Pott, to teach her English language and manners. But Nimi, who no longer felt any love and respect for her husband, stubbornly refused to learn English and resisted his attempt to Anglicize her. He lost his patience with his wife and found her 'rudely contradicting his ambition' (172). So ashamed was he of his illiterate wife that he did not take her anywhere. Unlike the wives of other officials, she did not play any role in Jemubhai's career. Neglected by her husband and insulted by the servants, Nimi led a lonely life within the confines of his official bungalow and gradually fell out of life. He found her a 'disruptive presence' (172) in his life and when his irritation became too much to bear, he resorted to physical violence. Made mentally invalid by misery and neglect, Nimi lost her once commended beauty and felt completely disoriented: "She peered out at the world but could not focus on it" (173). Before long they began to dread each other so severely 'as if they had tapped into a limitless bitterness carrying them beyond the parameters of what any individual is normally capable of feeling' (173).

This bitterness, distrust, and hatred began to snowball until they erupted in an amazing act of violence which led the judge to abandon Nimi for good. One morning, when he was away from Bonda on a tour, Nimi, the wife of a loyal servant of the Raj, participated half-heartedly in a rally of the Congress party organized to welcome Nehru at the railway station, an act of insubordination which seriously compromised the judge's career. He was enraged at her independence which had put him on the wrong side of history. When Jemubhai faced her with the evidence of her crime, she defied him: 'To his amazed ears and her own shocked ears, as if waking up to a moment of clarity before death, she said: "You are the one who is stupid"' (304). This resulted in a merciless physical torture by her male-chauvinist and Cambridge-educated husband: 'He emptied his glass on her head, sent a jug of water swinging into the face he no longer found beautiful, filled her ears with leaping soda water. Then, when this wasn't enough to assuage his rage, he hammered down with his fists, raising his arms to bring them down on her again and again, rhythmically. . . . "Stupid bitch, dirty bitch!" The more he swore, the harder he found he could hit' (304-5). Then he bought her a ticket and returned her to her family in Piphit because he realized that he could not bear her any longer and that if things went on like that, he would 'skid from control and jeopardize his career to commit a final violent act' (305). Six months later, a telegram came from Nimi's uncle (her father, Bomanbhai, had passed away in the meantime) to announce the arrival of a baby. Jemubhai did not go to see his daughter, nor did he take Nimi back when she was ready to return. Even his father's pleadings failed to change his mind: "Why are you talking like this?" he said to his father. "You're following the script of a village idiot. She is unsuitable to be my wife." (306)

Jemu, the best bet of his family, thus let down his father whose love and strength he had continuously fed on. He abandoned his family and betrayed it 'for the sake of false ideals': "He had been recruited to bring his countrymen into the modern age, but he could only make it himself by cutting them off entirely, or they would show up reproachful, pointing out to him the lie he had become."

(306) He had shamed his family, shamed the family of his wife, stolen her dignity, turned her into a human wreck—a very embodiment of her family's humiliation, and then abandoned her with the child he had begotten. Nimi's uncle, who had usurped Bomanbhai's property, turned her out of his house and she spent the rest of her life miserably with a sister. A few months after Independence, he received a second telegram informing him of the death of his wife (It was reported to the police that she had caught fire over a stove). Jemubhai chose to believe that it was an accident and so he did not suffer from any guilt. As the narrator puts it movingly: "Ashes have no weight, they tell no secrets, they rise too lightly for guilt; too lightly for gravity, they float upward and, thankfully disappear" (308). He did not accept his paternal responsibility of the girl whom he had accidentally begotten while engaging in one of those beastly sexual acts with his abhorred wife. He condemned her to convent boarding schools and never enquired after her whereabouts when as a college student she fell in love with and married an air force pilot, Mr. Mistry, who was a Zoroastrian and had grown up in an orphanage. They—the Hindu student and the Parsi pilot—met in a Delhi Park, 'each one empty with the same loneliness, each one fascinating as a foreigner to the other, but both educated with an eye to the West' (26). She agreed to this marriage, knowing perfectly well that nobody would be impressed by their 'secular romance' because 'This romance had allowed her to escape the sadness of her past and the tediousness of her current girlish life' (26).

The secular modernity of Sai's parents further alienated her mother from her family which felt disgraced and, therefore, disowned her. The hapless girl, who had never known her parents and had led a directionless life till her adult age, thus submitted herself to the dictates of an unknown fate which took her to Russia with her husband. Mr. Mistry, a competent pilot of the Indian air force, was selected for the Intercosmos Program by a visiting Soviet team of aeronautical and aviation experts. They left for Moscow, entrusting their six-year old daughter Sai to the care of a missionary boarding school in Dehra Dun. But even before the training for the joint space program was completed, Mr. and Mrs. Mistry were crushed under the wheels of a bus. So estranged had the daughter become from the father that he was not expected to pay any attention to the tragedy.

Meanwhile the British had lost their stomach for the empire and gone back to England, leaving the country to fate. All the Indian members of the ICS rose to very high positions because the absence of the colonial rulers had created a vacuum in the administration. Jemubhai, who had 'acquired a fearsome reputation for his speech . . and for his face like a mask that conveyed something beyond human fallibility' (62), rose all the way to become a judge in Lucknow high-court.

But the departure of the British and Independence created a new problem for the Anglicized Indians who had undergone white collar slavery in the hands of the colonial masters and seen the country through their eyes. The British had found India as a 'muddle' and left it 'messy.' A faithful servant of the English rulers, the judge found, after Independence, that the 'mess' was growing: 'India was too messy for justice; it ended only in humiliation for the person in authority' (264). Unable to unload the colonial legacy and adjust himself to the altered postcolonial scenario, the judge, who seemed to have had his heart frozen long ago and learned to despise his fellow Indians, decided to retire from service. Cut off from his family and community, he bought Cho Oyu—a sprawling bungalow with an elaborate colonial architectural pattern—from a Scotsman, who left India ten years after Independence. He withdrew himself from the outside world and began to live there with his devoted cook and faithful dog in a self-imposed exile.

His chosen isolation, continuation of the old life style (like preferring English food, scones, macaroons or cheese straws at tea, and powdering his face white), the recollection of the memories of his life as a touring official in the civil service—all these are artificial constructs with which he upholds his existence and tries to convince himself that nothing has changed. Outwardly, the judge has withdrawn from human contact (he lives with his cook no doubt but treats him as nothing better than a subhuman creature) into a solipsistic world consisting of memories of bygone days within the boundaries of his dilapidating house. Inwardly, his heart has become an arid desert zone that bars entry to any human being. The only living creature he loves and with whom he can relate meaningfully is Mutt—a dog of foreign breed and of very high pedigree. The fact that he prefers the company of this female canine to his human cook speaks volumes about his degraded humanity.

The guilt-ridden heart of the retired judge is assailed by 'burning memories' of his beginnings, of his student life in Cambridge, his experience of racial prejudice and his own cowardice that had prompted him to run away from a scene of racial violence, his betrayal with his family and community and his hatred for and violence against his wife, and finally his refusal to accept his own daughter, which are introduced in the novel through extended flashbacks. His attempts to chase these unpleasant thoughts back into their dark holes do not succeed. Even sleeping pills can not give him any respite from the seemingly endless chain of disquieting thoughts that fill his mind with memories of trauma and unredeemed guilt. Through the cracks and fissures of his famed 'mental steel' (113), these harrowing memories visit him at unguarded moments and remind him of the treasure he has lost and of the lie that his life has become.

It was at this stage that Sai, his teen-aged and orphaned granddaughter whom he had never seen before, arrived at his doorstep for shelter. Initially, the judge was disturbed by her presence and was 'worried that she would incite a dormant hatred in his nature, that he would wish to rid himself of her or treat her as he had her mother, her grandmother' (210). But ultimately he accepted her because he felt that the girl, in whom something of his past had survived, might be able to redeem his life. Sai turned out to be 'more his kin that he had thought imaginable' (210). He found something familiar about her. In more ways than one, the granddaughter continued the journey which had been started by him so long ago. She was, like him, 'a westernized Indian brought up by English nuns, an estranged Indian living in India' (210). She had the identical accent and manners as well as preference for European food. She had the same brooding habit and introspective nature as her reclusive grandfather. But while the judge, for whom time does not expand futuristically, prefers to live only in the past and is resigned to his claustrophobic and guilt-ridden world, Sai, who, soon after her arrival in Kalimpong, became conscious of having entered an enormous space that 'reached both backward and forward' (34), trundles, like the cook, towards the future. Again, unlike Jemubhai, Sai speaks Pidgin Hindi and evinces a marked dislike for the perversities of the convent education that smacks of colonial prejudice and is obsessed with the concepts of purity and sin. In the 'backwaters of his unconscious' (210), the judge realized that he had committed a serious mistake by refusing to accept his daughter and that 'an imbalance in his deeds [was] balancing itself out' (210). It struck him that this girl, whom he did not, surprisingly, hate, might be 'the only miracle fate had thrown his way' (210).

The meeting between the retired judge and his young granddaughter suggests, historically, the encounter between the past and the present, between discredited coloniality and secular/ hybrid modernity. The arrival of Sai from Dehra Dun to Kalimpong also implies the quest of an individual for her identity and familial root, which takes place in the backdrop of a disturbed political milieu.

Sai lives a sheltered life in the company of her grandfather, his cook, and a group of Anglophile neighbours who are mostly elderly persons living for old world charms. Her immediate neighbour is Uncle Potty, a gentleman farmer and drunk, who had come from a famous family in Lucknow and studied languages at Oxford. There is Potty's friend, a thoroughly Indianised Swiss priest named Father Booty who runs a dairy and dreams of teaching Indians how to make cheese. Apart from these two unusually friendly, old but nimble-spirited men who spend each evening drinking wine and reminiscing about bygone days, one finds garrulous Mrs. Sen whose daughter Mun Mun has gone to America and is now working with CNN; her rival Lola (Lolita) whose daughter Pixie (Piyali) has settled into a high profile assignment with the BBC, and Lola's sister Noni (Nonita). The rivalry between the neighbours is not just over their daughters but surprisingly over England and America. In Kiran Desai's novel, the memory of British rule clashes with the new American dream. But, ironically, the battle is fought neither in the U.K. nor in the U.S.A. but in India decades after independence. As the narrator humorously puts it: "Perhaps England and America didn't know they were in a fight to the death, but it was being fought on their behalf, anyway, by these two spirited widows of Kalimpong" (131).

The aged Bengali sisters—one widow and the other a spinster—hold the stories together with a chatter born of a security that comes from living on the fruits of blissful retirement. They sip tea and read Jane Austen and Trollope, safe within the confines of a rose-covered estate they call Mon Ami. Their bungalow is full of 'magpie things gleaned from a romantic version of the West' (238). Now and then Lola visits her daughter in London and when she returns, her suitcases are 'stuffed with Marmite, Oxo bouillon cubes, Knorr soup packets, After Eights, daffodil bulbs, and renewed supplies of Boots cucumber lotion and Marks and Spencer underwear—the essence, quintessence of Englishness as she under[stands] it (46-47). Like the judge, they live like foreigners in their own country. They have never tried to understand the sons of soil—in this case the ethnic Nepalis—and their problems or language. The Nepalis are indispensable for household jobs but they are held in distrust by people like Lola and Noni. The derogatory term 'Neps' is used by these wealthy people to describe the Nepali, who constitute the majority of Kalimpong's population, as a stereotype of generically uncivilized and violent people. As Lola says to her sister: "I tell you, these Neps can't be trusted. And they don't just rob. They think absolutely nothing of murdering as well" (45). Postcolonial India is nothing better than a 'sinking ship' (47) in the eyes of this privileged and class-conscious group of westernized Indians who advise their near and dear ones to leave the country 'sooner rather than later' (47).

Kiran Desai's novel seems to suggest that these Anglicised Indians, who are alienated from the people around them, are an 'unwanted anachronism in postcolonial India, where long-suppressed people have begun to awaken to their dereliction, to express their anger and despair.'[1] They are not aware how fragile their social standing is until a surge of political unrest terribly disturbs their settled existence obliging them to taste life without power and privilege. For some of the novel's characters, like Lola and Noni, the violent insurgence that sweeps up the entire population of Kalimpong in an eruption of extraordinary hatred, appears to be a bolt from the blue: "Just when Lola had thought it would continue, a hundred years like the one past—Trollope, BBC, a burst of hilarity at Christmas—all of a sudden, all they had claimed innocent, fun, funny, not really to matter, was proven wrong" (242). Their very wealth, which has so far protected them like a blanket or a talisman, now makes them vulnerable. They are shocked out of blissful ignorance and forced to pay attention to what happens around them.

It is this treatment of postcolonial chaos and despair that brings Kiran Desai closer to V.S. Naipaul whose shadow looms large in this novel. Very early in the story, the two Anglophile siblings—Lola and Noni—refer, while taking stock of the library books at their disposal, to *A Bend in the River*, Naipaul's predominantly pessimistic novel about the emergence of traditional Africa into the modern world, with its unsparing investigation into the wages of change. Lola, an ardent admirer of England and Englishness whose clothesline sags under the weight of Marks and Spencer panties, says to her sister who calls Naipaul a 'superb writer': "I think he's strange. Stuck in the past. . . . He has not progressed. Colonial neurosis, he's never freed himself from it." (46). She even accuses the London-based Nobel laureate of ignoring 'the new England' which has emerged as a 'completely cosmopolitan society' where 'chicken tikka masala has replaced fish and chips as the number one take-out dinner' (46). Her impatience with the postcolonial rage of Naipaul at first keeps Lola, and people of her ilk, in denial about the political ferment that is brewing in the hills and that will shock them out of gentle retirement. But growing violence in the town and land-grabbing by the Gorkhaland supporters ultimately make them conscious of this turmoil which is born of a desperation to find a better way of life and to settle the historical score.

Sai's life continues in Kalimpong in the presence of her maternal grandfather, who remains aloof, and his bandy-legged, chatty cook who loves her like his own daughter and calls her Saibaby or Babiji although his heart remains with his son in America. It is from the cook, with whom she develops a close friendship, that Sai learns the history of her family: the story of Jemubhai, his neglected wife and estranged daughter. The judge, however, hires Noni, the younger of the two Bengali sisters, as a tutor for Sai to teach her mathematics and science. He can not afford a convent school for his granddaughter. At the same time he is too high-browed to send her to a government school from where students 'come out speaking with the wrong accent and picking [their] nose' (34).

Over the years both the tutor and her sister grow very fond of Sai. The single biggest piece of advice that Noni, the spinster whom life has passed by and who has never experienced love at all, gives to Sai is: "if you get a chance in life, take it" (69). Noni, who discovers her younger self in the shy but sensitive girl, says to her: "Time should move. . . . Don't go in for a life where time doesn't pass, the way I did" (93). It is she who boosts Sai's urge for something beyond the ordinary and her desire to leave the claustrophobic world of Cho Oyu where time does not move. But before long Noni feels that she has exhausted her abilities in science and mathematics and requests the judge to find a tutor more qualified in these areas. The judge becomes angry with the 'irresponsible woman' (70) but he writes to the principal of the local college to send someone who can teach these subjects to his granddaughter. The principal recommends Gyan, a poor but promising Nepali youth who has just passed out of the college and is looking for a job. Gyan—the descendant of a Gorkha mercenary, arrives at Cho Oyu to replace Noni as Sai's tutor. Thus begins a tempestuous love-affair between the student who is sixteen and the teacher who is twenty.

The story of love between Sai and Gyan, which constitutes the nucleus of the Indian part of the narrative, is unfolded in the backdrop of a disturbed socio-political milieu when India faces the biggest challenge to her national integration. The time is mid-1980s and various separatist forces are attempting to attack and crumble the idea of India as a nation: "The country, Sai noted, was coming apart at the seams: police unearthing militants in Assam, Nagaland, and Mizoram; Punjab on fire with Indira Gandhi dead and gone in October of last year; and those Sikhs with their Kanga, Kachha, etc. still wishing to add a sixth K, Khalistan, their own country in which to live with the other five Ks" (108).

Things are falling apart under the impact of centrifugal forces and the centre can not hold the nation together. Different ethnic groups have started giving vent to their feeling of deprivation and sense of injustice in terms of militancy and bloodshed. In Kalimpong and the surrounding hilly areas, the Gorkhaland agitation under the leadership of Subhas Ghising and C.K. Pradhan is preparing to explode: "there was a report of new dissatisfaction in the hills, gathering insurgency, men and guns. It was the Indian-Nepalese this time, fed up with being treated like the minority in a place where they were the majority. They wanted their own country, or at least their own state, in which to manage their own affairs." (9)

The increasingly violent movement, which is born out of a demand for self-determination as well as recognition of racial identity of the Indian-Nepalese in narrow linguistic, ethnic and regional terms, plunges the entire Darjeeling district into an anarchic insurgency leading to the partitioning of people and their intertwined history, displacement, migration and loss. Sai and her lover are helplessly drawn, like many thousand ordinary people, into the vortex of larger politics. The insurgency threatens their new-sprung romance and causes their lives to descend into chaos until they too are forced to confront their colliding interests.

After their first encounter, both Gyan and Sai become conscious of the strong spell each exerts on the other. Sai finds the tutorial presence of Gyan—with his intense intelligence, serious eyes and curly hair—rather compelling. Gyan, on the other hand, runs away at the end of his tuition without looking at Sai who has 'produced such a powerful effect upon him' (73). She becomes acutely conscious of his gaze on her, of her appearance as a woman, and her physical beauty, and as days go on, she whets 'her appetite for something else' (74). Sai becomes 'interested in love' (87) and begins to think about her future: "if she continued forever in the company of two bandy-legged men, in this house in the middle of nowhere, this beauty, so brief she could barely hold it steady, would fade and expire, unsung, unrescued, and unrescuable" (74). She, therefore, decides that "she'd have to propel herself into the future by whatever means possible or she'd be trapped forever in a place whose time had already passed" (74). Although the judge warns her granddaughter against any romantic involvement with Gyan ('I hope that tutor of yours doesn't get any funny ideas' [93]), she eagerly and restlessly waits for him. A tension gradually builds up between the lovers until they can barely tolerate each other's absence.

Sai can no longer hide her deep concern for Gyan and finds herself protecting her tutor/lover from embarrassment in the face of the judge's 'sinister urge to catch the boy off guard' (109) by asking him supercilious questions. Gyan's feeling of unease makes her 'hot with shame' (113), and as she apologises for her grandfather's unpredictably arrogant behaviour, she finds 'his eyes rested directly upon her as if he were eating her alive in an orgy of imagination' (113) and comes by the incontrovertible proof of his love for her.

Throughout the rainy season when all over Kalimpong modernity fails and a series of road-blocks, strikes and processions by the Gorkha National Liberation Front indicate a 'growing political discontent' (107) in the hills, Sai and Gyan play 'the game of courtship.' They measure each other's limbs, exchange kisses and crave madly for physical intimacy: 'Just a week or two later, they were shameless as beggars, pleading for more' (125). Engrossed with themselves, the lovers in the beginning do not pay much attention to what is happening outside and their romance burgeons in the midst of the increasingly vehement demand of the Nepalese population for a separate state: 'Gyan was twenty and Sai sixteen, and at the beginning they had not paid very much attention to the events on the hillside, the new posters in the market referring to old discontents, the slogans scratched and painted on the side of government offices and shops. "We are stateless," they read. "It is better to die than live as slaves." "We are constitutionally tortured. Return our land from Bengal."' (126). Initially, it is dismissed as nothing more serious than the grievance of a handful of disgruntled students and agitators. But very soon the agitation assumes a grim dimension. One day fifty members of the Youth wing of the GNLF publicly take an oath to fight unto death for the formation of Gorkhaland and march down the streets of Darjeeling waving their unsheathed kukris. And quite suddenly, the term 'insurgency' begins to float in the air.

The political background of the Gorkhaland movement is provided in the novel through a conversation between Lola and Noni (127-29) which also evinces their attitudinal and temperamental differences. While Noni concedes that the Indian-Nepalis' demand for a homeland is partially justified, Lola dismisses it as 'nonsense.' She views the whole movement as a heinous conspiracy to disintegrate the country: "Those Neps will be after all outsiders now, but especially us Bongs. They've been plotting this a long while, Dream come true. All kinds of atrocities will go on—then they can skip merrily over the border to hide in Nepal. Very convenient." She traces the root of the demand for a separate state to Nehru's policy of re-organization of Indian states after Independence which she regards as the 'biggest mistake' committed by the country's first Prime minister. Because the political decision to divide and re-organize the states on the basis of language and other related issues has only encouraged fissiparous tendencies and secessionist forces which have posed a great threat to national integrity: '"This state-making," Lola continued, "biggest mistake that fool Nehru made. Under his rules any group of idiots can stand up demanding a new state and get it too. How many new ones keep appearing? From fifteen we went to sixteen, sixteen to seventeen, seventeen to twenty two." The present troubles in the hills, however, began with the accession of Sikkim to India during Indira Gandhi's final term in power. Nehru's scheming daughter had contrived a plebiscite in the Himalayan state to vote its sovereign ruler out of power. All the Nepalis, who had flooded Sikkim from every corner of India, were encouraged to vote against the king so that India could swallow 'the jewel-coloured kingdom,' whose blue hills they could see in the distance. Encouraged by the success of their 'dirty trick' in Sikkim, the Nepalis, according to Lola, began to have grand ideas and think of repeating the experiment in Darjeeling and Kalimpong which had always been highly sensitive areas, situated as these were near India's international border with Nepal, Bhutan and China. Like many Bengali-speaking people, Lola holds the Nepalis in distrust: "I tell you, these Neps can't be trusted." (45)

She tries to undermine the Gorkhas through her disparaging remarks and builds a hateful racial perspective for the GNLF movement: "These people aren't good people. Gorkhas are mercenaries, that's what they are. Pay them and they are loyal to whatever. There's no principle involved. . . . And what is this Gorkha? It was always Gurkha. And then there aren't even many Gurkhas here—some of course, and some newly retired ones coming in from Hong Kong, but otherwise they are only sherpas, coolies" (246-47). Noni, the spinster who represents the virtue of unprejudiced sanity and commonsense, takes a more lenient view of the worries of the

Nepalis about their long suppressed geo-ethnic identity and their demand for a separate state, Gorkhaland, which will include the three subdivisions of Darjeeling district, namely Darjeeling, Kalimpong and Karseong, as well as parts of Jalpaiguri and Cooch Behar districts. The difference in the attitudes of the two sisters to the knotty problem, which is about to engulf the entire region in an unprecedented outburst of violence, is evident from the following conversation:

> "But you have to take from their point of view," said Noni. "First the Neps were thrown out of Assam and then Meghalaya, then there's the king of Bhutan growling against—"
>
> "Illegal immigration," said Lola. . . .
>
> "Obviously the Nepalis are worried," said Noni. "They've been here, most of them, several generations. Why shouldn't Nepali be taught in schools?" (128)

Emboldened by the separatist movements in other parts of India, like Punjab, Kashmir, Tripura, Assam and the north-eastern states, the Nepalis had organized under the leadership of Subhas Ghising, an ex-army man-cum-poet, and formed the Gorkha National Liberation Front to achieve their aim. The GNLF had written letters to the British queen and the presidents of America and the Soviet Union requesting the foreign heads of states to interfere on their behalf and save them from 'colonial subjugation' (129) of the Indian state. As the ruling Marxist government took a very firm stand on the issue and refused to oblige Ghising and his people by conceding their demand, the GNLF resorted to a violent movement. Ignoring the intertwined histories of the mixed communities that comprised the diasporic hub in Kalimpong and Darjeeling, they waged a bloody war against the government to assert their narrow regional identity which left the hills terror-struck and caused indescribable hardship for the entire population.

It is interesting to note that Gyan and Sai's romance flourishes in the midst of growing unrest in the hills but the political turmoil remains in the background for them. They pass through the dumpling stage of love inventing nicknames and terms of endearments for each other. The lovers also go on excursions to the Mong Pong Nature

Reserve, to Delo Lake, to the sericulture institute and the Darjeeling zoo. They visit the Zang Dog Palri Fo Brang Monastery on Durpin Dara from where one 'could see so far and high, the world resembled a map from a divine perspective' (141). It is against this picturesque backdrop that they tell each other the stories of their families which span across generations and lead overseas. After her return late in the evening, Sai, who has grown up in her reclusive grandfather's walled-in bungalow, becomes 'conscious for the first time of the unbearable stickiness of family and friends' (143) and realizes that she has discovered the new, uncharted domain of love that provides her with infinite 'freedom and space' (143).

But the young lovers can not cling to their private world of fancy-free teenage romance for long. Because their nascent love is soon affected by the political disturbances in the outside world. Gyan is swept away with a group of GNLF members agitating for freedom from India. He decides that he needs to prioritise his identity as an ethnic Nepali and despise Sai and her bourgeois ways of life. One day after the new year, while returning from the market with rice, Gyan confronts a procession led by a group of young men including some of his college friends whom he has ignored since he started his romance with Sai. The youth hold their unsheathed kukris aloft and shout slogans in support of Gorkhaland, 'Jai Gorkha.' Gyan finds himself drawn into the procession effortlessly and as he floats through the market, he has 'a feeling of history being wrought' (157).

By participating in the procession and shouting slogans to assert his geo-ethnic identity, Gyan feels a relevancy and an affirmation he never felt before. He remembers the stories of Indian struggle for freedom from colonial rule and asks: "If a nation had such a climax in its history, its heart, would it not hunger for it again?" (158). While listening to the provocative harangue of a GNLF leader giving vent to the grievances of the Nepalis of India and their deep-seated sense of injustice, Gyan is shocked out of his selfish and romantic involvement with a girl at a time when his own community is fighting for freedom and dignity.

He is affected by the fervour as thirty supporters of GNLF step forward and draw blood from their thumbs with their kukris to write a poster demanding a separate homeland for the Gorkhas. He finally submits to the 'compelling pull of history and [finds] his pulse leaping to something that [feels] entirely authentic.' (160) Thus, Gyan, an educated and unemployed Nepali youth, gravitates to the first available political cause in his search for an authentic identity and a better way of living. He joins the ethnic-nationalist movement largely as an opportunity to express his long-suppressed rage and frustration:

> He told the story of his great grandfather, his great uncles, "And do you think they got the same pension as the English of equal rank? They fought to death, but did they earn the same salary?"
>
> All the other anger in the canteen greeted his, clapped his anger on the back. (160)

The movement provides people like Gyan with an occasion to unlade their age-old anger and despair. The narrator reminds the readers that 'old hatreds are endlessly retrievable' and they are 'purer . . . because the grief of the past was gone. Just the fury remained, distilled, liberating' (161). Gyan suddenly finds himself in a 'masculine atmosphere' (161) and feels ashamed of his irresponsible romance with Sai which now appears to him to be an impediment on his way to attain adulthood. He decides to join the GNLF and even voices 'an adamant opinion that the Gorkha movement take the harshest route possible.' (161)

This incident brings about a remarkable change in Gyan's attitude to Sai which results from his blurring of vision. Affected by the overwhelming fervour of the Gorkhaland agitation, he myopically prioritises his racial identity over his identity as a tutor-cum-lover. The very next day he arrives at Cho Oyu to give lessons to Sai in an unpleasant mood. He is 'restless' and angry: "This was a petty anger that pulled him back, curtailed his spirit, made him feel peevish" (162). He feels upset at the thought of having to undertake a long, arduous walk in the terrible cold to give tuition, for a small amount of money, to a rich and westernized girl like Sai who lives affluently in an enormous house, 'taking hot baths, sleeping alone in spacious rooms' (162). His annoyance and anger generate in him 'a self-righteous posturing, a new way of talking' (162) which surprises his student. When, in order to cheer him up, Sai tells him about the Christmas party at Mon Ami, Gyan strikes an aggressively nationalistic posture and severely criticizes her for her colonial hangover and psychological slavery of the West: "Why do you celebrate Christmas? You're Hindus and you don't celebrate Id or Guru Nanak's birthday or even Durga Puja or Dussehra or Tibetan New Year. . . . You are like slaves, that's what you are, running after the West, embarrassing yourself. It's because of people like you we never get anywhere" (163).

Sai's attempt to justify her action ('Nothing wrong in a bit of fun and Christmas is an Indian holiday as much as any other' [163]) only makes him feel 'anti-secular and anti-Gandhian.' He abuses his beloved for her lack of self-respect and condemns what he regards as her slavish imitation of the West: "It's clear all you want to do is copy. Can't think for yourself. *Copycat, copycat*. Don't you know, these people you copy like a copycat, THEY DON'T WANT YOU!!!!" (164). His inexplicable hatred (because he knows Sai is not the cause of what he feels but only its focal point) thus casts a dark shadow on their relationship. Worried about purity for the political cause, he feels that his romance with Sai has sullied him.

This concern for purity leads Gyan to dissociate himself from her with a fierce resolution: 'once again he felt the stir of purity. He would have to sacrifice silly kisses for his adulthood' (175). Their fledgling romance suffers a serious setback, for Sai retaliates his unexpected venom by saying, "You bastard. . . . My dignity is worth a thousand of you" (175). Gyan's annoyance with himself for giving in to a girl like Sai who can speak no other language but English and pidgin Hindi and who is not ashamed of her lack of Indianness, goes to such an extent that he does not hesitate to betray her and her grandfather by passing on the information of the judge's secret assets, including the guns, and of 'the lack of a phone and there being nobody to call for help' (117) to his GNLF comrades. This betrayal leads to a robbery at Cho Oyu and the humiliation of the proud judge who is forced to prepare the tea-table for the militants.

Meanwhile the trouble on the hillside begins to get worse. Strikes and roadblocks to paralyse economic activities are followed by boycott of elections and burning of the Indo-Nepal treaty of 1950.

Everybody—Nepali or not—is forced to contribute to the GNLF funds and purchase cassettes of fiery speeches made by Ghising and Pradhan. At first the privileged class of non-Nepali-speaking people tries to dismiss the growing insurgency as a 'tamasha' ('a few degenerate people [drumming up] the illiterates, all the no-gooders hanging about with nothing to do' [201]). But soon the agitation confronts them with all its fury and vengeance and compels them to take it seriously.

A few months after Gyan abruptly snaps his romantic involvement with Sai to join the movement for Gorkhaland full-fledgedly, the girl finds him at a GNLF rally near Darjeeling Gymkhana where she goes with her neighbours to exchange library books. But to her surprise, Gyan refuses to acknowledge her: "She opened her mouth to shout to him, but at that moment he caught sight of her, too, and the dismay on his face was followed by a slight ferocious gesture of his head and a cold narrow look in his eye that was a warning not to approach" (215). Sai feels so insulted at this rejection that she begins to scrabble for dignity and sense.

On their way back to Kalimpong, their vehicle is stopped and detained on the Teesta bridge for security check. Father Booty spots a remarkably beautiful butterfly fluttering beguilingly on a cable and in his enthusiasm snaps a photograph. It was out of his knowledge that photography is strictly prohibited, for reasons of security, on this bridge which is the country's link with her north-eastern states. The harmless photograph of a butterfly is regarded by the authority as an irrefutable proof of espionage and the photographer's house is ransacked for further evidence. In the end, Father Booty, who has lived in Kalimpong for forty-five years and made the place his home, is declared a foreigner residing illegally in India and summarily ordered to leave the country.

The forceful eviction of the old and amiable philanthropist, who regards himself as an 'Indian foreigner' (220) and has been working on a model dairy for the economic uplift of the people of Kalimpong, angers Sai who holds Gyan responsible for the whole thing: "This was Gyan's doing, she thought. This is what he had done and what people like him were doing in the name of decency and education, in the name of hospitals for Nepalis and management positions. In the end, Father Booty, lovable Father Booty who, frankly, had done much more for development in the hills than any of the locals, and without screaming or waving kukris, Father Booty was to be sacrificed" (223). Thus, the militant nationalism of the Indian Nepalis leads to the partitioning of people and puts an end to 'a grand civilization' (223) that had been created with music, alcohol and friendship over the years defying the shadow lines of race, religion, language and culture. It is a great loss that dejects Father Booty's friends and acquaintances including Sai and uncle Potty.

The situation in the hills deteriorates as a series of strikes called by GNLF affect business and disrupt normal life. There is acute scarcity of food, electricity, fuel and drinking water. Kalimpong is completely cut off from the outer world owing to roadblocks and tourism is seriously disturbed. The insurgents—mostly young boys who take their style from Rambo and whose heads are filled with karate and kung-fu—unleash a reign of terror by torturing random people all over the town and compelling everyone to contribute large sums of money to the GNLF fund. Police stations are attacked and power houses are gutted down. The police, unable to control the militants, practise their new torture techniques on the innocents. They pick up a miserable drunkard in connection with the gun robbery in the judge's bungalow and beat him mercilessly for a confession: "The more he screamed the harder they beat him; they reduced him to a pulp, bashed his head until blood streamed down his face, knocked out his teeth, kicked him until his ribs broke" (226). When the man crawls out of the police custody, his vision has been completely extinguished. His piteous screams, the narrator comments, announces the end of normalcy on the hillside.

The rising militancy, a violent expression of the long-suppressed anger of the ethnic Nepalis, shocks the rich and the privileged people who have never paid any serious attention to the sons of the soil and their problems, out of self-complacency. Depletions in their larder make them alert to this socio-political ferment which is born of a desperation to settle the historical ledger. The Bengali suffer the bad luck of being in the wrong place at the wrong time and they get embroiled in 'generations worth of trouble' (241). Lola and Noni wake up one morning to notice that their property has been forcibly occupied under the cover of night and a hut has been built up. Lola goes to Pradhan, the flamboyant chief of the GNLF's Kalimpong wing, to complain about the illegal encroachment on their property by his people. Instead of receiving any justice, the helpless and elderly widow is grossly insulted by him: "In fact . . . I am the raja of Kalimpong. A raja must have many queens . . . I have four but would you . . . dear Aunty, would you like to be the fifth?" Lola, the butt of a crude joke, leaves the place almost crying and helplessly shifts the oppressive burden of her humiliation on to her dead husband, Joydeep whose idea it had been to build the house in Kalimpong: "Joydeep. . . look at what you have done, you bloodyfool!!!. . . Look at what you've left me to! . . . Look what I have to deal with. . . . I don't even have my decency" (245).

As their world crumbles before them, the two sisters shockingly realize that they have been fools living in a realm of make-believe: "The two of them had been fools feeling they were doing something exciting just by occupying this picturesque cottage, by seducing themselves with those old travel books in the library, searching for a certain angled light with which to romance themselves." (247)

Thus, as the insurgency grows in strength, all these genteel lives are upended and those who have enjoyed power and privilege are compelled to taste life without it. While Kalimpong is rocked by sporadic fits of violence, Sai continues to smart from the insult caused by Gyan's refusal to acknowledge her in Darjeeling. She feels ashamed of his disgraceful behaviour with her in the presence of her friends: "She could not believe she had loved something so despicable. Her kiss had not turned him into a prince; he had morphed into a bloody frog" (249). She tries to console herself and accept the loss of love gracefully: 'There was grace in forgetting and giving up . . . it was childish not to—everyone had to accept imperfection and loss in life' (252). But her attempt fails and she can not either forget Gyan or combat her restlessness. So, as the curfew is lifted, Sai starts out on an 'undignified mission of searching for Gyan' in order to restore her broken relation with him and 'salvage her dignity' (252). But the mission proves to be disastrous. She is shocked by the dismal scene of abject poverty in Bong Busti where Gyan lives with his family: "There were houses like this everywhere . . . common to those who had struggled to the far edge of the middle class—just to the edge, only just, holding on desperately—but were at every moment being undone, the house slipping back, not into the picturesque poverty that tourists liked to photograph but into something truly dismal—modernity proffered in its meanest form, brand-new one day, in ruin the next." (256) She feels ashamed of herself for having been connected unknowingly with this poor enterprise and gets bitterly angry with her lover for his hypocrisy and pretension ('Pretending one thing, living another. Nothing but lies through and through' [257]). She encounters a stony Gyan who asks her in a frigid voice: 'What do you want?'

Astounded by the apparent indifference of the man who had ardently pursued her only a few months ago, Sai hides her real intention and asks him instead about the expulsion of Father Booty from Kalimpong. Evidently outraged by the injustice done to the philanthropic Swiss priest, who has been forced onto a police jeep leaving for the airport at Siliguri, 'having lost everything but his memories' (257), she tells Gyan: "You, for one, are better gone than Father Booty. . . . He's done much more than you ever will for people on this hillside" (258). At this, his nationalistic feelings are stirred and he responds angrily: "In fact, good thing they kicked him out . . . who needs Swiss people here? For how many thousands of years have we produced our own milk?" (258) Gyan's intolerance and uncivilized mode of conduct so enrage Sai that she anticipates the taste of blood which she wishes to draw by clawing him and plucking out his eyes. But apparently she remains cool and argues: 'Civilization is important' (258). He scoffs at her argument by saying: "That is not civilization, you fool. Schools and hospitals. That is" (258). Blinded by anger at his audacious attempt to trample upon her human dignity, Sai hits him below the belt: "But you have to set a standard. Or else everything will be brought down to the same low level as you and your family" (258). She accuses Gyan of unfairness, because he hates her for reasons which have nothing to do with her, and holds him responsible for the gun-robbery in their house.

Gyan, who has actually been frightened by the violent turn that the GNLF movement is taking and feels worried that he will not be able to live upto his revolutionary proclamations, is nonplussed by her irrefutable accusations which pose a serious challenge to his male chauvinist identity. His desire for adulthood is stirred and he feels that he 'owe(s) much to his rejection of Sai' who suddenly ceases to be a miraculous and inspiring person and appears to be a mirror that 'show[s] him himself far too clearly for comfort' (262). Unable to swallow the insult to himself and his family, he throws her into a lantana bush, beats her mercilessly with a stick and orders her never to come to his place again. In this way, their love is consumed by violence and hatred and their intercommunal romance is stymied by 'big reasons' beyond their comprehension and control. Sai returns home slowly, squirming in the pain of insult and unrequited love, and feels amazed to find how the history of her family repeats itself in her own life: 'Gyan would find adulthood and purity in a quest for a homeland, and she would be left forever adolescent, trapped in shameful dramatics. This was the history that sustained her: the family that never cared, the lover who forgot' (265). But she has an innate strength to rise above her personal sorrow and sympathise with other human beings in distress. Thus, when she finds that the father and the wife of the drunkard arrested and tortured by the police, who came to the judge to beg for mercy, have been turned out with inhuman indifference, she is overwhelmed by pity and enquires if the cook has given the helpless creatures anything.

After the terrible row over the issue of Father Booty, Gyan is locked up by his family in order to prevent him from mixing with Sai and participating in the violent movement. Although he pretends frustration at this familial ban, he feels relieved at the respite it offers. He even tries to rationalize his conduct and believes that no serious harm has been done: 'Let the world carry on outside for a bit, and then when it was safe, he'd visit Sai and cajole her into being friends again' (272). In the relative safety of home he evaluates his own action and arrives at the conclusion that his trouble had started when he tried to be part of politics and submitted himself to the pulls of history: "He wasn't a bad person. He didn't want to fight. The trouble was that he'd tried to be part of the larger questions, tried to become part of politics and history" (272). But after his failure to find a sense of purpose or direction in history and politics, he learns that 'Happiness [has] a smaller location' (272), that tiny joys can be found only by 'turning the wheels of a simple life' (273). But this rationalization only proves his own hypocrisy and cowardice which he seeks to camouflage as a longing for an 'ordinary existence situated between meek contours' (272). His disillusionment with the GNLF movement is followed by an overpowering sense of guilt. Gyan realizes that he will never be happy and innocent again after what he has done to Sai and her family. The guilt hangs heavy on his heart and makes him think seriously about a rapprochement with his estranged beloved. Thus, as Gyan and Sai remain confined in their rooms, suffering from remorse and pain of unrequited love respectively, they miss the defining moment of the Gorkhaland movement—the burning of the Indo-Nepal treaty of 1950—which leads to a volcanic eruption of violence and turns the picturesque hill town into a veritable inferno.

The Inheritance of Loss presents the apogee of violence when hundreds of GNLF supporters assemble at the Mela Ground of Kalimpong to consign the international treaty to flame and a gruesome battle ensues between them and the defenders of law, the policemen. The organization issued an edict that each home in the town must send a representative to the demonstration. The cook, who participates in the rally on behalf of the judge's family, watches a bizarre scene unfolding before his awe-struck eyes: "And then, BAM BABAM, the air was full of stones and bottles and brickbats and screaming. The crowd began to collect rocks, raided a building site for more; the police began to chase the crowd; the stones came down; everyone was being hit, people, police; they jumped on one another, beating with sticks, bashing with rocks; began to slash with their sickles—a hand, a face, a nose, an ear" (275). The police open fire to disperse the riotous mob, killing thirteen local boys, and the protesters retaliate by knifing some policemen to death: "One jawan was knifed to death, the arms of another were chopped off, a third was stabbed, and the heads of policemen came up on stakes before the [police] station." (276) The ghastly battle between an ethno-racial group fighting for autonomy and the custodians of law that culminates in the massacre elicits a wry, ironic comment from the narrator: "This was how history moved, the slow build, the quick burn, and in an incoherence, the leaping both backward and forward, swallowing the young into old hate. The space between life and death, in the end, too small to measure" (276).

The scene, depicting one of the most abominable explosions of hatred and violence that human civilization has witnessed in recent times, justifies Pankaj Mishra's observation in the *New York Times* that "despite being set in the mid-1980s, [*The Inheritance of Loss*] seems the best kind of post-9/11 novels."[2] As the cook, like everyone else, runs away from the blood-soaked streets of the burning bazaar, he is amazed by a view of the snow-white peaks of Kanchenjunga presenting a stark contrast to the scene of inhuman barbarity below: "Above was Kanchenjunga, solid, extraordinary, a sight that for centuries had delivered men their freedom and thinned clogged human hearts to joy" (277). But as he crawls his way back to Cho Oyu, crying inconsolably, with his heart being clawed at by panic like a rodent creature, he feels that the mountain will never be the same to him again.

The cook, who has already witnessed how the insurgency has overturned and discarded social hierarchy in the hills, now finds his life descending into chaos as the nation prepares, ironically, to fight itself: "army tanks rolling down from the cantonment area into the town. Instead of foreign enemies, instead of the Chinese they had been preparing for, building their hatred against, they must fight their own people" (278). Suddenly Kalimpong, an indivisible part of India, turns into an area where non-Nepalis like the cook feel they do not belong. They become unwanted foreigners in their own country. He finds the civilized place disintegrating and becomes apprehensive about his own son.

The incidents of horror continue uninterrupted through the cyclical change of seasons, 'through winter and a flowery spring, summer, the rain and winter again' (278). Kalimpong, 'trapped in its own madness' (278), remains completely cut off from the outside world. People are compelled to stay locked and barricaded. Those, who refuse to support the movement, are harassed and beaten by the GNLF men. The Bengali-speaking people become the obvious target of popular hatred. They are put on the other side of the argument and delineated as the enemy. Nobody acknowledges them publicly. Shopkeepers refuse to sell them goods and their neighbours begin to avoid them. Even children are affected by this communal hatred: "Little children lined up in rows to spit at Lola and Noni as they walked by" (280). In the aftermath of the Mela Ground massacre, the administrative backlash begins. The police are reinforced and they hunt down the GNLF members and comb the remote villages in order to weed out the Gorkhaland supporters. The state-sponsored terrorism is rivalled by the macabre atrocities perpetrated by the riotous insurgents:

> On the road to the market, the trees were hung with the limbs of enemies—which side and whose enemy? This was the time to make anyone you didn't like disappear, to avenge ancient family vendettas. Screams continued from the police station. . . . Injured men, their spilling guts wrapped in chicken skins to keep them fresh, were rushed on bamboo stretchers to the doctor to be stitched up; a man was found buried in the sewage tank, every inch of his body slashed with a knife, his eyes gorged out. (295)

Unnerved by the eruption of collective violence that betrays the aberrational psychology of both the mutinous mob and the insensitive police, the cook, who embodies the traditional human values of his own class, at first tries to seek consolation in the hope that "It will be all right, everything goes through a bad time, the world goes in a cycle, bad things happen, pass, and things are once again good" (281). But after realizing the frailty of his own life as a non-Nepali in Kalimpong, he loses his conviction and feels that his hope is devoid of wisdom. Suffering from acute scarcity of food, the judge's family survives on dalda saag, bhutiya dhaniya, ningro fiddle heads, churbi cheese and bamboo shoots—things they could not imagine before.

It is during this period of crisis that the father and the wife of the drunkard come back to the judge to seek his help and ask for some food so that they do not die of starvation. But he treats them again with inhuman apathy that amounts to cruelty and orders the cook not to give them anything but to herd them out. The judge's cruel indifference is his way of avenging his own humiliation at the hands of the Nepali hooligans during the gun-robbery, an incident which has shaken the very foundation of his smug socio-cultural superiority. A few days later, the desperate pair return again to Cho Oyu and when its residents are busy—the judge having his bucket bath, the cook churning butter in the kitchen and Sai smarting from the pain inflicted by her estranged lover—and do not notice them, they steal the judge's pet dog away.

The stealth of Mutt unhinges Jemubhai because the absence of the dog, whom he loves more than any of his human relatives, from his lonely and guilt-ridden personal world suggests the loss of the last vestige of existential meaning in his life. The crisis compels him to put an end to his self-imposed confinement within the boundary of the crumbling colonial edifice and venture out to the small busti houses in search of the expensive red setter. The judge, who has carefully avoided human company, now asks the plumber, the electrician, the milkman and the baker if they have seen his dog anywhere. He receives 'blank face' everywhere and 'some angry laughter': "Saala, Machoot . . . what does he think? We're going to look for his dog?" (289). His anguished search for Mutt ends in failure as he is not helped by anyone. The SDO snubs him: "A dog! Justice, just listen to yourself. People are being killed . . . we are in an emergency situation" (289). The officer even fixes the distraught judge with a 'gluey look' which convinces him that he means to be rude. The policemen, who used to feel awed in his presence only a few months ago, behave with him insolently and begin to snigger when he asks for their help: "Ha, ha, ha. Come about his dog! Dog? Ha, ha ha ha ha. . . . Madman!" (291). Convinced of the fact that the old world is disintegrating around him, that he has lost his earlier clout and his authority as well as privileged position has gone, 'frittered away in years of misanthropy and cynicism' (292), he breaks down and begins to shout pathetically 'all the language that was between Mutt and himself, sending nursery words of love flying over the Himalayas' (292).

The loss of the dog, which has so far defined and justified the judge's existence as a master, creates an acute sense of crisis about his identity that, in turn, leads to his self-humiliation. Undoing his education and the well-nurtured façade of his intellectual, rational and agnostic self, the Cambridge-returned member of the ICS gambles with fate and makes strange bargains with God: "If you return Mutt, I will acknowledge you in public, I will never deny you again,

I will tell the world that I believe in you—you—if you return Mutt" (301).

He is overcome with remorse and a sense of guilt. He now regrets that he had abandoned his family, tortured and returned his wife for the 'sake of false ideals' (308). The loss of his pet dog, he feels, might be a divine retribution for the "sins he had committed that no court in the world could take on." (301). Exhausted from endless waiting and fruitless search for Mutt, Jemubhai holds his cook responsible for the dog's disappearance and threatens him by saying: "If you don't find her RIGHT NOW . . . I'LL KILL YOU. That's it. I've had enough. It's your fault. It was your responsibility to watch her when I went for my bath" (312). The judge's insult makes Panna Lal feel terribly unhappy and he disappears into the forest in search of Mutt, ignoring Sai's request to come back: "Come home, it's all right, he doesn't mean it, he is so sad he's crazy, he doesn't know what he's saying" (313).

The search takes the distraught cook to Thapa's canteen where he tells a group of drunken men what has happened. But everyone ridicules him for raising such a commotion over the loss of a dog in a place where people die of starvation and disease without being given any attention. The only person who does not laugh at him is Gyan, who has again been let out of the house. Suffering from an overpowering sense of remorse for his abominable betrayal and maltreatment of Sai, Gyan, who has been a victim of temporary misjudgement and blurring of vision, avails himself of this opportunity to redeem his sin and effect a reconciliation with his alienated beloved. Thus, when the cook leaves the canteen, Gyan goes out after him to convey a message for Sai: "Tell her that I will look for Mutt. . . . Tell her that I promise. I will find the dog. Don't worry at all. Be sure and tell her. I will find Mutt and bring her to the house." (314)

Although the cook is not impressed by his assurance and is not sure of his ability to find out Mutt, Gyan is convinced that he will bring a present for Sai the next time he meets her. The hazards and risks involved in the quest will be an act of expiation for this disillusioned Gorkhaland supporter who has attained wisdom ('Gyan') through remorse, feeling of guilt and consequent emancipation from insularity of vision.

II

Interlaced with these dispatches from the hills are the meanderings of Biju, the son of the judge's cook, Panna Lal, through illegal employments in a succession of restaurants in New York. Biju's possibilities abroad mean the world to the cook. The prospect of having a son settled in the West gives him a unique sense of mooring and prestige. But Biju, an impoverished and struggling immigrant, actually falls through the cracks of the new power centre of globalization, America. While his father dreams of Biju making it big abroad (toaster ovens, electric shavers, digital cameras, and other glittering gadgets of modernity), the son is trying to stay afloat in the underground economy of New York city, bobbing from job to job, sleeping among rats, screeching subway trains and undocumented immigrants: "Biju joined a shifting population of men camping out near the fuse box, behind the boiler, in the cubby holes, and in odd-shaped corners that once were pantries, maids' rooms, laundry rooms" (51).

He belongs to a 'shadow class' (102) of illegal immigrants who are condemned to ceaseless movement in the new destination of global fortune-seekers, New York and spends much of his time dodging the immigration authorities, moving from one poorly paid job to another and desperately looking for a green card. Much of his savings are spent in bootless attempts to procure a green card that will not only legalize his immigration to America but also enable him to leave the country.

Biju's adventures in the underbelly of the American dream are presented in the novel as sharply observed vignettes about the price of immigration. The characters in this section are bright but ephemeral and shadowy. They are always on the run changing names, changing addresses, not sticking around long enough anywhere for their stories to set in. They keep floating in the mixed sea of humanity in this multicultural centre of global economy and politics. They are the human disposables of the new economic system which mercilessly uses them and throws them away according to its fast-changing rules and conditions.

Biju is a representative of these teeming millions who suffer due to continuing western hegemony in the late twentieth century discourse of global politics and economics and who crowd the American cities to realize their unfulfilled dreams of better life nurtured in the lap of third world poverty and superstitious backwardness. Everybody from every corner of the world rushes to this land of wish-fulfillment to share a fraction of its seemingly inexhaustible material resources, as a means of securing a better, more comfortable, and dignified living. They are prepared to do anything, go to any extent and suffer any kind of humiliation to gain an access to America where even 'poor people eat like kings' (49). As the narrative voice puts it: "But it WAS so hard and YET there were so any here. It was terribly, terribly hard. Millions risked death, were humiliated, hated, lost their families—YET there were so many here." (189).

In page after page Kiran Desai narrates the process of migration from the impoverished third world countries to the immigrant packed basements in New York city. Note, for example, the following scene in which Biju joins a long queue of Indians scrambling to reach the visa counter at the American embassy in Kathmandu:

> Biju, like half the room, didn't understand, but he saw from the ones who did, who were running, pleased to be given a head start, what they should do. Stink and spit and scream and charge; they jumped toward the window, tried to splat themselves against it hard enough that they would just stick and not scrape off; young men mowing through, tossing aside toothless grannies, trampling babies underfoot. This was no place for manners and this is how the line was formed: wolf-faced single men first, men with families second, women on their own and Biju, and last, the decrepit. Biggest pusher, first place; how self-contented and smiling he was; he dusted himself off, presenting himself with the exquisite manners of a cat. I'm civilized, sir, ready for the U.S. I'm civilized, mam. Biju noticed that his eyes, so alive to the foreigners, looked back at his own countrymen and women, immediately glazed over, and went dead. (183)

The Indian applicants' uncivilized behaviour and their willingness to demean themselves for an American visa leads Biju to contemplate: "In this room it was a fact accepted by all that Indians were willing to undergo any kind of humiliation to get into the States. You could heap rubbish on their heads and yet they would be begging to come crawling in" (184).

But what they achieve from this migration is the loss of human dignity and self-respect. There is certain sympathy in the novelist's tone when she describes the desperation experienced by Biju and people like him as they stand in line for a visa. What inspired her to describe the scene in such harrowing but credible details was the fact that she had 'stood in line [herself] at the American embassy many times over and witnessed the scene unfold.'[3]

The chapters which are set in New York are incredibly powerful and, in some cases, full of sad details. For example, the passages describing Biju's pain and homesickness and his desperate struggle to stay afloat in the dark and horrible basements of immigrant New York or the scenes describing Saeed Saeed—the man from Zanzibar Biju admires most in the U.S. of A—who ducks phone calls of people from his hometown because he can not provide food and shelter his mother bragged he could. The passages feel so realistic because they are based on real-life experience. Kiran Desai admits in an interview: "I actually lived with a man from Zanzibar for a year—a lot of [that part of the book] is taken from knowing him. It's true, that's how it works. Relatives arriving, but enough having them around, and then the terrible cruelty of the process of immigration; it seems to be about throwing people overboard, and breaking your connection with people who are hoping you will help them eventually."[4]

This alternately comical and contemplative novel, which constantly shuttles between the third and the first worlds, illuminates the blinding desire for a better life in a world where one person's wealth means another's poverty. The novelist explores the loneliness and pain of the immigrant and the inequity of a system in which, as Mr. Kakkar, an Indian travel agent in New York, says to Biju, "one side travels to be a servant, and the other side travels to be treated like a king" (269). *The Inheritance of Loss* raises some pertinent questions concerning the immigrant issue. The overwhelming impression that is left in the readers' mind is one of bitterness felt by most of the immigrants who leave their poverty-stricken country to pursue the glaring American dream. As the novelist herself has said,

"I also wanted to write about what happens when you take people from a poor country and place them in a wealthy one. How does the imbalance between these two worlds change a person's thinking and feeling? How do these changes manifest themselves in a personal sphere, a political sphere, over time?"[5]

But this is not a political diatribe. The epigraph to the novel, taken from Jorge Luis Borges's poem 'Boast of Quietness,' includes the lines which read: "They speak of humanity./ My humanity is in feeling we are all voices of the same poverty." The book examines the human loss suffered by lives that are forced by circumstances to be those of hypocrisy, of gaps and fear. There is always, Kiran thinks, "a degree of loss in being an immigrant. It feels as if one will never be able to tell an entire story. There'll be an aspect of living half a life, having only half a story to tell. We tend to hope for a simplicity of truth which is rarely delivered us."[6]

Kiran sympathetically portrays Biju's struggle for a bare existence in the busy and crowded city of Manhattan: "Biju on a bicycle with the delivery bag on his handlebars, a tremulous figure between heaving buses, regurgitating taxis . . . heckled by taxi drivers direct from Punjab. . . . They harassed Biju with such blows from their horns as could split the world into whey and solids." (49)

The novel depicts the profound sadness of Biju whose dream of a glamorous life turns into a nightmare while he ekes out a miserable existence in New York: "Biju put a padding of newspapers down his shirt—leftover copies from kind Mr. Iype the newsagent—and sometimes he took the scallion pancakes and inserted them below the paper . . . and once, on his bicycle, he began to weep from the cold, and the weeping unpicked a deeper vein of grief—such a terrible groan issued from between the whimpers that he was shocked his sadness was so profound." (51)

Desai's writing is suffused with humanism when she presents the life of illegal immigrants like Biju—the human victims of the new economic system—or when she describes the underside of opulence and development where homeless men winter out 'on a subway grate in a giant plastic-bag igloo that sag[s], then [blows] taut with stale air each time a train pass[es]' (52). The novel seems to suggest that the much flaunted economic development can never be a route to prosperity for the poor and underprivileged anywhere in the world. At one point in the novel, the narrator, while commenting on the rules of the new world order, says: "profit could only be harvested in the gap between nations, working one against the other' (205). Poor and lonely in a New York restaurant, Biju overhears the conversation of American businessmen who exult over the enormous profit to be gained in the new expanding markets of Asia:

> "We need to get aggressive about Asia," the businessmen said to each other. "It's opening up, new frontier, millions of potential consumers, big buying power in the middle classes, China, India, potential for cigarettes, diapers, Kentucky Fried, life insurance, water management, cell phones—big family people, always on the phone, all those men calling their mothers, all those mothers calling all the many, many children; this country is done, Europe done, Latin America done, Africa is a basket case except for oil; Asia is the next frontier." (136)

He also learns about the politics of migration to the new power centre of globalization. In a striking vignette of the western attitude to the endless human flux from the poor third-world countries, a couple, who own a restaurant called Brigitte's where Biju works for a brief period, echo the general fear of the American people of being inundated by the Asian, African and Latin American immigrants who flood their country "screaming colonialism, screaming slavery, screaming mining companies, screaming banana companies oil companies screaming CIA spy among the missionaries screaming it was Kissinger who killed their father and why don't you forgive third-world debt; Lumumba, they shouted, and Allende; on the other side, Pinochet, they said, Mobutu; contaminated milk from Nestle, they said; Agent Orange; dirty dealings by Xerox, World Bank, UN, IMF, everything run by white people." (134)

The couple, as representatives of the American society, counter the postcolonial complaints of the ex-European colonies thus: "Nestle and Xerox were fine upstanding companies, the backbone of the economy and Kissinger was at least a patriot. The United States was a young country built on the finest principles, and how could it possibly owe so many bills? Enough was enough." (34)

In the process of defending the U.S. of A against the concerted political blitzkrieg of the former slaves, they reiterate the policy of survival in the new world order: "Business was business. Your bread might as well be left unbuttered were the butter to be spread so thin.

The fittest one wins and gets the butter." (134)

Kiran Desai also distinguishes between the British and the American attitudes to immigrants. As Achootan, a fellow dishwasher in a New York restaurant, says to Biju: "But at least this country is better than England. At least they have some hypocrisy here. They believe they are good people and you get some relief. There they shout at you openly on the street, "Go back to where you came from" (135). And, in a brilliant example of the Empire striking back, Achootan, who had spent eight years in Canterbury, responded to the insults of the ex-colonizers by shouting on their face: "Your father came to *my* country and took *my* bread and now I have come to *your* country to get *my* bread back." (135)

Achootan does not need a green card in exactly the same way as Biju or Saeed Saeed does. He wants it as an act of revenge. His attitude to America is ambivalent. He hates the country but, at the same time, wants to stay there: "Well, he wanted it. Everyone wanted it whether you liked it or you hated it. The more you hated it sometimes, the more you wanted it." (135) Biju also shares the same ambivalent attitude to America. His failure to procure a green card made him restless sometimes and he "couldn't help but feel a flash of anger at his father for sending him alone to his country, but he knew he wouldn't have forgiven his father for not trying to send him, either." (82)

The more he grows desperate for a green card, the more envious he becomes of the legalized foreigners shopping at 'discount baggage stores for the miraculous, expandable third-world suitcase' (99) and senses the despair of others like him, some of whom 'lived and died illegal in America and never saw their families, not for ten years, twenty, thirty, never again' (99).

While back in Kalimpong, the judge's cook basks in a feeling of patronizing superiority over other fathers who seek his and his son's assistance to find jobs in America for their unemployed sons, and derives pleasure from the thought that his own son is earning a lot of money far away in New York, Biju is, in fact, not getting rich. In a city that offers so much to so many, he runs from one restaurant to another, always dogged by the nagging fear that he will be detected by the INS (Immigration and Naturalization Service) as an illegal worker and forcefully deported. Serving in upscale restaurants that are 'perfectly first world on top, perfectly third world twenty feet below,' he wonders that in a country of so much wealth, only so little is available to him. He wanders from place to place, seeking something reminiscent of home and feeling 'a pang for village life' (81). India is the place that Biju, like thousands of other compatriots, had dreamed of leaving. But once in New York he is not immune from nostalgia. He is assaulted by memory of home and can feel the pulse of the forest, the delicate gesture of the ferns, and smell the humid air.

Biju finds himself a foreigner in a world that is constantly in a flux and is devoid of any settled convention, where native rootedness is viewed as backwardness and any allegiance to communal customs is dismissed as superstition. With his poor adaptability and inhibitions inherited from his native culture, Biju continues his search for an elusive home while leading the wretched life of an illegal immigrant in the precarious anonymity of New York's restaurants and basement kitchens: "There was a whole world in the basement kitchens of New York, but Biju was ill-equipped for it." (22) In the new world, Biju—a good Hindu—feels everything that is authentically him inexorably leaching away as he learns to sear steaks. The cosmopolitan modernity of America stifles his native humanity and he clings more and more to his traditional Indian identity as a defence against a globalized homogeneity that tends to efface his inherited culture.

Biju can not forget the taboos and interdicts of his own culture. When, after a day's hard work, many of the restaurant staff visit the Dominican call girls in Washington Heights, he demurs and conceals his timidity behind manufactured disgust: "How can you? Those, those women are dirty. . . . Stinking bitches. . . . Fucking bitches, fucking cheap women you'll get some disease . . . smell bad . . . *hubshi*. . . all back and ugly. . . they make me sick" (16). He feels relieved when a Pakistani arrives in his restaurant. Because he knows what to do and how to behave with him. As advised by his father, he keeps away from the Pakistani and distrusts him. Biju finds his communal prejudice at work: 'He found he could not talk straight to the man; every molecule of him felt fake, every hair on him went on alert. *Desis* against Pakis. Ah, old war, best war' (22-23).

The Indians and the Pakistanis carry their old war to the new world (America) 'where every nationality confirm[s] its stereotype':

> '"Pigs pigs, sons of pigs, *sooar ka baccha*," Baju shouted.
> "*Uloo ka patha*, son of an owl, low-down son-of-a-bitch Indian."
> They drew the lines at crucial junctures. They threw cannonball cabbages at each other. (23)

Biju hates the Pakistani nationals and other black people. This habit of hatred is his inheritance. Like many Indians, he is awed by the white people who have done great harm to India but suffers from a lack of generosity for the poor people from the third world who have done no harm at all to his country.

Biju learns about the fast-expanding Indian diaspora (22) and about the tremendous popularity of Bombay film songs and actors (53) from fellow employees in a succession of restaurants and feels proud of his country's cultural heritage. From Saeed Saeed, the man from Zanzibar, he also learns that at the racial level Indians are hated by every other nation, from Tanzania and Uganda to Guadeloupe (77). Saeed is the most interesting character Biju comes across in America. He is overwhelmed by a desire to befriend Saeed because of his adaptability and confidence which prevent him from drowning in the sea of humanity that is America but helps him bob in the tide. Not only fellow Zanzibaris and fellow illegals but also white Americans wish to cling to him, 'like a plank during a shipwreck' (76), because of his generous nature and buoyancy of spirit. Biju is fascinated by Saeed's survival strategy and his enormous capacity for dodging the immigration authority: "He had an endless talent with doors, even though, two years ago during an INS raid, he had been unearthed and deported despite having been check-to-check, Kodak-proof, with the best of America" (78). But he was back in America in just two months' time with a new passport and a 'new name typed up with the help of a few greenbacks given to a clerk outside the government office' (79). Saeed jigs open every backdoor and spectacularly subverts the American immigration system but, paradoxically, pledges his emotional allegiance to the country. As the narrator puts it humorously: "The country recognized something in Saeed, he in it, and it was a mutual love affair. Ups and downs, sometimes more sour than sweet, maybe, but nonetheless, beyond anything the INS could imagine, it was an old-fashioned romance." (79)

The problems of Biju and Saeed are identical. Biju can identify himself with Saeed and his trouble caused by the desperate 'tribes' from Zanzibar who flock to New York in search of job and shelter. Because they remind him of his own experience of coming to America a few years ago: "Biju's sympathy for Saeed leaked into sympathy for himself, then Saeed's shame into his own shame that he would never help all those people praying for his help, waiting daily, *hourly*, for his response" (98). His reaction to a group of men ('tribes,' as Saeed calls them), 'looking weary as if they'd been travelling several lifetimes' (96), who have come all the way from Stone Town to the Queen of Tarts bakery in order to seek help from Saeed is deplorable. In response to Saeed's question: "What are they doing?," Biju, "feeling brave and excited by someone else's misfortune,'" replies: "They are still standing and looking." (97). Ironically, Biju suffered the same humiliation when he approached his father's friend Nandu for help on his first arrival in New York: "Nandu had also not answered the phone and had tried to hide when Biju arrived on his doorstep" (98). He even advised Biju to go back to India.

The novel depicts the 'meeting between Indians abroad of different classes and languages, rich and poor, north and south, top caste bottom caste.' (50) It also highlights the dismaying reality that while there is a lot of gloating about how the Indians are the richest minority group in America, it overlooks the fact that the poorest people of India are also in the United States who are betrayed not only by the westerners but also by the wealthier group of Indian immigrants. The class divide that exists in India continues overseas. At one point in the story, the narrator remarks: "It was horrible what happened to Indians abroad and nobody knew but other Indians abroad. It was a dirty little rodent secret" (138). While working in Harish-Harry's kitchen in Gandhi Café, one day Biju skids on some rotten spinach and breaks his knee. When he requests his Indian employer to call a doctor, the latter becomes angry and, instead of owning up any responsibility and arranging for his treatment, he begins to shout: "I take you in. I hire you with no papers, treat you like my own son and now this is how you repay me! Living here rent free. In India would they pay you? . . . Is it my fault you don't even clean the floor? YOU should have to pay ME for not cleaning, living like a pig. Am I telling YOU to live like a pig?" (188)

Biju vehemently retorts, exposing Harish-Harry's shameless exploitation of helpless compatriots who crowd the American cities, sometimes illegally, in search of jobs: "Without us living like pigs, . . . what business would you have? This is how you make your money, paying us nothing because you know we can't do anything, making us work day and night because we are illegal. Why don't you sponsor us for our green cards?" (188)

But even after this 'volcanic explosion' (188), Harish-Harry remains unperturbed. Instead of medicines, he brings Biju prasad from a temple. The wry authorial remark that follows unveils the actual relationship between the employer and the employed: "And in that *Prasad* Biju knew not to expect anything else. It was a decoy, an old Indian trick of master to servant, the benevolent patriarch garnering the loyalty of staff; offering slave wages, but now and then a box of sweets, a lavish gift." (189)

Biju had joined Harish-Harry's restaurant, Gandhi Café, because it was a Hindu establishment where beef was not cooked. He refused to give up his religion or compromise the principles of his ancestors. He saw the 'difference between a holy cow and an unholy cow' (136) and finally decided to 'live within a narrow purity' (137), even though he knew that it might be difficult for him to survive and succeed in America with that kind of attitude. Kiran Desai shows how immigrants like Biju and Saeed Saeed cling to their religious faiths and cultural taboos, unwilling to allow themselves to 'fall through the filthy differences between nations.' But even at Gandhi Café, all Biju finds is an owner who is lost between identities. Harish-Harry is an enterprising Indian-American businessman. He knows the secret of success in market economy: "Find your market. Study your market. Cater to your market. Demand-supply. Indian-American point of agreement. This is why we make good immigrants. Perfect match" (145). Though he has named his restaurant 'Gandhi Café' (thus capitalizing on the marketability of the Indian icon called Gandhi), he is not at all Gandhian in his treatment with his employees. In return of providing 'free housing' in the unhygienic kitchen of the restaurant, Harish-Harry compels them to 'work fifteen-, sixteen-, seventeen-hour donkey days' (146). He exploits the Indians but cringes before the Americans. His name is indicative of a deep rift within himself: "He tried to keep on the right side of power, tried to be loyal to so many things that he himself couldn't tell which one of his selves was the authentic, if any" (148). He represents the confused "*haalf 'n' haf*" crowd with 'one accent one side of the mouth, another the other side; muddling it up' (148). Biju, who has been seeking a clarity of principle, finds that 'there [is] no purity in this venture. And no pride' (148). By joining Harish-Harry's Gandhi Café, he has 'come home to no clarity of vision.' (148)

In a sense, Biju continues or re-enacts the journey of the judge to the affluent West which, as Kiran admits in an interview (*India Today*, Oct. 30, 2006, 83), had 'a darker side.' Biju is a postcolonial counterpart of Jemubhai, who does not, for a change, end in Cambridge but in New York. While the judge toiled over his academic endeavours in racist England, Biju struggles hard with his half-baked cooking skills to stay afloat in capitalist America. But both are stunned by their meeting with the West. One major thematic preoccupation of *The Inheritance of Loss* is the distance that its characters (like Jemubhai, Sai's parents and Biju,) travel as they pursue hopes of a glamorous life that inevitably eludes them. But whereas the judge consciously tried to forget his Indian identity and shamelessly aped the colonizers' culture, Biju desperately attempts to stay as much as possible within his cultural moorings. But his Indian-ness fails him miserably in America. While the Zanzibari Saeed Saeed succeeds in forging a perfect compromise between ethnic identity and the demands of urban modernity and the Gujarati Harish-Harry makes the best use of his hyphenated identity and canny survival instinct, Biju with his 'narrow purity' and inhibitions against 'unholy cow'—fails to make it in the cosmopolitan and multi-cultural city of New York. He cannot think, like Saeed and his friends, of conveniently marrying and divorcing American women for a green card. For him, the city's endless possibilities for self-invention become only a source of pain.

The growing sense of frustration caused by his failure to find a satisfactory job and the continuing green card problem makes Biju ill so much so that he begins to lose his temper: "The green card, green card, the *machoot sala oloo ka patha chaar sau bees* green card that was not even green. It roosted heavily, clumsily, pinkishly on his brain day and night; he could think of nothing else" (190). The gut annoyance at the green card combines with the irritation caused by his father's endless letters requesting him to find jobs for other people's sons to make him violently angry. His failure fills him with self-pity and the thought of going back to India crosses his mind: "Maybe . . . maybe he would return. Why not? To spite himself, spite his fate, give joy to his enemies, those who wanted him gone from here and those who would gloat to see him back—maybe he would go home." (191) As he stays back to lead a miserable and undignified life, his father draws a solid satisfaction from his son's misunderstood position in America. While he wants to get back, his father wants him to stay as long as he can: "Stay there. Make money. Don't come back here" (191).

It is at this stage that Biju learns about the eruption of trouble in the hills through an Indian news agent in New York, Mr. Iype, and feels worried about his father. He somehow establishes contact with him through the telephone of the Metal Box guesthouse. But the communication proves to be abortive, thanks to the poor telephone service in the conflict-torn district. He could only learn that his father was alive: "He could not talk to his father; there was nothing left between them but emergency sentences, clipped telegram lines shouted as if in the midst of a war" (232). The unfinished telephonic conversation with his father generates an unshakable unease in Biju. He is overwhelmed by the sheer emptiness of his life and feels burdened by his exaggerated sense of importance. Unable to look at America through the sanguine lens of Saeed's eyes, and unwilling to manufacture, like Harish-Harry, a fake version of himself and live a life that is not his own, Biju decides to return home. Although he is advised by well-wishers (like Mr. Kakkar) not to go back, he realizes that he has remained a foreigner in America and that his life is unreal, devoid of any meaning and purpose. He is assailed by self-doubt and self-questioning: "What was he doing and why?" (268). While walking back to Gandhi Café, Biju thinks: "he was emptying out. Year by year, his life wasn't amounting to anything at all; in a space that should have included family, friends, he was the only one displacing the air. And yet, another part of him had expanded: his self-consciousness, his self-pity" (268). This realization only makes him long to fade into insignificance and to return to a life 'where he might relinquish this overrated control over his own destiny' (268).

He feels neither dejected nor remorseful at the thought of going back. Once the decision to return home is taken by him, Biju begins to resuscitate the happy memory of the country. He does not 'think of any of the things that had made him leave in the first place' (270). He is not at all burdened by the memory of his stay in America: "Here he was, on his way home, without name or knowledge of the American president, without the name of the river on whose bank he had lingered, without even hearing about any of the tourist sights" (286). Instead, he begins to make plans for the future ('He would buy a taxi. . . . And he'd build a house with solid walls, a roof that wouldn't fly off every monsoon season' [286]) and play in his mind, again and again, the scene of his reunion with his father and weep 'at the thought of so much happiness and emotion' (286). The return to Calcutta feels like returning to his mother's lap. It is a real home-coming for him as he happens to discover his true identity after the prolonged humiliation and indignity of having to live as an illegal immigrant on the American soil: "Biju stepped out of the airport into the Calcutta night, warm, mammalian. His feet sank into dust winnowed to softness at his feet, and he felt an unbearable feeling, sad and tender, old and sweet like the memory of falling asleep, a baby on his mother's lap" (300). He feels relieved of 'the enormous anxiety of being a foreigner,' of the 'unbearable arrogance and shame of the immigrant,' (300) and realizes that he has regained the clarity of vision: 'He looked about and for the first time in God knows how long, his vision unblurred and he found that he could see clearly' (300). He feels so ecstatic and light-hearted at the prospect of going home and meeting his father again that the journey from Siliguri to Kalimpong with a group of GNLF men does not frighten him.

Riding high in a jeep on the thin road over the insane and unpredictable river Teesta surrounded by high mountains, Biju realizes that he has so far lived a divided life, having his heart always in other places, his mind thinking about people elsewhere—and it feels wonderful to have things different again. Having lived the shameful life of a fugitive in the inhospitable basement kitchens in New York, Biju is overwhelmed by the enormity of the mountainside and the wilderness and abundance of nature around him. Despite roadblocks and landslides, which impede their journey, he feels patient 'in the way one feels before the greatness of nature' (315), and waits to see his father. But before they reach Kalimpong, the GNLF men take a detour and, in the late evening, bring the jeep to a small village where Biju is robbed, at gunpoint, of everything he brought from America. Left almost naked, he is chased by a group of dogs set on him by the robbers so that he starts running through the dark forest 'without his baggage, without his savings, worst of all, without his pride. Back from America with far less than he'd ever had' (317). Biju is thus engulfed by the violent eruption of ethnic rage and frustration in the Darjeeling hills from where he has been physically removed in New York. He is completely dispossessed and made even poorer than when he left the country to pursue the dream of American affluence. No escape or withdrawal from violence is possible for Biju, and for others like him, in this globalized world. There is no evading the wages of terrorism, either of one's own choosing or on account of other people's compulsions, Desai's novel seems to suggest.

III

The two separate, though interlapping, threads of the narrative are superbly brought together in the concluding scene which is very skilfully handled by the novelist. In keeping with the surefooted confidence manifested throughout this immensely rich and riveting tale, the climactic scene treats the reader's heart to one last moment of wild and ecstatic joy. At the same time, it also satisfies his intellect by refusing to overlook the dark and depressing reality that constitutes the life of its characters.

The cook, Panna Lal, who had been threatened by the judge with dire consequences if he failed to find out Mutt, enters his master's bedroom in the dead hour of the night, wrapped in a haze of alcohol. He is hounded by a sense of guilt for having cheated Jemubhai in many different ways over the years. Deep within his conscience-stricken mind, he has an apprehension that unless he makes an atonement through a clean confession of his sins he may not see his son again. He approaches the foot of Jemubhai's bed and says: "I'm a bad man, beat me sahib, punish me" (319). Amazed by the cook's audacity to disturb him, the judge, who is also drunk, leaves his bed and begins to smack Panna Lal with his slipper. The more the cook confesses his varied acts of deception and theft and begs for punishment, the harder the judge kicks and hits him. Sai, awakened from sleep by the unusual sounds coming from her grandfather's room, rushes in to witness the bizarre spectacle and asks the angry master and the guilt-crazed servant to stop. But none of them pays any attention to her request. Helpless and distraught, she runs out of the room and stands alone in the 'humus dark.' While listening to the muffled thuds and subdued cries of the drunk old men, she feels 'her disgust at the cook, at his pleading, her hatred of the judge, her pitiful selfish sadness, her pitiful selfish pointless love' (321). But the noise of human violence is soon drowned by the sound of rain that begins to fall from an August sky, accompanied by the loud croaking of 'anthem singing frogs' (322). As she stands in the wet, with 'her heart lying in pieces' (322), Sai's personal suffering is sublimated into a genuine humanitarian concern 'for all the sadness in the world' (323) and she attains an inner illumination: "Never again could she think there was but one narrative and that this narrative belonged only to herself, that she might create her own tiny happiness and live safely within it' (323).

This realization, born out of profound sadness and mature wisdom, seems to sum up the central message of Kiran Desai's trans-continental romp about the globalized world in the new millennium. An incarnation of suffering, endurance and sympathy, Sai is no longer concerned about the future of Cho Oyu or about its inhabitants. Nor does she feel depressed by the untiring recurrence of abominable human cruelty and violence which have led to wars, destruction of civilizations, displacement, exile and misery:

> All night it would rain. It would continue, off and on, on and off, with a savagery matched only by the ferocity with which the earth responded

> to the onslaught. Uncivilized voluptuous green would be unleashed; the town would slide down the hill. Slowly, painstakingly, like ants, men would make their paths and civilization and their wars once again, only to have it wash away again. (323)

Because in the midst of all will stand nature unrestrained, pristine, and unconcerned with men's attempts to build and unbuild civilizations. The truth Sai learns is that whatever happens life will move on in its own rhythm: 'Breakfast, lunch. The judge would sit at his chessboard, and at 4-30, without thinking, from mere habit, he would open his mouth and say, as he always said, "Panna Lal, bring tea." (323) As she stands there, disconsolate but sober, Sai thinks of her father and his unfinished space programme, of the separate journeys undertaken by her grandfather, his cook, the cook's son, and finds a glimmer of strength within her to resolve that she must also leave the claustrophobic atmosphere of the decadent and antiquated colonial relic and embark on her own voyage into the world. With this resolution, a new dawn breaks out of the womb of darkness, spreading a 'whisky light' across the rain-drenched sky, even as the 'congress of hopeful frogs' (323) continues to sing. As she turns to go inside, Sai detects a small, almost indistinguishable figure labouring up the mountain slope and approaching Cho Oyu. The first thought that strikes her mind, is that of Gyan whom she has forgiven and continues to love: 'Gyan? She thought with a burst of hope. A message: I will love you after all' (324). Realizing her mistake, she goes into the kitchen and, out of compassion, offers to make tea for the cook who sits hunched up in a corner, covered in slipper marks. Just at that moment the gate of the bungalow is rattled and, out of habit, Panna Lal slowly walks out to open it. Moments later, Sai hears the demented voice of the cook calling loudly: "Biju!" She looks out and finds two shadowy figures leaping at each other as the gate swings open. Biju and Panna Lal—two inheritors of loss, who were separated from each other by the claims of modernity and the blinding desire for a better life—are finally united. At this climactic moment, Kanchenjunga appears above the parting clouds, as if, to witness the heart-warming re-union of the father and the son: 'The five peaks of Kanchenjunga turned golden with the kind of luminous light that made you feel, if briefly, that truth was apparent.' (324)

The truth that the novel conveys is that life comprises both hatred and love, justice and injustice, poverty and opulence, selfishness, cruelty and violence as much as sympathy, friendliness and charity, loss as well as gain, and that with all its inherent contradictions it will go on despite individual aberrations and socio-political upheavals. It is this profoundly humanistic and pro-life message that counterbalances the prevalent note of pessimism in the novel.

The Inheritance of Loss has undoubtedly an immense potential to sadden the readers. The book manifests divisions and differences in society which are so deeply entrenched that they can not be easily ironed out. All of the novel's characters eventually come to share Sai's realization that life is more often defined by loss than by fulfilment or gain. Living is difficult and full of uncertainty and unfulfilled longings. It can irremediably damage a person like the disaffected judge or his helpless wife. But neither the book itself nor its characters—who are buffeted by the winds of history, both personal and political, can be said to be particularly despairing. Hope prevails so much so that even the apparently irredeemable judge can think of Sai as the 'only miracle that fate had thrown his way' (210) and as his possible source of redemption. Hope sends Biju from India to seek his fortune in New York, and hope brings him back home. Hope of reunion with his son sustains the cook in his miserable life. Saeed Saeed hopes to receive a green card in near future. Gyan is optimistic of a reconciliation with estranged Sai who waits hopefully to follow the footsteps of her father. There is loss suffered by almost every character in the novel and it causes sadness. But since the novelist balances this saddening loss with enlivening humour and heartening wisdom, the readers do not close the book with a sense of gloom. *The Inheritance of Loss* is, in a sense, about finding one's way through the magical and blinding mist of life that blurs one's vision and often leads one astray. Sai, sobered and made wise by suffering and loss, learns: 'Life wasn't single in its purpose . . . or even in its direction. . . . The simplicity of what she'd been taught wouldn't hold' (323). And she gets ready to leave Kalimpong behind and continue her journey in the world. Due to temporary misjudgement, Gyan loses his love but he learns his mistake and sincerely longs for a rapprochement with her. Biju, defeated and disillusioned in New York, gives up his pursuit of the American dream and returns home, having lost the last vestige of civilized life. Despite the accumulation of little losses that constitute the only inheritance of its characters, the novel thus offers hope. Happiness, pursued by the little men and women who people this globalized novel, appears to be fleeting, like the glimpse of the golden peaks of Kanchenjunga through the parting clouds, but, like the luminous peaks, it is also infinitely beautiful. And the momentary glimpse of 'apparent' truth (about the riddle called life) that it offers is immensely valuable.

The novel is memorable for its humane breadth and mature wisdom. Starting from its epigraph from Jorge Louis Borges's poem 'Boast of Quietness': "They speak of humanity./My humanity is in feeling we are all voices of the same poverty," to its concluding sentence, Kiran's book shimmers with palpable humanity. With deeply-felt sympathy, she illuminates the pain of displacement and exile, the struggle of illegal immigrants for a bare existence (49), their deep vein of grief (15) and desperation (97-98), the exploitation of the poor and the downtrodden by the privileged and the wealthy (188-89), the ineptness and brutality of the police 'practising their torture techniques' (226) on innocent people and the helplessness of the victims' relatives begging for mercy (263-64). Her writing becomes suffused with humanism when she describes the underside of opulence and development where homeless men 'wintered . . . on a subway grate in a giant plastic-bag igloo' (52). It is this humanitarian concern that counterpoises poverty, inequality, cruelty and injustice, which form the only bequest of the novel's characters. Hermione Lee is probably correct when she says, "The book is movingly strong in its humanity and I think that in the end is why it won [the Booker]."[7]

IV

The Inheritance of Loss also examines at a deeper level the consequences of the introduction of a western element into a non-western country. The western element is so-called civilization, modernity, and the quest for a life of comfort, affluence and privilege. This is what happened during the British rule in India, as is evinced by the judge's story, and is happening again with the country's improved relationship with the United States in the era of globalization. And this is proved by Biju's narrative. After the dismantling of the Empire, people in the postcolonial world are left only with a promise of modernity which is 'proffered in its meanest form, brand-new one day, in ruin the next' (256). In fact, it is modernity—each character's understanding of it—that the little men and women in *The Inheritance of Loss* spend their life times trying to attain and come to terms with. Jemubhai Patel, the future judge, had studied his way out of the pettiness of family circumstances in Gujarat and found, by way of a lonely stint in racist England, a lucrative job in British India. He was the best bet of his family to bring his community into the modern age. Much was sacrificed for his success. But he could only make it himself by cutting his people off completely. In his attempt to ape the colonial masters, he consciously rooted out everything native from his personal system and developed a self-loathing as well as a loathing for his own people. But he could never achieve the confidence that could make him feel comfortable in the colonial high office. He suffered from a crushing sense of inferiority and defeat which resulted in a sadistic violence in personal sphere of life and turned him into a hated recluse in his own community. In the process of becoming equal with the British, he disowned his family, tradition and culture and inherited the loss of self-esteem, pride and vitality that left him emotionally paralytic and spiritually dead. So degraded he became that he hated the presence of humans and felt comfortable in the company of a pure bred bitch. Panna Lal, his cook, has also debased himself to fulfil his desire for modernity: "toaster ovens, electric shavers, watches, cameras, cartoon colours. He dreamed at night not in the Freudian symbols that still enmeshed others, but in modern codes, the digits of a telephone flying away before he could dial them, a garbled television." (55) He cheated his master in many different ways, conducted an underground liquor business, and sent his son to America to pursue this dream of a better life. In consequence, he lost his invincible honesty and integrity and developed a sense of guilt which generated an apprehension in his mind that he might not see his son again. Through penance, in the form of a confession and physical punishment by his master, the cook is cleansed of this feeling of guilt and rewarded with a re-union with his son who had been lured away from him by the trap of globalization. Biju was compelled to lead the humiliating life of an illegal immigrant in his search for American affluence. In the process, he lost his human dignity and freedom. His courageous decision to disregard the glitter of modernity and return home marks his liberation from spiritual bondage to the West and attainment of his true identity. Gyan, an educated, poor and unemployed youth, joined the Gorkhaland Movement in his search for an alternative way of life. He participated in the ethnic-nationalist movement of the disgruntled Nepalis mainly as an opportunity to give vent to his postcolonial rage and frustration. But in his enthusiasm he committed a blunder by betraying his beloved, Sai, and her family and forcing the philanthropic European entrepreneur, Father Booty, to leave Kalimpong. It did not take him long to get disillusioned with the increasingly violent movement and to realize that 'happiness ha[s] a smaller location.' (272) He suffered from a strong sense of remorse and seriously longed for a reconciliation with his estranged beloved.

While Gyan is drawn to a political cause in his frustrated quest for modernity, others like Pixie, Lola's daughter, and Mun Mun, the daughter of Mrs. Sen, try to escape from India, their native country, which is compared by Anglophile Lola to a 'sinking ship' (47), to the 'civilized' and affluent West in search of a life of prosperity, glamour and 'sanitized elegance' (47). In scene after scene, Kiran's novel delineates this endless process of migration from the third world to the first in search of modernity and the comforts that it offers, with 'a moral intelligence [which is] at once fierce and tender.'[8]

V

It has been remarked by John Sutherland that "Desai's novel registers the multi-cultural reverberations of the new millennium with the sensitive instrumentality of fiction. . . . It is a globalized novel for a globalized world."[9] The novel attempts to explore what it means to live between cultures, between East and West, the third world and the first. It is the feeling of being caught between two continents and cultures that infuses *The Inheritance of Loss*. At times, the book rejoices in the intermingling of cultures: "Above, the restaurant was French, but below in the kitchen it was Mexican and Indian. And, when a Paki was hired, it was Mexican, Indian, Pakistani." (281)

But at other times it seems to evoke a sense of wistful melancholy:

> Here Sai had learned how music, alcohol and friendship together could create a grand civilization. "Nothing so sweet, dear friends—" Uncle Potty would say raising his glass before he drank.
>
> There were concert halls in Europe to which Father Booty would soon return, opera houses where music moulded entire audiences into a single grieving or celebrating heart, and where the applause rang like a downpour. . .
>
> But could they feel as they did here? Hanging over the mountain, hearts half empty—half full, longing for beauty, for innocence that now knows. With passion for the beloved or for the wide world or for worlds beyond this one. (223)

The novel depicts 'a whole world' in the underground kitchens of New York restaurants or in the immigrant-packed basements of high-rise buildings at the bottom of Harlem where people speak English, Hindi, Gujarati, Spanish, French, Italian and Swahili. Biju finds himself at a loss in this sea of humanity. He wanders from place to place, hopping from one restaurant to another, seeking something that is reminiscent of home but only finding himself lost between conflicting identities and cultures. Pankaj Mishra has argued in his review of the novel in *The New York Times*, that Kiran Desai actually 'takes a sceptical view of the West's consumer driven multiculturalism, noting the 'sanitized elegance' of Lola's daughter's British-accented voice, which is 'triumphant over any horrors the world might thrust upon others.'[10] By doing so, Kiran distinguishes herself from diasporic writers like Hari Kunzru who seem to take an optimistic view of this intermingling of people and cultures, of what Salman Rushdie has described as 'the transformation that comes of new and unexpected combinations of human beings, cultures, ideas, politics, movies, songs.'[11] This kind of multiculturalism is totally confined to western metropolis and has only an academic value. It is unable to fathom the reasons of poverty, disease, famine and war in the present day world that compel people from Asia, Africa and Latin America either to take up arms or to migrate to the affluent countries of the West and embrace a dehumanizing existence there.

VI

The Inheritance of Loss is, also, a story of migration and lives being made over. Kiran takes on the experience of leaving one's own country and its accompanying sense of loss. Her approach is both novel and ambitious in the sense that she has expanded the scope of traditional immigrant literature by including the issue of imperialism as well.

About the issue of human migration—the history of human flux, displacement and exile in the colonial as well as the postcolonial period—that occupies a large portion of her narrative, Kiran says: "It is something that has been going on forever. I did not realize it as first. There are so many interlinked patterns that it becomes important to examine it. It is quite a pertinent issue. Politicians are still talking of taking non-westerners to western countries, people from poor countries to rich ones. It has a darker side. There is a reverse journey happening too, like in my grandfather's time, when they went abroad to study and then returned."[12]

The judge, like Kiran's own grandfather, went to England for higher education and then returned to India. This reverse journey reveals the 'darker side' of the early trend of migration during the colonial period from poor to rich countries. Biju's story reflects what is happening, again, in the postcolonial period with India's new and rapidly improving relationship with America. During his four years stay in Cambridge, the young Jemubhai took refuge in the library, dreading the ridicule of his peers and of young girls who giggled at his accent and smell. Unable to deal with the collision of identities, he became consumed by self-loathing. He returned to India a changed man: "He envied the English. He loathed Indians. He worked at being English with the passion of hatred and for what he would become, he would be despised by absolutely everyone, English and Indians, both" (119). The racial prejudice and rejection he experienced in imperial England had frozen his heart and had a devastating effect on him for the rest of his life. While the judge lost his Indian identity in his conscious attempt to Anglicize himself and became an abominable puppet in the hands of the colonial masters, Biju desperately tries to stay within his cultural moorings. He eventually becomes 'a man full to the brim with a wish to live within a narrow purity' (137). But his Indian-ness does not help him much in the new haven of globalization, where he feels defeated and frustrated at every step. Compelled to lead, as an illegal immigrant, an undignified, fugitive and divided existence in the underbelly of American opulence, Biju, with his native rootedness and poor adaptability, fails to assimilate and feels completely alienated in the multicultural ambience of New York. The immense possibilities of the city for self-invention generate only a sense of disappointment in him and he decides, finally, to return home.

According to Kiran Desai, imperialism and immigration are not very different experiences. Her novel reveals that both the experiences involve an internalized conflict of identities. The once-colonized country like India, negotiates between the modern way of living inherited from the imperialists and her national pride heaving with the uncontrollable but righteous rage of people feeling wronged and deprived. Likewise, the immigrant (like Biju) tries to adhere to his cultural moorings in a sea of foreignness, hoping desperately to assimilate and absorb but sticking to his native self fiercely. And both suffer from loss. It is the inheritance of little losses and failures accumulated from generation to generation that Desai has sought to chronicle through the parallel stories based in imperial England, postcolonial India and the centre of global politics and economy, the United States.

The novel also examines the new craze for migration to the United States from a humanitarian point of view. America has become, in the context of globalization, the most coveted destination for the worldwide fortune seekers. People from every corner of the globe rush to this new El Dorado in search of material prosperity and comfort. They are prepared to undertake any risk and undergo all sorts of humiliation to gain an access, sometimes illegally, to America. The price they pay for this perilous journey is the loss of authentic identity, dignity and basic human values. Still, the book views human migration not as a heroic venture but as a despicable act of cowardice committed by those who want to escape the pangs of conscience which they inevitably suffer from while living amidst dismal poverty and superstitious backwardness in their home countries. As the father of a Bengali gentleman who holds a green card and lives in Ohio says to his son,

> immigration, so often presented as a heroic act, could just as easily be the opposite; that it was cowardice that led many to America; fear marked the journey, not bravery; a cockroach desire to scuttle to where you never saw poverty, not really, never had to suffer a tug to your conscience; where you never heard the demands of servants, beggars, bankrupt relatives, and where your generosity would never be openly claimed; where by merely looking after your own wife-child-dog-yard you could feel virtuous. Experience the relief of being an unknown transplant to the locals and hide the perspective granted by journey. (299)

This disconcerting insight into the process of migration adds an extra perspective to the novel and marks it out from the general run of immigrant literature.

VII

Kiran tells the interconnected stories of migration and the loss it involves, the pursuit of a better life and the price it exacts, globalization and its discontents, and the postcolonial rage of an ethnic group struggling for self-determination in a highly distinctive and flexible style. The nimbly-paced story constantly shuttles between East and West, present and past, private and public histories, and the quick shift of narrational focus produces multiple narrative threads that lead to the inevitable division of the novel into so many chapters and sub-chapters. Each chapter is self-contained like a scene / frame in a film. Kiran uses extended flashbacks to the life in Kalimpong before the mobilization of the Nepalis for the Gorkhaland movement to explore the conflicting cultural identities of wealthy and educated Indians (like Lola, Noni, Joydeep and Uncle Potty) and to narrate the backstory of the retired and reclusive judge. With its cinematic techniques, picturesque locations, transnational cast of characters, sensational incidents of domestic and public violence, the novel reads like a perfectly made screenplay and is likely to tempt a cinematographer to select it for his film.

Critics and reviewers have compared Kiran Desai with Salman Rushdie. The energy and fecundity of her imagination, the vast scope of her 'globalized' novel that straddles East and West and incorporates individual / familial and national histories, and the nuanced complexities of its characters and their times make it somewhat akin to Rushdie's. Her style of writing with its compact paragraphs, plethora of exclamation marks, copious use of capital letters and unpunctuated words that often read like a breathlessly long sentence (64), the employment of slangs and swear words (181, 190), Hinglish (Hindi+English) jingles ('Shopping ke liye jayenge, bhelpuri khaenge . . . dollars me kamaenge, pum pum pum' [298]), lines from Islamic prayer (136), Bollywood film songs (51, 53) and advertising doggerel (194) exudes a vivacity and exuberance that unmistakably remind one of Rushdie's writing. But the tenderness, humour and grace as well as the human warmth one discerns in the work are characteristically Kiran's own. The beguiling story, its descriptions of scenes and incidents, and the images and emotions they evoke are undoubtedly inspired and they bear the stamp of her individual talent. Her prose exploits the extent to which punctuation and grammar can be used as means of expression. Passages like the following that describes the undocumented workers' fear of the US immigration department, are stunningly effective:

> They put down the phone hurriedly then, worried that immigration had a superduper zing bing beep peeping high-alert electronic supersonic space speed machine that could
> transfer
> connect
> dial
> read
> trace the number through to their—
> Illegality. (81)

The description of a young boy (Jemu) being prepared by his mother for school in the early morning brings to mind R.K. Narayan's unforgettable Malgudi characters, Swami or Raju for example:

> Fed he was, to surfeit. Each day, he was given a tumbler of fresh milk sequined with golden fat. His mother held the tumbler to his lips, lowering it only when empty, so he reemerged like a whale from the sea, heaving for breath. Stomach full of cream, mind full of study, camphor

> hung in a tiny bag about his neck to divert illness; the entire package was prayed over and thumb-printed red and yellow with tika marks. He was taken to school on the back of his father's bicycle. (58)

Kiran also proves herself to be equally adept in depicting scenes of domestic as well as political violence (169,304-5) and gross racial hatred (209), and in evoking the feel of colour, touch and smell of variegated natural objects with magical details. The novel resuscitates the hurrying scurrying sub-world of vegetables, insects and animals with telling images. The violence and atrocity that characterize the mode of civilized behaviour in the novel seem to pervade the world of insects and animals as well. With powerful images and pictures, the novelist brings to life the instinct of violence operating in the sub-human world: 'A dead scorpion being dismantled by ants' (250); 'Bees noosed by spiders' silk' (254), 'rats and snakes in the rafters fighting over insects and birds' eggs' (255), 'hens being hammered and pecked as they screamed and flapped, attempting escape from the raping rooster' (256). Kiran describes the onset of rain in the north-eastern Himalayas during the 'aqueous season' (105-7) and a rat in an underground bakery of Manhattan (75) with equal skill. She also employs physical descriptions to evoke complex psychological states as, for example, the winter landscape in New York reflecting the loneliness of the people: "On the Hudson, the ice cracked loudly into pieces, and within the contours of this gray, broken river it seemed as if the city's inhabitants were being provided with a glimpse of something far and forlorn that they might use to consider their own loneliness." (51) At the same time she can provide the readers with hilarious interludes like the one in which the Metal Box watchman's entire family listens to, and gives running commentary on, the telephonic conversation between the cook and Biju:

> "HELLO HELLO????"
> "???? HAH? I CAN'T HEAR. YOUR VOICE IS VERY FAR."
> "I CAN'T HEAR. CAN YOU HEAR?"
> "He can't hear."
> "WHAT?"
> "Still can't hear?" They asked the cook. (230)

In more than one interview, Kiran says that she has wavered to accept the American citizenship, just as she has been unwilling to embrace the American style of writing. Having attempted the creative writing programme at Columbia University, of which her debut novel *Hullaballoo* was a product, she decided to start afresh. In *The Inheritance of Loss* she writes in a distinctly un-American style and tells her diasporic story in a refreshingly new medium that has been forged in the crucible of her mixed heritage and borderless imagination. Kiran frequently incorporates *desi* (Hindi, Urdu and Gujarati), Tibetan, Nepalese, French, American and Swahili words, phrases and expressions into her English sentences; for example: 'haveli,' 'pallu,' 'tika marks,' 'dhuti, 'laddo,' 'jhora,' 'choorva,' 'huzoor,' 'paratha,' 'chapatis,' 'jalebis,' 'chaang,' 'sala,' 'choli,' 'lehnga,' 'kaju,' 'kishmish,' 'prasad,' 'bephkuph,' 'aayiye,' 'baethiye,' 'khaiye,' 'kakas-kakis,' 'masas-masis-phois-phuos,' 'chokra,' 'murga-murgi,' 'Hai hai, hamara kya hoga,' 'Dhanyavad,' 'Shukria,' 'namaste,' 'hubshi,' 'kangas.' 'haat,' 'atta,' 'srikhand,' 'eendu,' 'La ma,' 'zo-lungming,' 'bhai,' 'dekho,' 'aesa hai,' 'beta,' 'peepul,' 'choolah,' 'kemchho,' 'saaru cheho,' 'tene sanjo chho,' 'Hi fakey,' 'how ya doin,' 'wipe your ass,' 'the river full of dead fucking whales,' 'machoot sala.' 'oloo ka patha,' 'chaar sau bees,' 'Angrezi khana,' 'blanquette de veau,' 'Coquilles Saint-Jacques a la vapeur' etc. Such audacious mixing of English and other lexical items lends a diasporic feel to her language and makes it a suitable medium to evoke the multicultural and polyglossic reality that the novel depicts. But this multilingualism often appears to be playful and superficial. It does not have any deeper mediative engagement between different languages and cultures. In many places, again, the *desi* expressions are immediately translated into English for the benefit of the western readers in the manner of Rushdie; for example: 'No ghas phoos, no twigs and leaves' (212), 'Angrez ke tarah. Like the English' (105), 'Pigs pigs, sons of pigs, sooar ka baccha,' 'Ullo ka patha, son of an owl' (23). "Arre, Biju . . . to sunao kahani . . . batao . . . what's the story?" (146). But such bilingualism seems irritating to an Indian reader who is conversant with both the languages. There are also a few minor errors like 'Durga Puja goddesses being constructed in shacks' (31).

The Inheritance of Loss has a melancholy beauty particularly in its sensuous evocation of the natural world. The evocative natural setting, the mist that charges down like a dragon, 'dissolving, undoing, making ridiculous the drawing of borders' (9), and the snow-capped mountain peaks luminous in golden light—all bring to the minds of conscious readers the memory of Satyajit Ray's classic work *Kanchenjunga.* Ray's film provides a trenchant critique of the Anglicized and upper class Bengalis through the story of an apparently happy family that falls apart during its annual vacation in Darjeeling. Kiran Desai uses the same Kanchenjunga in her novel to deliver her final message. The five peaks of the mountain appear in the beginning, the middle, and the end of the book as if to remind the readers of the existence of something solid and permanent in contrast to what is happening in the ephemeral human world below. Her writing itself is like the far Himalayan peaks which are shrouded in mist but full of astonishing and alluring promise.

NOTES

1. Pankaj Mishra, Review of *The Inheritance of Loss, The New York Times,* Friday, February 10, 2006
2. Ibid.
3. 'Human warmth is such an innate part of India.'
4. file: //H: /kd-1/CRITICAL MASS Kiran Desai Q and A.htm
5. 'Human warmth is such an innate part of India.'
6. Ibid
7. file: //H: /kd-1/BBC NEWS Entertainment Kiran Desai claims Bookser title.htm
8. Pankaj Mishra, Review, *The Inheritance of Loss.*
9. *The Telegraph*, 12 October 2006.
10. Pankaj Mishra, Review, *The Inheritance of Loss.*
11. 'In Good Faith,' *Imaginary Homelands* (London: Granta Books, 1991), p. 394.
12. *India Today*, October 30, 2006, p. 83.

The Inheritance of Loss: A Critical Analysis of the Text

The Inheritance of Loss is an ambitious novel with a vast scope, spreading across two continents and several cultures. The novel consists of fifty-three chapters and tells parallel stories based in postcolonial India and in the United States, the new power centre of globalization. Briskly paced, the narrative constantly moves between Kalimpong in the north-eastern Himalayas, close to the Indian border with Nepal, Bhutan and China, and New York, the new haven of world-wide fortune-seekers. The Indian part, set against the backdrop of the violent agitation for Gorkhaland in the mid-1980s, deals with a Cambridge educated retired judge, who prefers to live in the past, in a world of guilt-ridden memories, and a coterie of Anglophile neighbours, who appear to be the last remnants of the British empire in independent India. The embittered judge, a musty relic of the Indian Civil Service, lives out a reclusive retirement in a crumbling colonial bungalow with his old, loyal cook, Panna Lal, and a purebred red-setter named Mutt, until his orphaned teenage granddaughter, Sai, comes to stay with him, and his existence—like that of the people he knows in the picturesque hill resort—is upended by the Nepalese insurgency. In extended flashbacks, the novelist also tells the judge's backstory—from his humble origin in Gujarat and higher education in Cambridge to his career in the Indian Civil Service before his premature retirement and arrival in Cho Oyu (the name of his bungalow)—and describes the life in Kalimpong with its inheritance of mixed culture before the Nepalis's mobilization for Gorkhaland that leads to the outburst of sectarian tendencies and the partitioning of people. The American part deals with the story of Biju, the cook's only son who struggles desperately to survive as an undocumented immigrant worker in New York, moving from one restaurant kitchen to another and con-

authority until his dream of possessing a green card and of a glamorous, affluent life turns into a nightmare and he feels humiliated by his undignified and demeaning existence. Rejected by America, he returns home only to find himself engulfed by the volcanic explosion of ethnic rage and frustration in the Darjeeling hills. The twin threads of the narrative are connected by Panna Lal who leads a miserable life as an underpaid cook in the judge's household and dreams of his son making it big in America. Alternately humorous and contemplative, this superbly crafted and riveting tale highlights the lingering effects of colonialism on certain sections of the Indian people, the difficulties of life in postcolonial India where lack of opportunities breeds discontent and despair, the problems and pains of illegal immigrants in America, the pursuit of a better life and the price it invariably exacts in a highly distinctive and graceful style. It ponders issues of nationalism and class, modernity and migration, globalization and economic inequality in a manner which is at once moving and revelatory, infinitely rich and tender.

Chapter I

The very opening sentence of the novel that introduces an evocative natural setting—the colour of dusk that permeates whole days, the mist that moves 'like a water creature across the great flunks of mountains' (1), and the grand peaks of Kanchenjunga briefly visible above the mist, 'gathering the last of the light' (1)—establishes the landscape as central in the story told from the omniscient narrator's point of view. In the foothills of the north-eastern Himalayas, where India unobtrusively blurs into Bhutan and Sikkim, is situated the picturesque town Kalimpong. Here, in an isolated and crumbling house named Cho Oyu lived a retired, Cambridge-educated judge with his orphaned granddaughter, Sai, his old, loyal and chatty cook, and his pet dog named Mutt. A shadow of his once imposing self, the reclusive judge and former member of the ICS, Jemubhai Papatlal Patel, had retreated from the messy human society outside to live in what was previously a magnificent colonial estate. Cho Oyu was as far away from the real world as the embittered and irascible judge could get. Owing to neglect and apathy, its once beautiful façade and interior had decayed; rickety furniture 'overlaid with termite cuneiform' stood in the shadows, and extreme cold and solitude permeate everything. The old man was not blind to the decay that surrounded him; he, in fact, embraced it. The judge seemed to prefer living in the past, in the old world charm. He spent his time within the confines of his house by regurgitating memories of bygone days and by playing chess against himself. He was withdrawn from the niceties of social interaction but clung to the fraying inheritance of old life. The old man still powdered his dark brown face white and liked 'cake or scones, macaroons or cheese straws' (3) at tea time. Any deviation from the routine which he had followed uninterruptedly from his days of colonial high office, annoyed him. His teenage granddaughter, Sai, who was a recent arrival in the make-shift family of the judge, waited in the half-shadows of the decayed house where time seemed to stand still, hungrily reading the old issues of *National Geographic* and longing to go out and see the world. She observed the magical phosphorescence of the Kanchenjunga, with its plumes of snow 'blown high by the storms at its summit' (1), thought about the profound solitude of the place that resembled the solitude of a giant squid described in the scientific journal, and felt the melancholy of the situation washing over her. She ached for Gyan, her mathematics tutor with whom she had fallen in love, and longed for fulfillment, even though she instinctively knew that love, like life itself, was more often defined by loss than by fulfillment. She restlessly waited for Gyan in the foggy February afternoon when the thickening mist replaced every solid object with shadow, but he did not turn up.

The cook, who looked after the judge and his dog, was an old man with bandy legs and arthritic knees. He spent most of his time in the 'cavernous kitchen' (1) at the back of the sprawling bungalow, preparing food with damp wood infested with a 'community of scorpions, living, loving, reproducing in the pile' (1) and in utensils 'as battered, encrusted as something dug up by an archeological team' (1). What sustained him in this miserable life was the thought of his only son Biju. As he said to Sai who often helped him in the kitchen: "My bones ache so badly, my joints hurt—I may as well be dead. If not for Biju . . . ' (3). Biju lived as an illegal immigrant worker in New York, hopscotching from one ill-paid restaurant job to another and constantly running away from the Immigration and Naturalization Service: 'Biju changed jobs so often, like a fugitive on the run—no papers' (3). The cook was the judge's only link with the world outside and the depletion in his store in the kitchen ('There's no more gas, no kerosene,' 3) was symptomatic of the imminent crisis in the hills that would lead to an acute scarcity of essential commodities.

The outside world intruded upon the judge's genteel retirement with the arrival of a band of robbers in Cho Oyu in the foggy February afternoon. The group consisted of some young Nepali boys dressed in cheap leather jackets, Khaki pants and bandanas tied on heads in the universal guerilla fashion. They were members of 'a ragtag army' collecting arms for an 'impoverished movement' (4) which had started brewing up in the mountains. They had come through the forest to loot the judge's hunting rifles that dated from his ICS days. Despite their clothes and apparent bravado, the boys did not seem convincing as robbers. Because, 'at one yelp from Mutt, they screamed like a bunch of school girls, retreated down the steps to cower behind the bushes' (4). But their embarrassment before the members of the family proved to be dangerous; it induced them to flex their muscles in the movie style. The leader, who carried a gun, sneered at the judge for his ignorance of the Nepali people and their language, and asked him to bring his guns. When the judge refused to oblige him and ordered them to leave his estate, he pointed his gun at Mutt and threatened to kill the dog. Terror-stricken Sai immediately brought the guns—three in number—that had been kept hanging on a wall at the end of the hall. With their first success, the boys' courage bloomed and they ordered Sai, who felt 'intensely, fearfully female' (5) before their adult gaze, to make tea for them. Meanwhile, the frightened cook had hidden behind the dining table. They dragged the cowering man out and asked him to cook some food for them. The boys ignored the plaintive appeal of the old man, who, out of sheer habit and accumulated wisdom of generations, had begun to beg for mercy. Finally, they humiliated the arrogant judge by forcing him to prepare the tea-table for them: "Wailing and pleading for his life, the cook fried pakoras. . . . The judge fumbled for a table cloth in a drawer stuffed with yellowed curtains, sheets and rags. Sai, her hand shaking, stewed tea in a pan and strained it, although she had no idea how to properly make tea this way, the Indian way. She only knew the English way" (6). The cook and Sai felt stunned to watch the judge's insult and witness the hierarchy being overturned and discarded: 'It came to them that they might all die with the judge in the kitchen; the world was upside down and absolutely anything could happen' (6). The robbers carried out an intensive survey of the decaying bungalow and looted every available thing, from food-stock to wine: 'Two trunks they found in the bedrooms they filled with rice, lentils, sugar, tea, oil, matches, Lux soap, and Pond's Cold Cream. One of them assured Sai: "Only items necessary for the movement." (7). Before leaving, they defecated in the toilet and compelled the judge to shout slogans in support of the Gorkhaland:

> '"Say, 'Jai Gorkha,'" they said to the judge. "Gorkhaland for Gorkhas."
>
> "Jai Gorkha."
>
> "Say, 'I am a fool.' "
>
> "I am a fool."
>
> "Loudly. Can't hear you, *huzoor.* Say it louder."
>
> He said it in the same empty voice. (7)

When the hooligans disappeared in the darkness, carrying away part of the judge's past (his guns and the trunk bearing his name and the name of the ship in which he had voyaged to England), the cook broke into a loud lament: "Humara Kya hoga, hai hai, hamara kya hoga." Jemubhai himself sat upright on a chair tightly gripping its arms to prevent a violent trembling, and felt as if the world was 'shaking with a ravaging force he was trying to hold himself against' (8). Both Sai and the cook averted their gaze from the humiliated judge because they instinctively knew that it was an 'awful thing, the downing of a proud man. He might kill the witness' (8).

The time was mid-1980s—February 1986 to be specific. Sai was seventeen years old and her burgeoning romance with her Nepali tutor was not even one year old. The newspapers were publishing reports of disturbances in Kalimpong and the adjoining areas of Darjeeling district, of 'gathering insurgency, men and guns' (9). The

Nepalese Indians, who were 'fed up with being treated like the minority in a place where they were the majority,' had started demanding an independent homeland, 'or at least their own state, in which to manage their own affairs' (9). Kalimpong, a beautiful but strategic locale in the north-eastern Himalayas where India indistinguishably merged with Bhutan and Sikkim and her army remained always alert 'in case the Chinese grew hungry for 9). The place had a long history of war, bargaining and betrayal between India and the bordering Himalayan states on the one hand and England on the other, even though the mist that always swept down from the mountains above like a dragon, made the drawing of borders meaningless and ridiculous.

Chapter II

The robbery was duly reported to the police the very next day. The cook, who was sent by the judge to police station to lodge the report, protested because he knew from experience that it would be useless, even dangerous, to inform the guardians of law. For, if they had been paid off by the robbers, they would remain inactive. If they had not, it would be even worse. The young boys, who had looted the house the previous evening, would definitely be tipped off by the police and they would take revenge by killing the members of the judge's family. And one way or the other, the police would extract a bribe. The thought of bribe reminded the cook of his own small savings from the sale of illicit liquor which he had put in a tin box and hidden under the judge's abandoned car in the garage. In a trembling voice he conveyed the judge's message to the police, emphasizing all the while that he was only a poor messenger and had nothing to do with anything. The policemen, who hated the cringing servant and his rambling talk, questioned him harshly to elicit more information because they were evidently disturbed by the report of gun robbery in the house of a retired civil servant and judge. They informed the superintendent of the incident and visited Cho Oyu that very afternoon to make an enquiry. The interview with the judge confirmed the complaint of robbery and trespassing. The police collected fingerprints and footprints of the robbers and carried out an inspection of the house in search of more evidence. The walled-in bungalow, isolated from the rest of the world, had long been an object of curiosity to the people of the town and the policemen took the opportunity to snoop around the crumbling estate: 'They surveyed the downfall of wealth with satisfaction, and one of the policeman kicked a shaky apparatus of pipes leading from the *jhora* stream, bandaged here and there with sopping rags. He shone his torch into the toilet tank and discovered the flushing contraption had been fixed with rubber bands and bamboo splints. "What evidence are you going to find in the toilet?" asked Sai, following him around, feeling ashamed' (12).

Cho Oyu had been built years ago by an adventurous Scotsman passionately pursuing the dream of romance in the far Himalayas. The price for such a romance was always very high but it had been paid for not by the dreamer but by others: "Porters had carried boulders from the riverbed—legs growing bandy, ribs curving into caves, backs into U's, faces being bent slowly to look always at the ground—up to this site chosen for a view that could raise the human heart to spiritual heights" (12). But the house, which had been built over the years, now contained marks of inevitable decay all over its crumbling structure: "A thousand deceased spiders lay scattered like dead blossoms on the attic floor, and above them, on the underside of the tin sieve roof, dodging drips, their offspring stared at the police as they did at their own ancestors—with a giant saucer-sized lack of sympathy" (12). After inspecting the main building, the police went to the cook's cottage because he was included in their list of suspects. They walked past the garage sheltering the judge's sinking car and a patch of clear and well-maintained ground where a saucer of milk and a pile of sweets had been placed as puja offerings by the superstitious cook to pacify a pair of black cobras living in a hole nearby. The police ransacked the cook's hut and scornfully scattered his belongings in search of a clue to the gun robbery. Sai, who accompanied the police, saw what her grandfather had neglected or learned to ignore—the cook's poverty exposed when the guardians of law searched his things—and felt almost physically hurt: "It pained Sai's heart to see how little he had: a few clothes hung over a string, a single razor blade and a sliver of cheap brown soap, a Kulu blanket that had once been hers, a cardboard case with metal clasps that had belonged to the judge and now contained the cook's papers, the recommendations that had helped him procure his job with the judge, Biju's letters, papers from a court case fought in his village all the way in Uttar Pradesh over the matter of five mango trees that he had lost to his brother" (13). There were two photographs hanging on the wall, one of the cook himself and his wife taken on their wedding day, and the other was that of their only child Biju taken before his departure from the country. His wife had died in an accident ('slipping from a tree while gathering leaves, to feed the goat' [14]) seventeen years ago. And Biju—of whom the cook was extremely proud—was now in America, serving Angrezi khana to white people. The policemen spilled the letters written by Biju from America which gave his father a unique sense of prestige in the eyes of the people he knew in the town.

Chapter III

The chapters, which are set in New York, delineate Biju's adventures in the underbelly of the American dream. Incredibly powerful and full of sad details, these sections are tartly observed vignettes about the price of immigration and the pain of exile. This chapter describes the early days of Biju in America which he spent standing at the counter of a junk food shop along with a row of men selling hot dogs, chilli dog, soft drinks and frankfurter to a mixed clientele. The shop, named 'Gray's Papaya,' was a well-run establishment and it sold the best frankfurter in the city. The indefatigable spirit of the men Biju worked with—mostly undocumented immigrants like him—both astonished and terrified him. The shop they worked in 'had a festive air with paper chains, plastic oranges and bananas' (15-16). But during summer it was too hot there, the temperature rising to over one hundred degrees. They became very tired in the extremely hot atmosphere of the sales counter and 'sweat dripped off their noses and splashed on their toes' (16). Even though Biju, like the other salesmen, energetically waved hot dogs to the customers in the multicultural and cosmopolitan ambience of the shop, he could not forget the inhibitions and taboos of his own culture. That was why he demurred when many of his fellow employees visited the Dominican call girls in Washington Heights after work. But he tried to conceal his timidity under artificial disgust: "How can you?

Those, those women are dirty. . . Stinking bitches. . . . Fucking bitches, fucking cheap women you'll get some disease. . . . smell bad . . . hubshi . . . all black and ugly . . . they make me sick" (16). The men laughed at his coyness and pusillanimity but forgave him because 'They were men, he was a baby' (16). Although Biju was nineteen years old, he looked and felt much younger. He refused to accompany them to the prostitutes on one pretext or another. He felt relieved when the manager of the shop, after receiving a memo from the immigration authority 'instructing him to do a green card check on his employees' (16), asked them to disappear. And the illegal workers, including Biju, quietly vanished in the grim underside of immigrant New York.

Chapter IV

While Biju was trying desperately to stay afloat in the underground economy of New York city, bobbing from one ill-paid job to another, the cook dreamt of his son making it big. He was sure that 'since his son was cooking English food, he had a higher position than if he were cooking Indian' (17). The police, ransacking the cook's hut, felt intrigued by the letters Biju had written to his father and began to read them avidly. The letters traced a succession of jobs Biju had accepted and chucked up and were repetitive in their content. The repetition provided the cook with a feeling of coziness and he derived a sense of satisfaction from the thought of his son's misconstrued position in America. Leading a miserable life in the judge's household, he imagined a different future for him.

The narrator presents the cook's dream about his son thus: "He imagined sofa, TV, bank account. Eventually Biju would make enough and the cook would retire. He would receive a daughter-in-law to serve him food, crick-crack his toes, grandchildren to swat like flies" (17). Unlike the judge who lived in the past in a house where time seemed to have stood still, the cook 'trundled toward the future' (17). In his carefully drafted letters to his son, Panna Lal gave some valuable and pragmatic advice (in a manner which is reminiscent of Polonius's advice to Laertes on the eve of the latter's departure to France in Shakespeare's *Hamlet*):

> Just make sure you are saving money. Don't lend to anyone and be careful who you talk to. There are many people out there who will say one thing and do another. Liars and cheats. Remember also to take rest. Make sure you eat enough. Health is Wealth. Before you make any decisions talk them over with Nandu. (18)

Nandu was Panna Lal's friend who hailed from the same village in Utter Pradesh and now worked in New York. The semi-literate cook did not know the location of the city where his son lived. It was Sai who had pointed it out to him on an inflatable National Geographic Globe and explained 'why it was night there when it was day here' (18). And, the narrator humorously remarks, the mystified cook 'found it strange that India went first with the day, a funny back-to-front fact that didn't seem mirrored by any other circumstance involving the two nations' (18).

After completing the investigation, the police left the cottage. They had found no clue to the gun-robbery but, in the process of examining his belongings, 'exposed the cock's poverty, the fact that he was not looked after, that his dignity had no basis' (18). His bed with its frayed mattress had been overturned. The letters lay scattered on the floor along with his few items of clothing. The law-keepers had mercilessly ruined the façade of his dignity and thrown it on his face. Sai was shocked to discover that the cook whose son worked in America, possessed so little. She felt embarrassed as she watched him collecting his messily dispersed belongings from the ground. Although the cook loved her very much, Sai rarely entered his hut and even when she did come looking for him, both of them felt ill at ease. They could never completely overcome the social gap that existed between them and something about their intimacy ultimately proved to be phoney: "their friendship composed of shallow things conducted in a broken language, for she was an English speaker and he was a Hindi speaker' (19). Because of the broken nature of their conversation, they could never go beyond the superficies and 'enter into anything that required an intricate vocabulary' (19). Yet Sai always felt tender toward this aged man who spoke to her affectionately and called her 'Babyji or Saibaby.' She had first seen him nine years ago when she arrived at Cho Oyu from St. Augustine's Convent in Dehra Dun. As the taxi driver, who had dropped her off, rattled the locked gate and shouted for the servant/ khansama, Sai—'a little stick figure'—waited silently with a tin trunk by her side, her 'smallness emphasizing the vastness of the landscape' (19) which was overlooked by Kanchenjunga glowing macabre above. After what seemed to be a long while, she heard the sound of a whistle and saw the bandy-legged cook approaching with a lantern to open the gate, 'looking as leather-visaged, as weathered and soiled as he did now. . . . A poverty-stricken man growing into an ancient at fast-forward' (19).

Sai felt angry with the police for the terrible mess they had left in the hut and expressed profound sympathy for the poor and helpless man. But ironically her attempt 'to console his dignity' (20) only served to highlight its ruin. As she bent on the floor to help the cook to collect his belongings, she found him carefully placing the letters in the correct envelopes in the hope that 'One day he'd return them to Biju so his son would have a record of his journey and feel a sense of pride and achievement' (20).

Chapter V

Described as 'a globalized novel,' *The Inheritance of Loss* records the multi-cultural reverberations of the globalized world in the new millennium. Living a downtrodden life as an illegal immigrant in the restaurant kitchens of New York, the power centre of global economy and the destination of worldwide fortune seekers, Biju came into contact with the multicultural ambience of the new world: 'Above, the restaurant was French, but below in the kitchen it was Mexican and Indian. And, when a Paki was hired, it was Mexican, Indian, Pakistani' (21). Always dogged by fear that he would be discovered as an illegal worker, he hopped from one restaurant to another and was acquainted with the glaring inequality of economic globalization and the sharp divide between the first world and the third, the colonial and the native, the rich and the poor: "Biju at Le Colonial for the authentic colonial experience. On top, rich colonial, and down below, poor native Colombian, Tunisian, Ecuadorian, Gambian" (20). He also came to learn from fellow workers about the fast expanding Indian diaspora and felt amazed by his own ignorance:

> "Where is Guyana?"
> "Don't you know?" The Guyanese man said, "Indians everywhere in Guyana, man"
> "Indians in Guam. Everywhere you look, practically, Indians."
> "Trinidad?"
> "Trinidad full of Indians!! . . ."
> Madagascar—Indians Indians.
> Chile . . . Indians, whiskey, electronics.
> Kenya. South Africa. Saudi Arabia. Fiji. New Zealand. Surinam.
> In Canada . . . Indians, yes in Alaska; a *desi* owned the last general store in the last town before the North Pole. . .
> On the Black Sea, yes, Indians, running a spice business.
> Hong Kong. Singapore.
> How had he learned nothing growing up? (22)

Kiran Desai brilliantly charts the map of Indian diaspora in her novel but her focus shifts mainly between the sleepy Himalayan burg of Kalimpong with its colonial heritage and New York, the post-imperial centre of global politics and economics.

Biju found himself cast in a world which was constantly in a flux and devoid of any settled conventions. With his poor adaptability and native rootedness, he found himself an ill-equipped foreigner in the new world and clung more and more to his traditional Indian identity as a defence against the globalized as well as homogenized reality. "There was a whole world in the basement kitchens of New York," the narrator remarks, "but Biju was ill equipped for it" (22). He felt relieved when a Pakistani worker arrived in the kitchen. Because he knew what to do with him. As advised by his father, who was alarmed by the news of the arrival of a Pakistani national in his son's restaurant, Biju distrusted and kept away from him: 'He found he could not talk straight to the man; every molecule of him felt fake, every hair on him went on alert' (22). His communal prejudice was at work. The Indians and the Pakistanis carried their old war to America where 'every nationality confirmed its stereotype' (23). Biju and his inimical neighbour turned the underground kitchen into a battlefield and vigorously hurled expletives at each other:

> '"Pigs pigs, sons of pigs, *sooar ka baccha*," Biju shouted.
> "*Uloo ka patha*, son of an owl, low-down son-of-a-bitch Indian."

> They drew the lines at crucial junctures. They threw cannonball cabbages at each other.' (23)

But the owner of the establishment, a Frenchman was not amused by this Indo-Pak war of words. Angry at the noise made by the trouble-some pair which, he feared, might disturb the delicate balance in his upscale restaurant that was 'perfectly first world on top, perfectly third-world twenty-two steps below' (23) and scare away its patrons, he bluntly asked them to leave. Thus the Indian and the Pakistani lost their jobs in their attempt to be true to their racial and communal stereotypes: "Paki one way, Biju the other way. Rounding the corner, meeting each other again, turning away again' (23).

Chapter VI

When Sai, the teenage and orphaned granddaughter Jemubhai had never seen before, arrived at his doorstep for shelter, she was received by the bandy-legged cook. He appeared at the gate with a lantern, 'blowing on a whistle to warn away jackals, the two cobras, and the local thief, Gobbo, who robbed all the residents of Kalimpong in rotation and had a brother in the police to protect him' (24). He was disappointed to learn that she had come neither from America nor from England, nor even 'from foreign' (24) but from Dehra Dun at the other end of the Indian Himalayas. He asked about her parents and was shocked when Sai told him that she was an orphan and that both her parents had died in Russia where her father was a space pilot. The story of the ill-fated couple is told by the narrator in a cinematic flashback:

> The cook turned back: "How did they die?"
>
> Somewhere above, there was the sound of an alarmed bird, of immense wings starting up like a propeller. (25)

The accident had occurred in Moscow, near the Society for Interplanetary Travel where Sai's father, Mr. Mistry, a pilot of the Indian Air Force, was undergoing rigorous training as a probable candidate for the 'Intercosmos Program' during the last days of Indo-USSR political romance. Like many other Indians, Sai's parents had grown up during those exciting years in 1950s and early 1960s when the friendship between the two nations 'had been cemented by weapon sales, sporting competitions, visiting dance troupes, and illustrated books that introduced a generation of Indian school children to Baba Yaga [and] . . . to the troubles of Prince Ivan and Princess Ivanka' (25). They had met each other in a Delhi park. Mrs. Mistry—then Miss Patel—was an 'astonishingly pretty' (26) college student and Mr. Mistry—a Zoroastrian—was a handsome air force pilot. Within a year, Mr. Mistry proposed and she agreed to this marriage because the 'romance had allowed her to escape the sadness of her past and the tediousness of her current girlish life' (26). The Hindu student and the Parsi pilot knew that nobody would be amused by their 'secular romance.' Still the lovers 'considered themselves lucky to have found each other, each one empty with the same loneliness, each one fascinating as a foreigner to the other, but both educated with an eye to the West' (26). The secular modernity of Sai's parents alienated her mother from her family which felt disgraced and disowned her. The hapless girl, who had never seen her parents and had led a directionless life till her adult age, submitted herself to the whims of an unknown fate which took her to Russia with her husband. Mr. Mistry, a competent pilot of the Indian Air Force, was selected for the joint space programme by a visiting Soviet team of aeronautical and aviation experts. The couple left for Moscow, entrusting their six-year old daughter, Sai, to the care of the same convent in Dehra Dun her mother had attended. But even before his training was completed, Mr. Mistry and his wife were crushed under the wheels of a bus one afternoon while they were crossing the square to the Society for Interplanetary Travel. When the shocking news reached Sai in Dehra Dun, she tried to cry but she found that she could not. She had not seen her parents for two whole years and so 'the emotional immediacy of their existence' (28) had vanished from her mind. Resting in the infirmary of the convent and being consoled by the nuns, the girl could only whisper to herself: "My parents are dead. I am an orphan" (27).

The death of her parents created a special problem for the convent authorities because they found that in 'a country so full of relatives, Sai suffered a dearth' (28). The senior nuns remembered the girl's mother and the fact that her keep had been paid for a judge who had never visited the school. They also knew that her father had been brought up in an orphanage and had no relative in the country. There were other threads of the girl's story which none of them could piece together because 'some of the narrative had been lost, some of it had been purposely forgotten' (28). They found no other alternative but to expel Sai from the convent and send her to her grandfather, retired Justice Jemubhai Patel, whom she had never seen before and who had been living in Kalimpong since 1957 in a house bought from a departing Scotsman. After visiting Cho Oyu, Jemubhai was deeply impressed ('He had felt he was entering a sensibility rather than a house,' [28]) by the colonial mansion which had been built on a mountain ledge from where 'the Himalayas rose layer upon layer until those gleaming peaks proved a man to be so small that it made sense to give it all up, empty it all out' (29). He decided to give up his job and live 'in this shell . . . with the solace of being a foreigner in his own country,' (29) for he decided not to learn the language of the local people.

Sai was glad to be expelled from the boarding school because she hated the perversities of convent education that smacked of colonial prejudice and was unduly obsessed with purity and sin. She was entrusted to a visiting nun, who had been learning convent finance systems, and was now on her way to Darjeeling. They took a taxi from Siliguri and parted company on the bank of the Teesta river where their paths diverged. Sai became conscious of 'the enormous space she was entering' (31) as the taxi corkscrewed on the precipitous mountain road along the insane river until it reached, through the darkness of night, Kalimpong and stopped before the gate of a house situated in the middle of a wilderness.

Chapter VII

Sai instinctively disliked her grandfather as she met him in the dining table on the day she had arrived at Cho Oyu. While the cook fashioned a celebratory motor car with mashed potatoes to welcome her, Sai looked at the judge and his dog and felt: 'Grandfather more lizard than human. Dog more human than dog' (32). With his shrivelled figure dressed in frazzled but clean and ironed clothes, his dark face whitened by powder, his lack of movement and fixed gaze, Jemubhai appeared more like 'a reptile' than a human in her eyes and reminded her of a creature of the past: "Like other elderly people, he seemed not to have travelled forward in time but far back. Harking to the prehistoric, in attendance upon infinity, he resembled a creature of the Galapagos staring over the ocean." (33)

The first encounter between the judge and his granddaughter did not appear to be very auspicious. He seemed not to have noticed her arrival in his house. When he did, at the dinner table, he looked at her with a fixed gaze and dispassionately asked her name:

> "Well, what is your name?"
> "Sai."
> "Sai?" he said crossly, as if angered by an impudence. (33)

He was immensely pleased—although he tried not to show it—by her complimentary remark about his pet dog, a purebred and cute-looking red-setter with an elegant snout whom she compared to 'a film star' (33). But his mood was soon soured by the bumbling cook, who in his excitement over the mashed potato car, had forgotten to serve him the soup before the main course and by the power failure that plunged the house in semi-darkness. The judge, who did not tolerate any break in the routine he had followed since the days of his colonial high office, was upset by the cook's carelessness. And the 'electricity fell abruptly to a lower strength as if in accordance with [his] disapproval' (33). In the uneven light produced by a single bulb, the four members of the makeshift family looked like 'four shadow puppets from a fairytale flickering on the lumpy plaster of the wall—a lizard man, a hunchbacked cook, a lush lashed maiden, and a long-tailed wolf dog' (33). Mutt, the pet canine, was shocked by the buzzing sound produced by an upturned beetle on the dining table. When her master overturned the insect with his knife, the bitch 'gazed at him like an adoring spouse' (34). As the old and underpaid cook brought the forgotten tomato soup from the kitchen and placed it on the table, complaining all the while about his poverty and poor health, the judge calmed down and chalked out, over the dinner, his plan for the orphaned granddaughter. He told Sai that she could stay there but she should not disturb his privacy and that he would hire a tutor for her because he could not afford to send her to a convent school. At the same time, the Anglophile ex-judge was too highbrowed to think of a government school for the girl because she would 'come out speaking with the wrong accent and picking [her] nose' (34).

While lying on her bed later that night the sensitive girl realized that she 'could sense the swollen presence of the forest,' and hear 'the sound of the *jhora* that ran deep in the décolleté of the mountain' (34). She was assailed by a 'fearful feeling of having entered a space so big it reached both backward and forward' (34) and by a secret knowledge that the colonial relic that housed her grandfather was decaying at a frightening pace. Before falling into sleep, Sai felt that she could hear 'the sound of microscopic jaws slow-milling the house to saw-dust' (34).

Chapter VIII

The arrival of the teenage granddaughter upset the balance of the judge's life. It opened the floodgates of memories, compelling him to think 'of his own journeys, of his own arrivals and departures, from places far in his past' (33). His attempts to chase those unpleasant thoughts away from his mind did not succeed. Even sleeping pills could not give him any respite from the seemingly endless chain of disquieting thoughts that filled his mind with shame and guilt. Lying awake in bed, with Mutt by his side, he revisited the past and was assailed by searing memory of his first journey from his ancestral home at Piphit in Gujarat to England for higher education. The revisitation of the bygone days was triggered by the black tin trunk which Sai had brought with her and on which her name and the name of her convent were inscribed. It was with a similar trunk Jemubhai Papatlal Patel had left home and journeyed to Liverpool via Bombay, by a ship, SS Strathnaver. The time was 1939. It was British India and Jemubhai was twenty years old. In a cinematic flashback, the narrator describes the ill-fated voyage to imperial England that changed the course of the future judge's life.

Jemubhai had left home a month after his marriage. He had barely seen the face of his newly wed wife who was fourteen years old at the time of his departure. Serenaded at the railway station by a military band hired by his rich father-in-law, Jemu travelled to Bombay with his father and a tin trunk that contained, among other things, a sweater knitted in a fanciful pattern by his mother 'to express the extravagance of her affection' (36), a new *Oxford English Dictionary* and a decorated coconut to be tossed into the sea waves to bring good luck to his journey. But even before he left the shore of the country, the would-be judge felt ashamed of his parents, his culture and tradition. When his father, who saw him off at the Bombay dock, instructed him to throw the coconut into the sea from the deck of the ship, he felt pity and shame for him: "Jemubhai looked at his father, a barely educated man venturing where he should not be, and the love in Jemubhai's heart mingled with pity, the pity with shame. His father felt his own hand rise and cover his mouth: he had failed his son" (37). So ashamed did Jemu feel of his superstitious progenitor that he did not throw the coconut into the sea and he refused to cry. He would never again experience love for any human being 'that wasn't adulterated by another, contradictory emotion' (37). He was further humiliated when his cabin mate, a man from Calcutta who could compose sonnets in Latin, twitched his nose at the stench of the food that Jemu's mother had carefully prepared in case her son felt hungry on the way but which had been spoilt by heat in the course of the journey. He was furious at the ignorance of his inconsiderate mother, who could thus precipitate his humiliation among strangers, and threw the packet of food into the sea. In doing so, he not only rejected the love of his parents as well as the immense sacrifice they had made for him but also exposed his own loneliness and fear:

> Jemu picked up the package, fled to the deck, and threw it overboard. Didn't his mother think of the inappropriateness of her gesture? Undignified love, Indian love, stinking, unaesthetic love—the monsters of the ocean could have what she had so bravely packed getting up in that predawn mush.
>
> The smell of dying bananas retreated, oh, but now that just left the stink of fear and loneliness perfectly exposed. (38)

The ship anchored at Liverpool to the accompaniment of a band music welcoming the passengers to the "Land of Hope and Glory." While his brown cabin mate hired a white porter to pick up his bags, Jemu carried his own luggage and stumbled on to a train that took him to Cambridge.

The Anglophile future judge was stunned by his encounter with the West. It was a time when people of colour were not particularly liked in Britain. Jemubhai, who was refused to rent a room because of his dark complexion and Indian origin, was himself amazed to discover poverty in imperial England where people lived 'unaesthetic lives' (38) in tiny gray houses. He visited a score of homes in search of a room before he met an elderly and financially constrained lady—Mrs. Rice—who allowed him to stay in her house as a paying guest. But the stay in Cambridge proved to be disastrous. Jemubhai, who had registered at Fitzwilliam—a third grade college by British standards—with the help of an essay he had written for the entrance examination, immediately settled down in his rented room to study. Because it was the only skill he had carried from his native land. As a student, isolated in racist England, Jemu experienced a remarkable change in his personality:

> He worked twelve hours at a stretch, late into the night, and in thus withdrawing, he failed to make a courageous gesture outward at a crucial moment and found, instead, that his pusillanimity and his loneliness had found fertile soil. He retreated into a solitude that grew in weight day by day. The solitude became a habit, the habit became the man, and it crushed him into a shadow. (39)

His loneliness left an indelible mark on his appearance that unsettled others. People began to shun him: "For entire days nobody spoke to him at all . . . and elderly ladies, even the hapless—blue haired, spotted, faces like collapsing pumpkins—moved over when he sat next to them in the bus" (39). Under the unbearable pressure of solitude his mind began to 'warp.' He became a stranger to himself and even forgot how to laugh. For five long years he did not make a single friend and see anything of the English countryside. He took refuge in the library, dreading the ridicule of young girls who giggled at his curry smell and of peers who laughed at his accent. Unable to cope with the conflict of identities, young Jemu was consumed by self-loathing. The prejudice and rejection he experienced in England froze his heart and fuelled in his soul a shame and a dislike for his heritage, his culture and the colour of his skin: "He began to wash obsessively, concerned he would be accused of smelling. . . . To the end of his life, he would never be seen without socks and shoes and would prefer shadow to light, faded days to sunny, for he was suspicious that sunlight might reveal him, in his hideousness, all too clearly" (40). In the end, Jemu 'felt barely human at all' (40). He leaped 'when touched on the arm as if from an unbearable intimacy' and broke into 'tears of self pity' (40) at the casual gesture of affection.

When the judge met his granddaughter again at the breakfast table next morning, he ordered the cook to take her to her tutor, a Bengali lady named Noni (Nonita) who lived an hour walk's away from Cho Oyu. On the way, the cook showed Sai the houses of their neighbours, a group of Anglophile and mostly retired people living for old world charms. Their immediate neighbour was Uncle Potty, a 'gentle man farmer and a drunk' (41), who had purchased the land from the judge. There was Potty's friend, a thoroughly Indianised Swiss Priest named Father Booty, who ran a dairy and dreamed of teaching Indians how to make cheese. Apart from these two unusually friendly old men who spent each evening drinking wine and reminiscing about bygone days, Sai found two Afghan princesses, whose father had been dethroned during his holiday at Brighton and who had been given refuge in India by Nehru himself, and a garrulous widow, Mrs. Sen, who lived in a small dingy house and whose daughter Mun Mun had gone to America to work with the CNN. Finally they reached Mon Ami, a picturesque rose-covered cottage where Noni, a spinster, lived with her sister Lola (Lolita), who was a widow. She had moved in after the untimely death of Lola's husband. They lived on his pension. In order to make her own contribution to the family income, Noni had accepted the judge's proposal to teach his granddaughter both science and Shakespeare. Over the years both the tutor and her sister grew very fond of Sai whom they regarded as the 'orphan child of India's failing romance with the Soviets' (42).

Chapter IX

Lola, the older of the two Bengali sisters who had a stronger personality, was shocked at the news of gun robbery in Cho Oyu and became apprehensive about their own safety. When Sai reminded

Lola that they had a watchman to protect them, she told her that he was a Nepali and so he could not be trusted. The Nepalis were indispensable for household works but they were held in general distrust by the non-Nepali-speaking people. In order to substantiate her allegation she recalled an incident of dacoity in the house of a Tibetan neighbour—Mrs. Thondup who also had a watchman. But the Nepali fellow did not come when the dacoits looted every single thing from the house and disappeared into Nepal. Noni—the tutor—told her sister not to be panicky because their guard, named Budhoo, had given them no reason for distrust so far. In truth, the man was a reassuring presence for the two aged sisters who had lived long without any male guardian in Mon Ami, a rose-covered estate modelled on European cottage which afforded a brilliant view of Kanchenjunga and whose vegetable patch contained 'the country's only broccoli grown from seeds procured in England' (44). They enjoyed a security that came from living on the fruits of blissful retirement. Like many Anglicised Indians, they were alienated from the local people—in this case the ethnic Nepalis—and their desires and aspirations, hopes and despair. Like the judge they lived like foreigners in their own country, their attention and interest being always focused on the West. Their tastes and colonial life-style made them appear to be an undesired anachronism in post-Independence India where, as the brewing trouble in the Darjeeling hills indicated, long suppressed ethnic groups had begun to awaken to their feelings of injustice and deprivation. "Their washing line sagged under a load of Marks and Spencer panties," the narrator says, and the Tibetan *choksee* tables in their drawing room are piled with books, "including a volume of paintings by Nicholas Roerich . . . Salim Ali's guide to birds and all of Jane Austen" (44). To protect the treasure trove in the house, and also their dignity, they had employed Budhoo, an ex-army man with an experience of fighting against the insurgents in Assam. At night, when the sisters wrapped in expensive shawl, sat up on their beds and sipped Sikkimese brandy, either listening BBC news on the radio or watching British T.V. serials on Doordarshan, the faithful guard kept vigil in the biting cold outside: "At intervals through the night Budhoo also marched about Mon Ami, banging a stick and blowing a whistle so Lola and Noni could hear him and feel safe" (45). Still, the sisters had no trust in him; they even believed that he might murder them in their sleep. The derogatory term 'Neps' was used by Lola to describe the ethnic Nepalis, who constituted the majority of Darjeeling's population, as a stereotype of generically uncivilized and violent people: "I tell you, these Neps can't be trusted. And they don't just rob. They think absolutely nothing of murdering, as well" (45). She was not, however, surprised by the new troubles on the hillside because Kalimpong had always been a politically volatile area due to its strategic location in India's border with her neighbouring states. When they had first come to live in the town, the whole place was 'upside down' in the wake of Chinese occupation of Tibet. They had seen hordes of refugees 'streamed through the forests, garnet lines of fire pouring down the mountains, as they escaped from Tibet along the salt and wool trade routes' (45). In anticipation of political disturbance, the first thing they thought about was their larder as well as their library books. Interestingly, while taking stock of the books they had borrowed from the Gymkhana library in Darjeeling, the siblings refer to V.S. Naipaul's novel *A Bend in the River* which deals with the emergence of traditional Africa into the modern world and the high wages of this change. Lola, a spirited supporter of England and Englishness, said to Noni who called Naipaul a 'superb writer': "I think he's strange. Stuck in the past. . . . He has not progressed. Colonial neurosis, he's never freed himself from it" (46). She accused the London-based Caribbean Nobel Laureate of ignoring the 'new England' which had emerged as a 'completely cosmopolitan society' where, according to the report of the *Indian Express*, 'chicken tikka masala has replaced fish and chips as the number one take-out dinner' (46). It was this impatience with the postcolonial rage and despair of the representative third world writer that ironically kept Westernized people like Lola in denial about the political storm that would soon burst on the hills and shock them out of genteel retirement. She thus felt proud of her daughter, Pixie (Piyali Banerji), a BBC reporter who, according to Lola, did not 'have a chip on her shoulder' (46). Every year this Anglophile lady, who lived in postcolonial India but mimicked the colonial life style, visited her daughter in London and retuned with British goods to make everyone sick with her praise of the ex-masters' country: "Her suitcases were stuffed with Marmite, Oxo bouillon cubes, Knorr soup packets, After Eights, daffodil bulbs, and renewed supplies of Boots cucumber lotion and Marks and Spencer underwear—the essence, quintessence, of Englishness as she understood it" (47). Her daughter had inspired her to prefer the BBC news to the bulletin of All India Radio. When she listened to Pixie reading 'in pucca British accent,' the news of disease, war and famine in the poor third world countries, her heart was filled with pride. While her sister felt outraged and exclaimed in horror, Lola could hear 'nothing but the sanitized elegance of her daughter's voice, triumphant over any horrors the world might thrust upon others' (47). It was she who had advised Pixie to think only of her own happiness and thus to leave her country of birth which appeared nothing better than 'a sinking ship' (47) to the privileged class of Westernized Indians.

Chapter X

Biju, an impoverished and struggling immigrant in New York, was still on the run, moving from one ill-paid job to another and eking out a bare existence. He started his second year in the new world as a cook in an Italian restaurant, stirring vats of Bolognese in the kitchen and listening, over a speaker, an opera singer's song about 'love and murder, revenge and heartbreak' (48). He experienced the difference of treatment meted out, by American citizens, to immigrants from the poorer countries of Europe, like Bulgaria and Czechoslovakia, who shared with them common religion, skin colour and ancestry, and those who arrived desperately and in great number from the poverty-stricken third world nations. The wife of the restaurant owner resented the cook's smell so much that her husband bought soap, shampoo and deodorant and told Biju to use them. He even intimately asked him questions about his country to raise his self-respect. As things did not change and they found no difference in Biju, the owner asked him to quit.

After temporary unemployment, Biju again found a job in a place named Freddy's Wok where he was required to deliver ordered food to customers on a bicycle. Kiran Desai sympathetically portrays an illegal immigrant's struggle for a mere living on the busy streets of Manhattan: "Biju on a bicycle with the delivery bag on his handlebars, a tremulous figure between heaving buses, regurgitating taxis—what growls, what sounds of flatulence came from this traffic. Biju pounded at the pedals, heckled by taxi drivers direct from Punjab. . . . They harassed [him] with such blows from their horns as could split the world into whey and solids." (49) The novel depicts, with unsparing irony, the 'meeting between Indians abroad of different classes and languages, rich and poor, north and south, top caste bottom caste' (50). It exposes the despicable attitude of the wealthier group of Indian immigrants to their poor compatriots and reveals how the class divide that exists in India continues overseas. One evening Biju was sent to deliver the food items ordered by three Indian girl students who lived in a neighbourhood apartment. One of the girls took the bag and went inside to bring the money. As Biju waited outside the room, which was "suffused with Indian femininity' (49), he overheard their conversation about a common friend who preferred to date with an American, a 'Marlboro man with a Ph.D.' (50) rather than with a smart Indian boy. The talk is followed by an authorial comment that highlights the hypocrisy and self-righteousness 'common to many Indian women of the English-speaking upper educated' who were 'eager for Western style romance, and happy for a traditional ceremony with lots of jewellery' (50). Kiran Desai's humorous remark exposes these high-browed, self-conscious and all-knowing women who 'considered themselves uniquely positioned to lecture everyone on a variety of topics: accounting professors on accounting, Vermonters on the fall foliage, Indians on America, Americans on India, Indians on India, Americans on America' (50). The girl returned with the money and paid Biju an extra tip to buy warm clothes for the coming winter, with an excessive display of friendliness to the lower class Indian menial: "*Dhanyawad. Shukria.* Thank you" (50). As he stood on the threshold and watched the privileged girls checking the savoury eatables on their dining table, Biju 'felt a mixture of emotions: hunger, respect, loathing' (50). Before mounting his bicycle he impulsively put his fingers to his lips and whistled into the open window of the room, like a typical Indian male whose repressed libido led him to tease the opposite sex, and then pedalled very fast into the roaring traffic of Broadway, singing wistfully a popular Hindi melody: '*O, yeh ladki zara si deewani lagti hai.*' Biju, whose native humanity was smothered by the urban modernity of cosmopolitan New York, thus tried to cling more and more to his traditional Indian identity as a defence against a reality that threatened to rub out his inherited culture for a globalized homogeneity.

Desai also explores the pain of the undocumented immigrant in America and delineates his profound sadness through the meanderings of Biju whose dream of a dignified and glamorous life turned into a nightmare while he, lonely and forlorn, led a miserable existence in the precarious anonymity of New York: "Biju put a padding of newspapers down his shirt—leftover copies from kind Mr. Iype the newsagent . . . and once, on his bicycle, he began to weep from the cold, and the weeping unpicked a deeper vein of grief—such a terrible groan issued from between the whimpers that he was shocked his sadness was so profound" (51). After hours of donkey work he returned to his den in the grim underbelly of immigrant New York and fell asleep. Biju had taken shelter in the basement of a building situated at the bottom of Harlem, which had been illegally rented out by an unscrupulous superintendent to fellow illegals, and joined 'a shifting population of men camping out near the fuse box, behind the boiler, in the cubby holes' (51). Kiran's writing is suffused with humanism when she describes the subhuman life led by illegal immigrants and portrays the underside of opulence and development where a homeless man marked his 'hunting and gathering territory' with his own pee and 'wintered . . . on a subway grate in a giant plastic bag igloo that sagged, then blew taut with stale air each time a train passed' (52). Biju soon lost his job because the customers began to complain that the food ordered by them arrived cold and he could not pedal his bicycle faster as the owner of Freddy's Wok wanted him to do.

It was spring when he found an employment again. As the ice melted on the Hudson and the cherry blossoms made the narrow pavements of the busy streets look picturesque, people came out of their homes in large numbers to enjoy the brief interval between winter and summer, both extreme as hell, and flooded the city's cafes and restaurants. Biju joined the Queen of Tarts bakery and met Saeed Saeed, 'the man he admired most in the United States of America'

(53). Saeed hailed from Zanzibar, a place full of Indians. It was Saeed who told Biju about the tremendous popularity of Bollywood films and actors in Stone Town. As he wiggled his hips to the tunes of riveting dance numbers like, '*Mera joota hai japani*' or '*Bombay se aaya mera dost*,' a feat in which other employees of the bakery also joined, Biju felt immensely proud of his country's cultural heritage.

Chapter XI

Sai was tutored by Noni on three days a week. On those days the cook dropped Sai off and collected her at the rose covered cottage called Mon Ami. He spent the time, when the girl took tuition on science, in the market, selling his home made liquor, *chhang*. It filled his heart with pride to watch 'men sitting in the steam and smoke with their bamboo mugs full of his grain topped with hot water' (54). The ill-paid cook had started the liquor business for the sake of Biju because his salary had hardly been increased in years and the judge refused to pay for his son's keep. The success of the *chhang* venture had encouraged him to conduct another lucrative, though clandestine, business of army liquor from his own quarters in Cho Oyu. The cook thus debased himself and compromised his honour and integrity to fulfill his desire for modernity: 'toaster ovens, electric shavers, watches, cameras, cartoon colours' (55). Unlike others, he—a widower—'dreamed at night not in the Freudian symbols . . . but in modern codes, the digits of a telephone flying away before he could dial them, a garbled television' (55).

The cook was not proud of being in the service of the parsimonious judge. When he compared himself with other servants on the hillside, who always boasted 'how well they were treated by their employers—money, comfort, even pensions in special bank accounts' (55), he felt ashamed. The rivalry among the servants had led the cook to tell lies about himself and his employer: 'He fanned a rumour of the judge's lost glory, and therefore of his own, so it flamed and prospered up and down the market' (55). Everyone in Kalimpong knew that the judge had been a great 'statesman' and a rich landowner who gave away his family property and left his position of power as a High Court judge because of his patriotic zeal, and that this 'inspiring man' had been 'brought to knees, to austerity and philosophy' (56) by sorrow at his wife's untimely death. The cook had never seen the judge's wife. But he insisted that his information about her, which had been handed down from the older servants in the family, was accurate. Over the years he had grown to believe in his own 'marvellous story' (56) because it boosted his sense of self-respect. When Sai came to stay in Cho Oyu, she learnt the same story from him. The cook told her his version of her grandfather's past as she gave him company in the kitchen and watched him making chapatis.

The rambling voice of the cook reached the judge as he sat over his chess in the drawing room and made him revisit his past. The regurgitation of the past was not a pleasant experience for him but he could not resist the flood of memories that inundated him: 'When he thought of his past, he began, mysteriously to itch. Every bit of him filled with a burning sensation. It roiled within until he could barely stand it' (56).

Jemubhai had been born in 1919 to a family of peasants in Piphit, a seemingly ageless and sleeping Gujarati town, near Baroda. It had been transformed into a thriving business centre under the impact of colonial rule. Jemu's father had a modest business of supplying false witnesses to the court of law. He trained the poor scoundrels how to tell lies before the judge and thus subvert justice: "He was proud of his ability to influence and corrupt the path of justice, exchange right for wrong or wrong for right; he felt no guilt' (57). The business succeeded so much that when his first and only son, Jemu, was old enough to go to school, he decided to give him English education. From his early student life Jemubhai had developed a profound respect for the English and all they stood for: "In the entrance to the school building was a portrait of Queen Victoria in a dress like a flouncy curtain, a fringed cape, and a peculiar hat with feathery arrows shooting out. Each morning as Jemubhai passed under, he found her froggy expression compelling and felt deeply impressed that a woman so plain could also have been so powerful. The more he pondered this oddity, the more his respect for her and the English grew' (58). It was here—in this mission school—he rose to the promise of his gender. Jemu was the first son of the Patel lineage whose intelligence seemed 'modern in its alacrity' (58), and his parents deprived their daughters to ensure that he received the best of everything in the family, from love to food. He was the chosen son of the family and much was sacrificed for his success. When he matriculated at the top of his class, the father's ambition began to soar the sky. He ignored the Principal's suggestion that Jemu should sit for the local pleader's examination to find a job in the lower courts, because he had other plans for his son: "The father walked out thinking, Well, if he could do that, he could do more. He could be the judge himself. . . His son might, *might, could*! occupy the seat faced by the father, proud disrupter of the system, lowest in the hierarchy of the court. . . . Father below, son above, they'd be in charge of justice, complete" (59). The intensity of the father's fantastic dream touched the son so much that 'it took form, began to exert palpable pressure' (59). They aimed for the I.C.S. examination. Jemu attended Bishop's College on a scholarship and then left for Cambridge. When he came back, as a member of the ICS, he was posted in a remote district of Uttar Pradesh.

The rest of the chapter describes Jemubhai's life as a touring official in the civil service. Here again the cook's reminiscence merges with his master's recollection. But after the 'burning memory of his beginnings' (61), the judge experienced a sweet relief by remembering the happiest period of his professional life as a civil servant in colonial India. He followed a very tight schedule, from bed-tea ('pronounced as 'bad tea' by the cook who served it) at five forty-five in the morning to eleven at night when he went to sleep. In between he rode into the villages with local officials to measure the fields and checked the crop in order to make sure that his yield estimate matched the statements provided by the village headmen. He also heard cases and recorded the proceedings in English. In the afternoon he took tea with drop scones and went into the countryside with guns to hunt birds although he was a poor shot and on most occasions he returned empty-handed. And finally at night he filled out the registers and recorded, in his diary, his random observations. Jemubhai enjoyed 'the constant exertion of authority' and immensely 'relished his power over the classes that had kept his family pinned under their heels for centuries' (61). Over the years he acquired a formidable reputation that carried him all the way to Lucknow high court where 'he would preside, white powdered wig over white powdered face, hammer in hand' (62). The cook, however, felt disappointed to be serving the judge. He regarded it as a comedown from his father who had worked only for the white men. The old servants who had experienced the glamour of British civil servants, were generally disheartened by the Indianization of the ICS. But the cook had no option but to accept his position because he had no training or experience for the job and all the recommendations his father had procured for him were false.

Chapter XII

Sai's uneventful life continued in Kalimpong in the company of her grandfather, his cook, and their Anglophile neighbours until she met an ethnic Nepali youth, Gyan. She met Gyan, a brilliant student of science, because one day her tutor, Noni, realized that she had exhausted her capacity to teach her physics. It was an unusually hot afternoon in summer. The heat had induced a stupor in the people of the neighbourhood all of whom had retired inside their houses, all except Mrs. Sen and Lola. The former had left her home, undeterred by the sweltering atmosphere, and set out for Mon Ami to give Lola the news that her daughter Mun Mun, a green card holder in America, would soon be hired by CNN. The rivalry with her neighbour had prompted Mrs. Sen to brave the searing heat which roasted dozens of snakes on stones: 'She reflected happily on how this would upset Lola. Hah, who did Lola Banerjee think she was? Putting on airs . . . always showing off about her daughter at the BBC' (66). Lola—unaware of the disturbing news—was working in the garden, picking caterpillars off the English broccoli and throwing them to a bird which pecked and ate them. Noni and Sai sat on the veranda with an open physics book before them. They were discussing the structure of atom but Noni soon found that she could not concentrate on the topic. A sudden exhaustion seemed to have come over her. So she put the book aside and began to chat with her student.

Sai, who was sixteen years old, 'looked far older in some ways, far younger in some' (66) than her actual age. She appeared younger because of the 'sheltered life' she had lived since her childhood, and older because her time was spent in the company of retired people. Noni examined Sai critically and felt worried about her. She and her sister believed that it was not good for the girl to continue to grow up like this: "She won't pick up social skills . . . nobody her own age . . . house full of men" (66). They did not approve of the manner in which Sai's grandfather had abandoned her to the care of his cook and of the way the teenage girl spent her days in the company of the old, loquacious and socially inferior servant who told her stories about his village, his dead wife, his litigation with his brother, and about his son Biju who was in America, earning a lot of money. The bourgeois sisters insisted on drawing a line of demarcation between the classes—the master and the servant. Otherwise, 'it harmed everyone on both sides of the great divide' (67). They always discouraged their own maid, Kesang, from disclosing her personal information to them. But it was difficult to restrain the talkative woman. Whether they liked it or not, she would always 'slide into areas of the heart that should be referred to only between social equals' (67) and tell them about her romance with a milkman. They were shocked by this uninhibited revelation of the most personal relationship. Lola had always believed that servants could not experience love in the same way as their masters. As she told her sister: "Their entire structure of relationships is different, it's economic, practical—far more sensible, I'm sure, if only one could manage it oneself" (68). But Kesang's affair had compelled her to wonder 'if it were she who had never experienced the real thing' (68) with her husband, Joydeep. Noni, on the other hand, had never experienced love at all. Hers had been an emotionally barren life: 'She had never flown the brief glorious flag of romance, bright red, over her existence, not even as an episode of theatre, a bit of pretence to raise her above her life' (68). She was shocked to find that the maid's love had actually made her feel jealous: 'The lines had blurred, luck had been misassigned' (68).

Noni wondered whether anyone would love Sai, given the extraordinary circumstances of her life. She had discovered her younger self in the shy and introverted girl when she had first arrived in Mon Ami. She realized that her diffidence was the unfortunate outcome of 'committing a sensitive creature to a mean-spirited educational system' (68) where one could remain untrapped only 'by going underground, remaining quiet when asked questions, expressing no opinion, hoping to be invisible—or they got you, ruined you' (68). Noni herself had been subjected to such a system by her father, with the same consequence. It was too late when she regained her confidence and she realized to her dismay that she had lost the chance: 'Life had passed her by' (68). In reply to a question, Sai informed her tutor that she did not want to meet people of her own age so much as she wanted to travel. In fact, she had started reading frantically and books had made her restless. She had inherited her father's wanderlust, his 'urge for something beyond the ordinary' (69). She felt suffocated in the claustrophobic atmosphere of her grandfather's house where time did not move. Noni not only boosted her student's urge for going beyond the ordinary but also gave her a valuable piece of advice: "if you get a chance in life, take it. Look at me, I should have thought about the future when I was young. Instead, only when it was too late did I realize what I should have done long ago. . . . You must do it on your own, Sai" (69). On that very afternoon she wrote to the judge that she could no longer teach Sai science and mathematics and requested him to engage a more qualified tutor for the girl. The judge was angry with the spinster for her irresponsible behaviour. Nevertheless, he sent a letter to the principal of the local college requesting him to find a good science instructor for his granddaughter.

Chapter XIII

Within a few weeks, Gyan—a poor but promising student of science—appeared at Cho Oyu on the recommendation of the principal to replace Noni as Sai's tutor. He was a Nepalese youth who had just passed out of the college and was looking for a job. Gyan took the teaching assignment seriously. He enjoyed the walk to the judge's imposing colonial bungalow that gave him 'a refreshing and simple happiness' (71), although it was two hours' uphill journey from the unhygienic and poverty-stricken Bong Busti where he lived. At first, Sai was reluctant to be pulled out of her absorption in *National Geographic* and to be forced to sit in the dining room with the young student. But somehow she submitted to the incarceration that marked the beginning of a tempestuous love-affair between her, who was seventeen, and the tutor, who was twenty.

They sat in the dining room facing each other, with the equipments of study like ruler, pens, globe, graph paper and geometry box neatly arranged on the table before them. The instruments created a clinical ambience in the room which reminded the aged cook of the atmosphere in the chemist's shop where he occasionally went to seek advice and bring medicines for a variety of ailments he suffered from. His desire for modernity had prompted the cook to invest his trust in medical science and when he emerged from the clinic with the prescribed medicines, he felt 'virtuous': 'Oh yes, he awaited modernity and knew that if you invested in it, it would inform you that you were worth something in this world' (72). But the moment he met a person of his class, the Mon Ami maid Kesang or the Metal Box watchman or the hospital cleaner outside the clinic who would declaim against modernity and propel him towards superstitious mumbo jumbo ("Now there is no hope, now you'll have to do puja, it will cost many thousands of rupees"), he would begin to vacillate and doubt the efficacy of medicines. By the time he reached home, his faith in modern science would have completely vanished and he would have to return to the chemist the next day 'to recover his good sense' (72).

From their first encounter both Gyan and Sai become conscious of the strong spell each exerted on the other. While the cook sat on a stool outside the room, keeping a discreet eye on the student and the teacher and nodding his head approvingly at the latter's teaching skill, their minds, apparently engrossed in the discussion of atoms, would slowly begin to deflect and, 'like the evening hour opening to deeper depths outside, they would be swallowed into something more treacherous than the purpose for which Gyan had been hired' (73). Sai found the tutorial presence of Gyan—with his 'intense intelligence,' curly hair and serious eyes—rather compelling. Gyan, on the other hand, virtually ran away at the end of two hours' tuition without looking at Sai who had 'produced such a powerful effect upon him' (73). She became acutely conscious of his gaze on her and of her own appearance as a woman. For the first time in life, Sai undertook a thorough investigation of her physical beauty. But she 'found it was a changeable thing, beauty. No sooner did she locate it than it slipped from her grasp; instead of disciplining it, she was unable to refrain from exploiting its flexibility' (74). Standing before the mirror she rolled her eyes and smiled charmingly that 'transformed her expression from demon to queen' (74). She examined her small, jiggling but firm breasts and wondered whether they would 'give her a certain amount of bartering power' (74). As days went on, Sai became more and more obsessed with her appearance and whetted 'her appetite for something else' (74). She thought about her future in the company of two aged men in a disintegrating house and began to feel worried about her beauty: 'But if she continued forever in the company of two bandy-legged men, in this house in the middle of nowhere, this beauty, so brief she could barely hold it steady, would fade and expire, unsung, unrescued, and unrescuable' (74). The thought of being 'trapped forever in a place whose time had already passed' (74) filled her mind with sadness and fear so much so that she decided to 'propel herself into the future by whatever means possible' (74). Like her mother, Sai, too, sought an escape from the tediousness of her insignificant life through a romance.

Chapter XIV

Biju's struggle for a bare living in New York continued. He set out for the Queen of Tarts bakery from his basement shelter in Harlem very early in the morning. He remained always on alert, watching for the immigration cops who sometimes appeared from nowhere and interrogated illegal aliens like him. He somehow fell again and again through the cracks in the American immigration system. The bakery was located beneath a subway. As the underground trains passed with a deafening sound, their wheels sparking 'firework showers that at night threw a violent jagged brightness over the Harlem projects' (75), Biju and some others like him made 'a start on miniature lives' (75). He was greeted by the man from Zanzibar, Saeed Saeed, who was the most interesting character Biju had come across and admired in America. He was overwhelmed by a desire to befriend Saeed Saeed because of his confidence and adaptability which prevented him from drowning in the sea of humanity that was New York but helped him bob in the tide. Not only fellow illegals and Zanzibaris but also white Americans 'wished to cling to him like a plank during a shipwreck' (76). He teased the Americans who dined alone in a restaurant, and the 'overweight confidence-leached citizens' of the global superpower confided in him their secrets. Biju's admiration for Saeed Saeed, a black African and a Muslim, brought to the fore an inherent contradiction in his attitude and conduct. He remembered his earlier fight with a Pakistani national whose religion he had grown up to hate. But he could not bring himself to hate Saeed. Amazed by this attitudinal inconsistency he asked himself: "Saeed was kind and he was not Paki. Therefore he was Ok? The cow was not an Indian cow; therefore it was not holy? Therefore he liked Muslims and hated only Pakis? Therefore he liked Saeed, but hated the general lot of Muslims?" (76)

Biju was reminded of the prejudice of his villagers against black people—'the hubshi'—which he also shared and it only accentuated his dilemma: 'Therefore he hated all black people but liked Saeed?' (76) This habit of hatred was Biju's cultural inheritance and it had accompanied him to America. Like many Indians, he was awed by the white people who had done great harm to India but suffered from 'a lack of generosity regarding almost everyone else' (77), who had done no harm at all to his country. Saeed Saeed had also faced an identical dilemma about Biju. He had learnt from other restaurant kitchens how at the racial level, Indians were hated by every other nation both in the third and the first worlds, from Tanzania and Uganda to Guadeloupe. He had doubtlessly been warned about Indians but, unlike Biju, he did not suffer from any contradictions. His generous nature and buoyancy of spirit always kept him above such dilemmas. Saeed had many a girl friend. With his vivacity and dreadlocks, he won the hearts of white American girls who found him 'cute' and irresistible: 'Saeed described the beauty and the poverty of Zanzibar, and the girls' compassion rose like leavened loaf—how they wanted to save him, to take him home and lull him' (78). Biju was fascinated by Saeed's survival strategy and his enormous capacity for dodging the immigration authority: 'He had an endless talent with doors, even though, two years ago during an INS raid, he had been unearthed and deported despite having been cheek-to-cheek, Kodak-proof, with the best of America' (78). Even his photographs with the famous Americans like Mike Tyson and Naomi Campbell, which he had taken himself in a disposable camera while waiting outside nightclubs, could not prevent his deportation. Back in Zanzibar, where he was greeted as an American, he lazed on the sand and flirted with the rich and the beautiful girls who gave him their kangas to remember them by. But he returned to America in just two months' time with a new passport and a 'new name typed up with the help of a few greenbacks given to a clerk outside the government office' (79). Saeed 'jigged open every back door' and 'spectacularly sabotaged' (79) the American immigration system but, paradoxically, he also pledged his emotional allegiance to the country. As the narrator puts it humorously: "The country recognized something in Saeed, he in it, and it was a mutual love affair. Ups and downs, sometimes more sour than sweet, maybe, but nonetheless, beyond anything the INS could imagine, it was an old-fashioned romance" (79).

But no such romance was in store for Biju who drudged away at the bakery and, often shaken by the terrible noise of extra heavy transport passing the subway overhead whose 'jolting rhythm travelled up through his defenceless shoes' (79), felt apprehensive about his father His innocence was destroyed by the panicked thoughts ('Ill. Dead. Maimed') of his old father whom he had left behind to pursue his American dream.

Back in Kalimpong, the cook basked in a feeling of patronizing superiority over other fathers who sought his—and Biju's—assistance to find jobs in America for their unemployed sons. He was initially disturbed by such requests and suffered from a conflict within him 'between generosity and meanness' (80). But ultimately his munificence got the better of his selfishness and, in order to 'bolster his son and his own pride' (80), he agreed to write to Biju requesting him to help others to migrate to and find employment in America: "Dear beta, please see if you can help" (80). The very fact that he had a son in America improved his status in the eyes of the people. He felt 'snug and glad' to be able to help others and the letters 're-established Biju in his father's eyes as a fine-suited and booted success' (80). Meanwhile, the craze for a green card made Biju restless in New York. But he could not apply for naturalization like other illegal immigrants like Saeed because Indians were brazenly discriminated against: "Saeed applied for the immigration lottery each year, but Indians were not allowed to apply. Bulgarians, Irish, Malagasys—on and on the list went, but no, no Indians" (81). He watched how his fellow workers at the bakery called the immigration hotline at night to know the results of the lottery and, confronted with questions regarding their status, put down the telephone quickly 'worried that immigration had a super duper . . . high alert electronic supersonic space speed machine' (81) that could trace their number and detect their illegality. The failure to procure a green card made him so fretful that he would often cross to the river bank and loiter alone in 'a dense chamber of green' which had grown from the 'fertile city crud' (81) and which made him feel strangely nostalgic about his village life. At such moments he suffered from an ambivalent attitude towards America and gave vent to his contradictory feelings for his father: "Biju couldn't help but feel a flash of anger at his father for sending him alone to this country, but he knew he wouldn't have forgiven his father for not trying to send him, either" (82).

Chapter XV

This chapter introduces the readers to the picturesque town of Kalimpong and some of its important landmarks. The novelist presents a sketch of the mossy Indian hill station on a busy market day to suggest the peaceful co-existence of its mixed population before the Gorkhas' mobilization for a separate state that would become increasingly militant and engulf the quiet Himalayan burg in an unprecedented outburst of violence. Kiran Desai wrote these sections of the novel in Kalimpong, staying in a wild and beautiful house lent to her for the period and learning the hard and lonely way to be a writer. Her descriptions of both the place and its people thus come across as authentic. More so because when she had been growing up, Kiran briefly went to school in Kalimpong's St. Joseph's Convent and she knew some of the characters who figure in this novel. The narrative traces, like a cinematographer's camera, all the places the cook visits and all the people he meets in the town. The cook's experience in the bazaar is interspersed with his memories of the time when he had first come to Kalimpong with the judge and witnessed some historic incidents like the arrival of the deposed Dalai and Panchen Lamas from Chinese occupied Tibet, presenting thereby a contrast between the previous glory of the town where wool caravans arrived, 'chaperoned by Tibetan muleteers in furry boots' (84), and people used to come from outside to sample the 'exquisite scent of pine' (84), and its present-day squalor evoked by the 'greasy bus station with its choking smell of exhaust' and 'the dark cubbyhole where, behind a soiled red curtain, [one] could pay to watch on a shaking screen such films as Rape of Erotic Virgin and SHE: The Secrets of Married Life' (84). The cook came to the town on a 'haat day' when 'a festive crowd thronged to the market in a high pitch of excitement, everyone in their best clothes' (83). He sat on a bench beneath a flowering plum tree and, disregarding the jovial crowd around him, began to read Biju's letter which had just arrived from America with the news that he had found a new job in a bakery where the owner left them in complete charge. Ecstatic at the news, the cook carefully put the letter in his pocket and plunged into the bustling haat, which is described very realistically by the narrator:

> he descended steeply into the *haat*, pushing his way between bent and bowed Nepali ladies with golden nose rings dangling and Tibetan women with braids and prayer beads, between those who had walked from faraway villages to sell muddy mushrooms. . . . Powders, oils, and ganglions of roots were proffered by Lepcha medicine men; other stalls offered yak hair, untidy and rough as the hair of demons, and sacks of miniature dried shrimp with oversized whiskers; there were smuggled foreign goods from Nepal, perfumes, jean jackets, electronics; there were kukri sickles, sheets of plastic rainproofing, and false teeth. (83-84)

The cook boastfully divulged the news of Biju's success to everyone he met in the market and added for the listener's edification his own version of affluent America where his son lived: "New York. Very big city. The cars . . . and buildings are nothing like here. In that country, there is food for everybody" (84). He even hoped that one day his son would take him from this poverty-ridden country to that land of wish-fulfilment. He thus derived immense satisfaction from Biju's misconstrued position in America and the hope of getting united with him sustained the aged and infirm cook in his miserable life as an underpaid menial in the judge's family. The thought of his son's success even made him magnanimous, so much so that when the manager of Snow Lion Travel Agency, which sold tourists trips to the neighbouring states of Sikkim, Nepal and Bhutan, told him half jokingly: "When you go to America, take me along also" (85), he readily agreed. Without any idea of the country and its harsh treatment of illegal immigrants, he promised the manager: "Yes, yes. I will take us all. That country has lots of room. It's this country that is so crowded" (85). His confidence seemed to stem from Biju's assurance that he had been saving money to buy an air ticket for his father. The cook felt proud of his son, who had enhanced his prestige in the eyes of the people, and he believed that 'One day his son would accomplish all that Sai's parents had failed to do, all the judge had failed to do' (85). He walked past the Apollo Deaf Tailors without saying anything because 'they would literally turn a deaf ear just as they did to customer complaints' (85), and entered into Lark's store to buy tea, noodles and condensed milk for the judge's kitchen. There he encountered the most important person in the town, the doctor who also had her son in America, and informed her of Biju's new job. On his way back home in the dusk, the proud and joyful father broke the news even to the labourers 'carrying heavy loads uphill.' He told both Mrs. Sen and Lola, unaware of the bitter rivalry between the neighbours over England and America. It is interesting to note that in Kiran Desai's novel, the lovers of British colonial rule in India clash with the followers of the new American dream. But, ironically, the battle of the empires is fought not in the West but on the Indian soil years after the country's emancipation from foreign rule. The cook also told the news of his son's achievement to the Afghan princesses, who gave him money to bring them a chicken each time he went to the market, to the monks who played football outside the monastery, and, finally, to drunk Uncle Potty and his friend, the Swiss Priest Father Booty who were dancing on the former's veranda. Before returning home, he stopped at the last stall on the road to buy some groceries and found the owner's daughter at the counter, a lovely and plump girl. The thought of negotiating Biju's marriage with the girl crossed his mind: 'Surely Biju would like her?' (86). There was a rumour in the town that the girl's father had made a lot of money. But to the cook 'money wasn't every thing' (86). He was more interested in the 'simple happiness' of life that could he obtained through 'looking after someone and having someone look after you' (88).

Chapter XVI

The journey of orphaned Sai from the boarding school in Dehra Dun to the crumbling bungalow of his retired grandfather in Kalimpong implies, in a sense, a cognitive journey of a hapless and sensitive individual in search of identity and familial roots. It is only natural, therefore, that the teenage girl should feel curious about her origin, her grandparents who had brought her mother on this earth. As Sai fell in love with Gyan, she became interested in the love affair of the judge with his wife and began to pester the cook to tell her about it. At first the cook gave her his own fantastic version of his master's relationship with his wife, one he had told other servants of the town to enhance his prestige in their eyes. Sai's grandmother, he said, was a great lady who was very kind to her servants and her husband loved her so much that the sorrow of her death made him a cruel man. Sai was amazed by the incredible story because such love was unexpected from a selfish man like her grandfather who had thoughtlessly disowned his own daughter. At her insistence, the cook finally came out with the truth and told her what he really knew: 'He did not like her at all. She went mad' (88). The judge's wife was the daughter of a rich man who hailed from a very distinguished family, one of much higher standing than that of Jemubhai. They married only among fifteen families of Gujarat but her father made an exception for Jemubhai because he was an ICS. She was a very beautiful woman with delicate features and her complexion was so fair that one could easily have mistaken her for a foreigner.

Sai was not satisfied with this meagre information; she wanted to know more about her family and its tradition. So she mustered courage and confronted her grandfather, 'sitting poised like a heron over his chessboard' (88), with a straightforward question: "Who was my grandmother?" Her query discomposed the guilt-ridden judge and compelled him to think about his wife whom he had wanted to forget: "He didn't want to think of her, but the picture that came to mind was surprisingly gentle" (89). Jemubhai was the first boy of their community who had studied his way out of the pettiness of family circumstances and was preparing to go to an English university. His father, who had been dreaming to send him to England and make him an ICS, borrowed money from rapacious money-lenders at an excessively high rate of interest to meet the expenses. Since that was not enough, the family began to search for a bride with lucrative dowry bids: 'The dowry bids poured in and his father began an exhilarated weighing and tallying: ugly face—a little more gold, a pale skin—a little less. A dark and ugly daughter of a rich man seemed their best bet' (89). Instead they found the beautiful daughter of a very rich merchant and financier, Bomanbhai Patel, who lived in the posh area of Piphit. Bomanbhai was the inheritor of a thriving business started by his father who had prudently helped the British in a skirmish with the Gaekwads and, in return, received from the colonial rulers a contract to supply horse feed to their army cantonment. In course of time, the family amassed immense wealth by monopolizing the delivery of all dry goods to the army. Bomanbhai had extended the business, for greater profit, by supplying unauthorized women to the sex-starved British soldiers. But he kept his own wife and daughters strictly behind the purdah in a fortified haveli which enhanced his honour within his community. While his womenfolks led an idle, extravagant but orthodox life inside the zenana, flooded with costly silk and rare pieces of jewels sold by foreign traders and bankrupt maharajas, Bomanbhai 'began to acquire little fancies and foibles, to cultivate certain eccentricities that, just as he plotted, reiterated the security of his wealth and reinforced his honour all over again' (90). He exhibited his wealth and expensive habits to the people in a casual, though carefully planned, manner. He reached the acme of his triumph when he, a bania by origin, hired a Brahmin cook for his kitchen. This clever and unscrupulous merchant was filled with ambition when he got the wind of Jemubhai's imminent departure to England for the ICS examination: 'Ambition still gnawed at him, and Brahmin cook he might have, but he knew that there was a wider world and only very rarely did history provide a chink allowing an acrobatic feat' (90). Without wasting any time he met Jemubhai's father and stunned him with the offer of his most beautiful daughter, Bela, for his son. It was a marriage of convenience. Jemu married Bela (her name was changed into Nimi after marriage by his family according to its custom) for the money he required for his passage to England. His family had agreed to the proposal in the hope that the boy, their best bet, would bring his community into the modern age, while the calculating father of the girl thought: 'If Jemu succeeded in his endeavour, she would be the wife of one of the most powerful men in India' (91). The lavish wedding party lasted for a week and the bridegroom received a huge dowry that included, among other valuable things, 'a ticket for passage on the SS Strathnaver from Bombay to Liverpool' (91). Jemu left for England within a month of his marriage, even before he could know his wife well. Despite the prodding of his younger uncles and 'a focused and defined urge in himself' (92), he could not bring himself to deflower the fourteen-year-old girl and felt genuinely sorry when she started crying at his attempt to pull off her sari. The only happy memory of his married life was a cycle ride together. One day, when his family was out selling the jewels given by Bomanbhai as dowry to collect extra money for him, he carried her on his father's Hercules bi-cycle and pedalled very fast along the village path, between trees and grazing cows. As the cycle flew down a slope, 'their hearts were left behind for an instant, levitating amid green leaves, blue sky' (92).

When the judge's mind returned from recollection of the past to his chessboard, he found that his granddaughter had climbed up a tree at the end of the garden to catch a glimpse of her tutor's approach. A curious tension had started growing between Sai and Gyan with each succeeding week of science teaching so much so that 'they could barely sit in the same room without desiring to flee' (92). But the moment they separated from each other, they began to feel restless and wait for the next meeting with increasing anticipation. The judge ordered Sai to get down from the tree and warned her against any possible emotional involvement with Gyan: "I hope that tutor of yours doesn't get any funny ideas" (93). She carried out her grandfather's order without protest but revolted against him inwardly. As she went indoors to shut herself up in her room, she remembered the advice of her former tutor Noni ("Don't go in for a life where time doesn't pass" [93]) and decided to leave the place where time stood still. Sai's desire to leave Cho Oyu and move on was thus prompted by her grandfather's retrogressive attitude which she detested. The judge was a guilt-ridden soul who lived exclusively in the past. For him time did not move towards the future and the only spatial expansion that his troubled psyche could experience was in terms of repetitive revisitations of the past that only contributed to his irremediable sense of guilt.

Chapter XVII

While Biju felt angry with his father for sending him alone to America, back in Kalimpong the cook felt a sense of positional superiority over, and adopted a condescending attitude to, those who had 'sons in the queue ready to be sent' (94). He was 'besieged by requests for help' (94) from the desperate fathers who brought him small gifts and offered him drinks until 'he was beginning to feel as if he were a politician, a bestower of favours, a receiver of thanks' (94). But gradually his smugness was sublimated into a genuine philanthropic ardour and he requested his son to help others and find jobs for them in America: "Biju beta . . . you have been fortunate enough to get there, please do something for the others" (95). He sent him 'a whole shoal of letters' many of which were lost on the way but enough reached Biju's address in Harlem that he felt he 'might drown' (95). Saeed sympathized with Biju and shared his helplessness because their problems were identical. His mother too dispensed his address and telephone number to everyone who sought them in Stone Town. And the desperate young men from Zanzibar arrived at John F. Kennedy airport with one dollar bill and his phone number in their pockets, seeking shelter in his small apartment that was already filled with men, 'every scrap rented out' (95). The flow of immigrants continued uninterrupted in spite of the fact that the American authority had introduced such strict regulation that it was very hard to get a visa. He admitted his helplessness to Biju, "More tribes, more tribes. I wake up, go to the window, and there—MORE TRIBES. Every time I look—ANOTHER TRIBE" (96). One day Saeed was telling stories of Stone Town to his fellow workers at Queen of Tarts when he looked out of the window and in a second slipped under the counter, whispering in an alarmed voice: 'Oh my-eeee God! Tribes, man, it's the tribes. Please God. Tell them I don't work here" (96). Biju's reaction to the group of men, 'looking weary as if they'd been travelling several life times,' who had come to the restaurant to seek assistance from a compatriot in the alien country was deplorable like that of Omar who asked Saeed annoyingly: "Why do you help? I stopped helping and now they all know I won't help and nobody comes to me" (96). While Omar's remark smacked of abject selfishness, Biju's response evinced his abominable delight in his friend's predicament. In reply to Saeed's question: "What are they doing?," he said, "They are still standing and looking," 'feeling brave and excited by someone else's misfortune. He was almost hopping' (97). He even felt 'a measure of pride in delivering this vital news' (97), just as he nourished a sense of privileged superiority over those acquaintances of his community in Kalimpong who sought his assistance for migrating to America. Ironically, Biju had experienced the same humiliation when, after his arrival in New York, he approached his father's friend Nandu, who lived with taxi-drivers in Queens, for help: 'Nandu had also not answered the phone and had tried to hide when Biju arrived on his doorstep, and then when he thought Biju had left, had opened the door and to his distress found Biju still standing there two hours later' (98). Instead of offering any help, he advised Biju to go back to India, and finally he brought his friend's son to the basement in Harlem and abandoned him among foreigners. Biju never saw him again. Saeed's generosity did not let him to be selfish like Omar and Biju and refuse help to the desperate tribes from Zanzibar. Despite his own precarious position, he could not help sharing his food and shelter with those men who had fled from poverty and deprivation in their native country to the affluent West in search of a better living. As he says to his friends: "You can't say this is my food, like Americans, and only I will eat it. . . . In Zanzibar what one person have he have to share with everyone, that is good, that is the right way—"

"But then everyone have nothing, man! That is why I leave Zanzibar." (98) Biju was filled with profound sympathy for this humanitarian soul and felt ashamed 'that he would never help all those people praying for his help, waiting daily, hourly, for his response' (98).

His sense of uppish superiority over the young men of his community who could not manage to migrate to America was swamped by this feeling of shame which was further intensified by his failure to procure a green card without which he would not be able to return home: 'The green card the green card. . . . Without it he couldn't leave. To leave he wanted a green card. This was the absurdity' (99). The more he grew desperate for a green card, the more envious he became of the 'legalized foreigners' whom he found shopping at 'discount baggage stores for the miraculous, expandable third-world suitcase' (99), and sensed the despair of 'those who lived and died illegal in America and never saw their families, not for ten years, twenty, thirty, never again' (99). Kiran Desai authentically depicts the craze for legalized citizenship in America among illegal third-world nationals who could contemplate marrying a deformed person holding a green card: 'Even a disabled or mentally retarded green card holder would be fine' (100). Biju, like his co-workers at the bakery, spent his spare hours in futile attempts to obtain a green card which emptied his savings. Led by Saeed Saeed, they went to Washington Heights and waited on a street corner till 'a battered van came by and they paid into the cracked open door, handed over their photographs taken according to INS requirements . . . and were thumb printed through the crack' (101). Week after week they waited but the 'van did not come back' (101). In order to console themselves, some of them visited whores but Biju abstained from such ventures for lack of courage and adaptability and his ingrained cultural taboos.

Before long they lost their jobs as the Queen of Tarts bakery was closed by health inspectors on receiving complaints from its customers that they had found dead rats inside loaves. Saeed Saeed soon found employment in a shop ironically named 'Banana Republic' which was 'synonymous with colonial exploitation and the rapacious ruin of the third world' (102). Biju joined the 'shadow class' of illegal immigrants who were condemned to ceaseless movement: 'The men left for other jobs, towns, got deported, returned home, changed names. Sometimes someone came popping around a corner again, or on the subway, then they vanished again. Addresses, phone numbers did not hold' (102). He returned to his basement shelf at night with a feeling of emptiness and reminisced about his peaceful village life spent in the company of his grandmother and the simple happiness it offered. It is interesting to note that India was the place that Biju, like many others, had dreamed of leaving for its backwardness and lack of opportunities. But once in New York, he was not immune to nostalgia. Jobless and disappointed, he was assaulted by memory of home so powerfully that he could feel the pulse of the forest, smell the humid air, hear the sound of silver grasses, and visualize enkindled earthen lamps floating down the river on Diwali night.

Chapter XVIII

Kiran Desai's novel delineates a world in which almost all the characters are shown to either betray or fall victims to a bestial instinct which is absolutely unbecoming of human beings and their civilized mode of conduct. This bestiality is symbolically represented in the beginning of this chapter through a striking posture of a subhuman creature, the pet dog of the reclusive judge. It was the end of the prolonged summer, with visible signs of the approach of storm clouds in the sky and a peculiar tension in the air which Sai had confused with Gyan's presence. She sat out on the lawn with his grandfather when the dog started behaving strangely: 'Mutt, catching sight of the shadow of her own tail, leapt and caught it, began to whiz around and around, confused as to whose tail it was. She would not let go, but her eyes expressed confusion and beseeching—how could she stop? What should she do?—she had caught a strange beast and didn't know it was herself. She went skittering helplessly about the garden' (105). Mutt fought with her own shadow which she confused with a 'strange beast.' Kiran Desai brilliantly traces the source of the pervasive savagery that marks her fictional world to the instinctive bestiality in man, the civilized and rational animal who resorts to violence when he becomes confused and fails, like the dog, to know that it is himself he is fighting with. Equally commendable is the ingenuity with which the novelist describes the advent of the storm and the onset of rain in Kalimpong.

> Then, in a flash, it was upon them. An anxious sound came from the banana trees as they began to flap their great ears for they were always the first to sound the alarm. The masts of bamboo were flung together and rang with the sound of an ancient martial art. . . . The sky gaped, lit

> by flame; blue fire ensnared the pine tree that sizzled to an instant death leaving a charcoal stump, a singed smell, a crosshatch of branches over the lawn. An unending rain broke on them. (105)

The arrival of monsoon after the searing heat of summer elicited different responses from the judge, his pet dog and his granddaughter. While Mutt was panicked by the storm and rain that changed her into 'a primitive life form' (105), the judge hated 'the dingy season' because it 'made a mockery of him [and] his ideals' (110). But Sai remained 'calm and cheerful' during the 'aqueous season' (106) because it was 'the only time when her life in Kalimpong was granted perfect sense' (106). She rode the changing moods of the season when all over the town 'modernity began to fail' (106). She found release from the stranglehold of tension that had been built up between Gyan and her as the tutorial session was interrupted by continuous rain which also temporarily subdued the mounting political unrest in the hills.

Yet, it was during this 'wet diarrheal season' (106) that the green romance of the student and the tutor burgeoned. The story of love between Sai and Gyan that constitutes the nucleus of the Kalimpong part of the narrative, unfolded in the grim backdrop of a politically disturbed milieu when India was virtually reeling under the biggest and the most formidable challenge to her integration after independence. The time was mid-1980s and various separatist forces attempted to disintegrate the country: "The country, Sai noted, was coming apart at the seams: police unearthing militants in Assam, Nagaland and Mizoram; Punjab on fire with Indira Gandhi dead and gone in October of last year" (108). Things were falling apart as the centre could not hold the nation together. But Sai and Gyan's romance continued to intensify despite the geo-political upheavals. Between storms, when the rain paused and the sun appeared in the sky, Gyan—worried about the tuition—arrived at Cho Oyu to pick up the discontinued thread of mathematics lesson. Sai could no longer hide her deep concern for Gyan. One afternoon, after an hour of teaching, Gyan wanted to leave in the midst of torrential rain and thunder but she prevented him, saying: "Don't . . . you might get killed by lightning" (108). He was persuaded by Sai and the cook to spend the night at Cho Oyu as it would be difficult for him to find his way home through the stormy night. But her grandfather was annoyed by the tutor's presence which he felt to be an "insolence, a liberty driven if not by intent then certainly by foolishness" (109). Gyan's unease at the dinner table reminded him of his own diffident youth: 'He detected an obvious lack of familiarity, a hesitance with the cutlery and the food' (109). But the resemblance proved to be deeper than mere lack of confidence. For, Gyan 'carried an unmistakable whiff of journey, of ambition—and an old emotion came back to the judge, a recognition of weakness that was not merely a feeling, but also a taste, like fever' (109) The embittered old man could not resist 'a sinister urge' to catch the naïve youth off guard by asking him a slighting question: "so, what poets are you reading these days, young man?" Sai's concern for her tutor again betrayed itself when she hastened to protect him from the embarrassing situation and defended him by saying, "He is a science student" (109). Gyan, however, obliged the old man by reciting a poem from Tagore's *Gitanjali*. His recitation unlocked invisible and firmly closed doors in the troubled mind of the judge and he went down memory lane to his own student life in England.

The judge led a solitary life in Cambridge. Unable to bear the ridicule of peers and British girls, who laughed at his imperfect pronunciation and his smell, he took refuge in the library. There he spent the day time, reading extensively about the British account of India—the expedition to Gujarat and the arrival of the East India Company in Bombay—which made him feel 'greedy for a country that was already his' (110). He left the books only to go to the lavatory for 'the daily trial of his digestion' (110). The English food did not suit Jemubhai's digestive system and he had developed a painful constipation. Nevertheless, he worked very hard, almost eighteen hours a day to equip himself for the ICS Examination: 'He measured out a reading calendar, listed each book, each chapter in a complex chart' (111). He read late into the night in his rented room. He shunned human company and developed friendship only with the landlady's dog who begged him for a share of his food, 'drooling damp patches on to his lap, raking an insistent paw across his knees and wrecking the pleat of his corduroys' (111). But despite such hard labour and meticulous preparation, he could not fare well in the viva voce of the Open Competitive Examination. He failed to answer some of the questions he was asked but pledged his unquestioned allegiance to the colonial administration and recited one of his favourite poems (Tennyson's 'Lochinvar') for his examiners. While most of the Indian candidates for the ICS 'had crisp-ironed their speech' (112) before the examination, Jemubhai's English 'still had the rhythm and the form of Gujerati' (112) because he had barely communicated with anybody for whole years. Thus, when he finished his recitation and looked up, he found that all his examiners were giggling. The memory of the humiliating experience now made the judge angry, so much so that he stood up, put down his fork and knife 'in devastating judgment upon himself' (113) and left the dinner table abruptly, uttering loudly: "Damn fool." Gyan's unease at this unexpected turn of events mortified Sai and she became 'hot with shame' (113). She apologized repeatedly for her grandfather's behaviour and 'his eyes rested directly upon her as if he were eating her alive in an orgy of the imagination' (113). Sai felt relieved because she found '[at] last the proof' (113) of his love. Left alone in the drawing room amidst hammering rain and howling wind that made speech impossible, they began to examine and measure each other's limbs which led to a strange physical intimacy between the two. But Sai could not stand when Gyan touched her lips and traced them with his fingers. She leapt up suddenly and, like her grandfather, left for her own room after finally wishing him good night. She made her way to the door like a drunk and vanished into the dark 'with Gyan's bereft eyes following her' (116). Meanwhile, the judge could not sleep in the privacy of his bedroom and the comforting company of his pet dog, because the memory triggered by the tutor's recitation continued to chase him. Even a calmpose failed to drive away the unpleasant thoughts unleashed at dinner from his mind. He was compelled, against his wishes, to revisit the past. As the three other inhabitants of the bungalow—Sai, Gyan and the cook—lay awake in their respective rooms pursuing their own thoughts amidst the deafening sound of wind and rain and the blinding flash of lightning that 'shamelessly unzipped the sky' (120), the judge picked up the lost thread of memory and ruminated about the last phase of his student life in England. Jemubhai passed the ICS examination by securing the lowest qualifying marks and was placed at the bottom of a supplementary list of successful candidates. Having discovered his name in the list he, 'the newest member . . . of the heaven-born' (117), sent a telegram to his father and ran straight back to his rented room. While his father, whose dream had come true, 'exploded with joy' (118) and distributed sweets among neighbours and acquaintances, Jemubhai lay on his bed 'crying for three days and three nights' (117). He soon moved to a new and more expensive lodging where he met his only friend in England, a Bengali ICS with the surname Bose. They had a lot of similarities between themselves: 'similar inadequate clothes, similar forlornly empty rooms, similar poor native's trunks' (118), but Bose differed from the judge in one major respect: he was an incorrigible optimist. He became Jemubhai's mentor during the years of probation. Bose not only corrected his pronunciation but also refined his taste. It was during this period that the judge's personality underwent a complete transformation. He rooted out the last remnant of ethnicity and native culture from his system and shamelessly aped the English: 'the judge eventually took revenge on his early confusions, his embarrassments gloved in something called "keeping up standards," his accent behind a mask of a quiet. He found he began to be mistaken for something he wasn't—a man of dignity. This accidental poise became more important than any other thing. He envied the English. He loathed Indians. He worked at being English with the passion of hatred' (119). But this ill-conceived attempt to emulate the colonial masters and hate the native people eventually backfired. Because, 'for what he would become, he would be despised by absolutely everyone, English and Indians, both' (119).

Chapter XIX

The American part of *The Inheritance of Loss* comprises tartly observed sharp vignettes about the price of immigration from the poor third world to the affluent West more than a plot-driven narrative with real suspense. In scene after scene, the novel depicts how people from every corner of this globalized world rush to America, the new El Dorado, to share its opulence and plentiful material resources as a means of living a more comfortable and dignified life. In the process, they fall victims to the terrible cruelty of the system of immigration and lose their innocence, honesty and basic human dignity. The novel examines lives which are forced, by circumstances, to be those of uncertainty, fear and hypocrisy. The happiness they seek proves to be elusive and their adventures in the grim underbelly of the American dream do not add up to anything worth inheriting. This chapter shows how some of Biju's acquaintances like Saeed, who fail to secure American citizenship through legal means, adopt a dishonest strategy and unconscientiously play the game of marrying and divorcing white women for a green card which sustains their life and fulfils their dream of earning dollars.

Biju—still jobless—met Saeed on the street. Saeed was oddly dressed, 'wearing a white kurta pajama with sunglasses, gold chain, and platform shoes, his dreadlocks tied in a ponytail' (121). He informed Biju that he had given up the job at Banana Republic because its owner was a gay who made indecent approaches ("My boss, I swear he keep grabbing my ass," he said.), and that he had married a white American girl who was a waitress in the restaurant where he now worked as a cook. It was a marriage of convenience, because he had wed the girl for a green card. He himself admits, in reply to wonder-struck Biju's question: "Who did you marry???," that he had married 'Toys': "All of a sudden they ask for my green card, say they forget to look when I apply, so I ask her, 'Will you marry me for papers?" (121). He was now practising with his paper wife for the INS (Immigration and Naturalization Service) interview. The marriage had proved expensive for Saeed because the girl preferred costly dress and fast-food. He had visited her family of 'long-haired Vermont hippies,' who fed on organic and unprocessed food, and had taken pictures with them for the INS photo album. They loved him as their son-in-law but also pitied him for his obvious dislike for their food. Saeed, who relished white rice and white bread, had to join their dog that 'shared his dislike for the burdock burger [and] the nettle soup' (122). But this humiliation could not diminish his admiration for the United States, which was 'a wonderful country' in his eyes, and her people whom he regarded as 'the most delightful in the world' (122). The family became happy to learn about his attempts to sabotage the immigration system in the country with 'faked-up papers' and passports (he had two passports, one for Saeed Saeed and the other for Zulfikar) and promised to help him in any 'subversion against the U.S. government' (122). The girl's grandmother had even written a letter to INS authority certifying that they knew Zulfikar from Zanzibar who was 'a cherished new member of their family that belonged to 'the ancient clan of Mayflower Williams' (122). Biju was stunned by Saeed's marital adventure to hoodwink the system but he could not bring himself to follow the strategy. On his way back home, he tried to smile at some American women and draw their attention by saying: "Hi, Hi." But they did not look at him. America thus rejected Biju as England had rejected Jemubhai Patel years ago.

Meanwhile, modernity had completely collapsed in Kalimpong due to continuous and heavy rainfall. No letters could come from the plains due to landslides and telephones did not work for the failure of microwave. The cook uselessly visited the post office to see if Biju's letters had come and Lola's hysterical efforts to make a phone call to her daughter from a STD booth did not bear fruit. The two melancholy souls met in the market, commiserated with each other for a moment and then parted ways. The cook left for the butcher while Lola went to buy some Baygon spray for her home. Throughout the 'fecund season' (123) she killed scores of tiny insects by applying this spray. But even her poison could not destroy the fertility of the insect world: 'Each day a thousand new ones were born. . . . Entire nations appeared boldly overnight' (123).

Chapter XX

The newly sprouted romance of Gyan and Sai blossomed with the passing weeks. Throughout the rainy season they developed a physical intimacy by examining and measuring each other's limbs. Sai presented the 'world's most astonishing tongue display' (124) while Gyan showed her how he 'could wiggle his eyebrows, slide his head off his neck from left to right to left like a Bharat Natyam dancer, and . . . could stand on his head' (124). Very often she would remember certain aspects of her beauty she had noticed during her own examination of her body before the mirror and display them to her tutor-lover 'like items taken from under the counter and put before a discerning customer in one of the town's curio shops' (125) But he could never measure the depth of her large and beautiful eyes because 'her glance proved too slippery to hold' (125). With the discovery of 'the newness of landscape between them' (124), they started playing, under the tutorial pretext, 'the game of courtship, reaching, retreating, teasing, fleeing' (125). The exploration of their anatomies ate up the hours until 'the situation was driven to the same desperate pitch of the days when they sat forcing geometry' (125). Emboldened by her compliance, Gyan pleaded her to kiss him one day. Though she was frightened at first by the request, Sai finally obliged him: 'she closed her eyes and felt the terrified measure of his lips on hers, trying to match one shape with the other' (125). Soon they became shameless like beggars and craved madly for more. The lovers kissed each other's parts from nose to toes, and 'linked word, object and affection in a rediscovery of childhood, a confirmation of wholeness' (126).

Engrossed with themselves, Sai and Gyan did not notice what was happening outside and their romance burgeoned amidst growing discontent of the ethnic Nepalis of the Darjeeling hills who were agitating for a separate state: 'Gyan was twenty and Sai sixteen, and at the beginning they had not paid very much attention to the events on the hillside, the new posters in the market referring to old discontents, the slogans scratched and painted on the side of government offices and shops. "We are stateless," they read, "It is better to die than live as slaves." "We are constitutionally tortured. Return our land from Bengal" (126). Initially it was dismissed as nothing more serious than the usual grievance of a handful of unemployed students and disgruntled agitators. But before long the movement took a concrete shape and assumed a grim dimension. One day fifty members of the youth wing of the GNLF publicly took an oath to fight unto death for the formation of their own state, Gorkhaland, and marched down the streets of Darjeeling, waving their unsheathed kukris. And quite suddenly, the term 'insurgency' began to float in the air. The political turmoil that broke out in the hills would soon draw the young lovers into its vortex and stymie their fledgling romance.

Chapter XXI

The political background of the GNLF movement for a separate state is provided in this chapter through a conversation between the two aged Bengali sisters, Lola the widow and Noni the spinster. The discussion, which also revealed the attitude of the privileged community in Kalimpong to the new trouble in the hills, took place one afternoon when they were sipping tea in their drawing room after Sai's lesson. While Noni conceded that the Indian Nepalis' demand was partially justified ("They have a point," said Noni, "maybe not their whole point but . . . half to three-quarters of their point" [127]), Lola, dismissed it as 'nonsense' and unjustified. She constructed a hateful, racial perspective for the movement and viewed it as a heinous conspiracy to disintegrate the country: "Those Neps will be after all outsiders now, but especially us Bongs. They've been plotting this a long while. Dream come true. All kinds of atrocities will go on—then they can skip merrily over the border to hide in Nepal. Very convenient" (127). Lola traced the root of the demand for a separate state to the Nehruvian policy of re-organization of Indian states after Independence which she regarded as the 'biggest mistake' (128) committed by the country's first prime minister. Because the political decision to divide and re-organize the bigger states on the basis of language and other related issues had only encouraged fissiparous tendencies and secessionist forces which posed a great threat to national integrity: '"This state-making," Lola continued, "biggest mistake that fool Nehru made. Under his rules any group of idiots can stand up demanding a new state and get it, too. How many new ones keep appearing? From fifteen we went to sixteen, sixteen to seventeen, seventeen to twenty two." Lola made a line with a finger from above her ear and drew noodles in the air to demonstrate her opinion of such madness' (128).

Through this disparaging remark she made it clear what she thought of Nehru and his policy. The present trouble in the hills, however, had begun with the accession of Sikkim to India during the final term of Indira Gandhi in power. Nehru's scheming daughter had contrived a plebiscite in the Himalayan state to vote its sovereign ruler out of power. All the Nepalis, who had flooded Sikkim from every corner of India, were encouraged to vote against the king so that India could swallow 'the jewel-coloured kingdom' (128). Encouraged by the success of their 'dirty trick' in Sikkim, the Nepalis, according to Lola, had begun to have grand ideas and think of repeating the experiment in Darjeeling and Kalimpong which had always been highly sensitive areas situated as the places were near India's international border with Nepal, Bhutan and China. Noni, the younger sister who represented the virtue of unprejudiced sanity and commonsense, took, on the other hand, a more lenient and sympathetic view of the worries of Indian Nepalis about their long-suppressed geo-ethnic identity and their demand for self-determination through the formation of a separate state, Gorkhaland. The difference in the attitudes of the two sisters to the knotty problem, which was about to engulf the entire region in an unprecedented eruption of violence, was also evident from the following talk:

> "But you have to take it from their point of view," said Noni. "First the Neps were thrown out of Assam and then Meghalaya, then there's the king of Bhutan growling against—"
>
> "Illegal immigration," said Lola. . . .
>
> "Obviously the Nepalis are worried," said Noni. "They've been here, most of them, several generations. Why shouldn't Nepali be taught in schools?"
>
> "Because on that basis they can start statehood demands." (128)

By giving arguments both in favour of and against the Gorkhaland agitation, Kiran Desai proves that she does not take political sides. Emboldened by the separatist movements in other parts of India, like Punjab, Kashmir and the north-eastern states, the Nepalis had organized themselves and formed the Gorkha National Liberation Front to achieve their aim. They had written letters to the British queen and the presidents of America and the Soviet Union requesting those foreign heads of states to interfere on their behalf and save them from the 'colonial subjugation' (129) of India.

Mrs. Sen, Lola's neighbour and rival who joined the discussion later, further problematized the issue of national integration by examining it from a communal perspective. A Hindu chauvinist herself, she hated Pakistan and viewed the vivisection of India to create the land of the pure as the origin of all the problems in the sub-continent: "Pakistan! There is the problem. . . . First heart attack to our country, no, that has never been healed—" (129). Muslim-bashing was one of her favourite pastimes and with her 'ready-made thoughts and opinions' she gave vent to her unabashedly communal prejudice whenever she found an opportunity. Mrs. Sen ascribed the country's ills to the explosion of Muslim population: "More Muslims in India than in Pakistan. They prefer to multiply over here" (130). For this, she held the ignorance of the community and their lack of modernity responsible: "They have nothing better to do, you know. Without TV and electricity, there will always be this problem" (130). She even called the Muslims hypocrites ('two faced') and her argument that comprised 'a central pillar of Hindu belief' was that: 'so strict was the Koran that its teachings were beyond human capability. Therefore Muslims were forced to pretend one thing, do another: they drank, smoked, ate pork, visited prostitutes, and then denied it' (130). Lola felt uneasy at Mrs. Sen's crude remark because the exaggerated complaint about the multiplication of Muslims sounded 'vulgar and incorrect' (130) to the class of Anglicized and privileged Indians like them who read Jane Austen. She, therefore, strongly protested against her neighbour's attempt to confuse the Indian Muslims with the Nepalis and communalize the issue. '"It's quite another matter with Muslims," she said stiffly. "They were already here. The Nepalis have come and taken over and it's not a religious issue"' (130). Both Lola and her sister despised Mrs. Sen as 'a low calibre person' (131) who had proved her inferiority by allowing her daughter to settle in America instead of England. They laughed at her rustic pronunciation of English words ('POEtatto' for potato, for example) and their contempt for the woman, who was rumoured to have once earned a living by peddling confiscated customs goods from door to door, had intensified when her daughter, Mun Mun, found a job with CNN, thus 'placing her in direct opposition to Pixie at B.B.C.' (131) In order to divert her attention from the disconcerting topic of Pakistan and Muslim that had derailed their conversation, Noni asked her about Mun Mun. Mrs. Sen was all praise for her daughter: 'Oh, they keep begging her to take a green card. She says, "No, no." I told her, "Don't be silly, take it, what harm is there? . . .

How many people would kill for one. . . . Silly goose, isn't it so? What a bee-oo-tee-ful country and so well organized"' (131). Her rival's admiration for America provoked Lola and the two neighbours were locked in a bitter argument over the relative superiority of the country they loved:

> Lola: "But don't you find them very simple people?"
> Mrs. Sen: "No hang-ups, na, very friendly."
> "But a fake friendliness I've heard, hi-bye and no meaning to it."
> "Better than England, ji, where they laugh at you behind your back—" (131)

Thus, the battle of the empires—the old British one (where marmalade was labelled "By appointment to Her Majesty the Queen") and the nouveaux riche American one (where jam was called 'Smuckers')—was fought by third parties in post-Independence India. The narrator's ironic comment that follows highlights the slavish mentality of a section of Indians who suffered from colonial hang-over and were more loyal to England and America than the British and the Americans themselves: "Perhaps England and America didn't know they were in a fight to the death, but it was being fought on their behalf, anyway, by these two spirited widows of Kalimpong' (131). Embarrassed by the fight, Noni desperately tried to change the topic again and asked Sai to give her news. While the elders had been discussing politics, she remained self-absorbed, thinking about 'how she turned to water under Gyan's hands' and about 'those indolent afternoons they spent together' (129). She looked 'out of focus' so much so that the three ladies could not 'read her expression clearly' (132). Lola and Mrs. Sen forgot their rivalry for the time being and directed their frustration with each other to the girl. They were surprised to learn that Sai had found no boy-friend yet and advised her to make hay while the sun shone. "Wait too long and the craze will go," one of them said to the introverted teenager.

Chapter XXII

This chapter delineates Biju's problem of identity, which seemed to stem from his failure to forge a compromise between his ethnicity and demands of American urban modernity, and his search for an elusive home in the precarious anonymity of the glamorous new world. He also learnt about the politics of migration to the new power centre of globalization while eking out a miserable life as an illegal immigrant and moving from place to place like a beast continually driven by its hunters. In a striking vignette of the Western attitude to the endless human flow from the poor third world countries, mostly former colonies, a couple—Odessa and Baz—who owned a restaurant (named Brigitte's after their dog) where Biju worked for a brief period, echoed the general fear of the American people of being inundated by the Asian, African and Latin American immigrants who flood their country. While drinking the best Darjeeling tea in the morning at a corner table of the restaurant amidst the bustling of the staff, they read in the *New York Times* how the once colonized people from all over the globe came to America "screaming colonialism, screaming slavery, screaming mining companies screaming banana companies oil companies screaming CIA spy among the missionaries screaming it was Kissinger who killed their father and why don't you forgive third world debt" (134). They also read how the natives of the decolonized nations accused the Americans for their political ills and continued Western hegemony in the discourse of postcolonial politics and economics: "Lumumba, they shouted, and Allende; on the other side, Pinochet, they said, Mobutu; contaminated milk from Nestle, they said; Agent Orange; dirty dealings by Xerox. World Bank, UN, IMF, everything run by white people" (134). The couple, as representatives of the American society, countered the postcolonial complaints of the ex-European colonies thus: "Nestle and Xerox were fine upstanding companies, the backbone of the economy, and Kissinger was at least a patriot. The United States was a young country built on the finest principles, and how could it possibly owe so many bills?" (134). In the process of defending the US of A against the concerted political blitzkrieg of the former slaves, they reiterated the policy of survival in the new world order: "Business was business. Your bread might as well be left unbuttered were the butter to be spread so thin. The fittest one wins and gets the butter." (134)

Kiran Desai also distinguishes between the American and the British attitudes to immigrants. As Achootan, a fellow dishwasher in Brigitte's said to Biju: "But at least this country is better than England. At least they have some hypocrisy here. They believe they are good people and you get some relief. There they shout at you openly on the street, 'Go back to where you came from" (134-35). And, in a brilliant example of the Empire striking back, Achootan, who had spent eight years in Canterbury and experienced British racial hatred, responded to the insults of the ex-colonizers by shouting on their face: "Your father came to my country and took my bread and now I have come to your country to get my bread back" (135). Achootan did not need a green card in exactly the same way as Biju or Saeed did. He wanted it as an act of revenge. His attitude to America was ambivalent. He hated the country for political reasons but, at the same time, wanted to stay there for the material comfort it provided. In reply to a question Odessa asked him angrily when he sought sponsorship: "Why do you want it if you hate it here?," Achootan admitted this ambivalence: "Well, he wanted it. Everyone wanted it whether you liked it or you hated it. The more you hated it sometimes, the more you wanted it" (135). His attitude is symptomatic of the inherent contradiction in many third world immigrants whose hatred for America is inextricably mixed up with an irresistible longing to be there. Odessa and Baz failed to grasp this ambivalence just as they did not understand Biju's fetish of holiness and impurity. The restaurant specialized in steak, and although Biju knew that his reasoning about 'holy cow' and unholy cow' would not work there, he could not help fixing the Indians, who came to eat beef, with 'a concentrated look of meaning' as he cleared their plates. He found himself in a world which was devoid of any settled convention, where his native rootedness was viewed as backwardness and his adherence to traditional/ communal customs and beliefs was dismissed as superstition. With his poor adaptability and inhibitions against eating the flesh of 'holy cow,' he continued to search for an elusive home in the alien world. Lonely and unhappy in Brigitte's which was situated in the financial district of New York, he overheard the conversation of American businessmen who gloated over the enormous profit to be gained in the newly expanding markets of Asia: "We need to get aggressive about Asia. . . . It's opening up, new frontier, millions of potential consumers, big buying power in the middle classes, China, India, potential for cigarettes, diapers, Kentucky Fried, life insurance, water management, cell phones" (136). Echoing the frontier thesis of Frederick J. Turner, they said: "this country is done. Europe done, Latin America done, Africa is a basket case except for oil; Asia is the next frontier" (136). But Biju was not enlightened by this talk; nor could he compromise his ethnicity with the demands of cosmopolitan modernity of America. He refused to give up his religion or discredit the principles of his ancestors because he believed: "You had to live according to something. You had to find your dignity" (136). He saw the 'difference between a holy cow and an unholy cow' (136) and decided to 'live within a narrow purity' (137), even though he knew that it might be difficult for him to survive and succeed in America with that kind of attitude. He was reminded of Saeed Saeed who had also refused to eat a pig and proudly proclaimed: "First I am Muslim, then I am Zanzibari, then I will BE American" (136). Kiran Desai shows how immigrants like Biju and Saeed clung to their religious faiths and cultural taboos so that they 'might not fall through the filthy differences between nations' (136). Biju gave up the job at Brigitte's and left the place 'as a new person' (137). While looking for an employment in places where beef was not served, he came to learn about the contemptuous attitude of some immigrant Indians towards their compatriots as well as their homeland. In a restaurant called Marilyn, he heard the Indian owner—a Gujarati—talking to a travel agent who offered special concession rates in air tickets to India. The moment the owner learnt that the agent was an Indian, he affected American accent and told him straightaway: "You canaat pay me to go to that caantreey agaen!" (138) The narrator, who unambiguously depicts in the novel the plight of Indian diaspora in America, reveals the shameful betrayal of the poorest Indians by their weaker compatriots in the following terms: "It was horrible what happened to Indians abroad and nobody knew but other Indians abroad. It was a dirty little rodent secret" (138). Biju's quest for a home in America, where he could live within 'narrow purity,' ultimately brought him to a Hindu establishment named 'Gandhi Cafe' where beef was not cooked and Gandhiji's favourite tunes were always played over a sound system. Its owner Harish-Harry, ran, along with his two brothers both bearing hyphenated names like him: Gaurish Garry and Dhansukh-Danny, a triplet of Gandhi Cafés in New York, New Jersey and Connecticut and donated money to help a Hindu cause like protection of cows.

Chapter XXIII

Gyan and Sai's romantic affair continued to flourish in the midst of growing unrest in the hills. The political turmoil remained in the background for them. They passed through the 'dumpling stage of love' (140), inventing nicknames and terms of endearments (like 'momo,' 'Kaju' and 'Kishmish') for each other. The lovers went on excursions to the Mong Pong Nature Reserve and to Delo Lake. They picnicked on the banks of the Teesta and the Relli rivers. The pair went to the sericulture institute whose manager showed them 'piles of yellowy cocoons moving subtly in a corner' (141) and shared his dream of producing a water-proof, stain proof 'new millennium sari' (141). They travelled by the toy train and went to the Darjeeling zoo. They also visited the Zang Dog Palri Fo Brang Monastery situated on Durpin Dara from where they 'could see so far and high, the world resembled a map from a divine perspective' (141). It was against this idyllic backdrop that they told each other the stories of their families which spanned across generations and led overseas. Sai heard from Gyan the interwoven stories of the Royal Army and the Nepalis of Darjeeling who had joined over the generations the Gorkha regiment, swore allegiance to the crown and fought around the world the wars of the British. His ancestors had left their village in Nepal and come to Darjeeling in the 1880s, lured by promises of job in the tea plantations. They settled in a small hamlet, bought a buffalo and started a profitable milk business. In course of time the Imperial Army arrived in the hills to recruit potential soldiers from among the Nepali youth. Gyan's great-grandfather was the first in the family to join the British army which offered him more money than his father, who laboured as a runner for the tea plantation, had ever earned. It was 'the beginning of over a hundred years of family commitment to the wars of the English' (142). He led a prosperous life, acquiring a wife and three sons, until he was sent to the battlefield in Mesopotamia where 'Turkish bullets made a sieve of his heart and he leaked to death' (142). Out of kindness to his family, the army recruited his eldest son who was spindly and was killed, before his twenty-third birthday, in Burma while resisting the Japanese offensive against the British. His brother was also employed and he died in Italy. The last of the family recruit, who survived the war, was an uncle of Gyan's father. He returned to Kalimpong when Gyan was a small child, and lived with them until his death. Their family had since stopped sending their boys to the army and invested their fortunes in teaching. Gyan's father was a school master who taught in a tea-plantation school. Sai was curious to know more about his father but she did not press him because she 'knew about stories having to stop' (143). After her return to home late in the evening, Sai, who had grown up in the claustrophobic atmosphere of her reclusive grandfather's walled-in bungalow, 'became conscious for the first time of the unbearable stickiness of family and friends' (143) and realized that she had discovered a new, uncharted domain of love that held the promise of infinite space and freedom.

Chapter XXIV

This chapter depicts yet another meeting between Indians of different classes, rich and poor, master and servant, in America. It highlights the disappointing truth that while there is a lot of gloating about how the Indians constitute the richest minority group in America, it glosses over the awkward fact the poorest people of India are also found in the United States who are exploited and betrayed not only by the unsympathetic Americans but also by the wealthier group of Indian immigrants. The class divide that exists in the home country continues overseas.

Biju joined Harish-Harry's restaurant because it was a Hindu establishment whose ambience reminded him of home and where he would be able to preserve his traditional if conservative identity. But his expectations were not fulfilled because all that he found was an owner who was lost between identities. Harish-Harry was an enterprising Indian-American businessman who knew the secret of success in the competitive market economy. As he used to say, '"Find your market. Study your market. Cater to your market." Demand-supply. Indian-American point of agreement. That is why we make good immigrants. Perfect match' (145). He also intellectually countered the claim of superiority in the world affairs made by capitalist

America with a naïve but emphatic valorisation of Indian civilization. As he said to his American customers: "In fact, dear sirs, madams, we were practising a highly evolved form of capitalism long before America was America; yes, you may think it's your success, but all civilization comes from India, yes" (145).

Although he had named his restaurant 'Gandhi Café' to capitalize on the sale value of the great Indian icon in the international market, he was not at all Gandhian in his treatment with his employees, who were all illegal immigrants. In return of providing 'free housing' in the incapacious and unhygienic kitchen of the restaurant, Harish-Harry, at the advice of his calculating wife who assisted him to run the business and looked after its finance, compelled them to 'work fifteen-, sixteen-, seventeen-hour donkey days' (146). Biju had left the basement in Harlem that provided him with a façade of respectability and set up his new life in the kitchen of 'Gandhi Café,' 'amid oversized pots and saw-dusty sacks of masalas' (147). The narrator describes the 'free housing' given by the exploitative Indian businessman to Biju and his fellow workers, all undocumented immigrants from India desperately looking for jobs, thus: "The men washed their faces and rinsed their mouths over the kitchen sink, combed their hair in the postage stamp mirror tacked above, hung their trousers on a rope strung across the room, along with dishtowels. At night they unrolled their bedding wherever there was room" (147). Disturbed by rats at night they often slept on the dining tables but would shuffle back down at daybreak before the arrival of the Harish-Harry with his wakening call: "Chalo, Chalo, another day, another dollar" (147). Towards his employees he was 'avuncular,' 'jocular' but he could also become suddenly very 'angry and disciplinary' (147). He was not 'above smacking their heads' (147). But his manner changed dramatically when an American customer walked in the restaurant. Overcome by a panic, he 'smiled and genuflected' (147). Harish-Harry abused and exploited Indians but cringed before the Americans. His name was indicative of a deep rift within himself. As the narrator trenchantly remarks about his halfway identity that tried to make the best use of the twin worlds of the East and the West: "He tried to keep on the right side of power, tried to be loyal to so many things that he himself couldn't tell which one of his selves was the authentic, if any" (148). But it was not Harish-Harry alone. Kiran Desai shows the prevailing confusion 'among the "haalf 'n' haf" crowd' (148) of whom Harish-Harry was a representative. It was rampant among the desis who romanced with the Americans, and among 'the Indian students coming in with American friends, one accent one side of the mouth, another the other side; muddling it up' (148). Biju, who had been seeking a clarity of principle, found that there 'was no purity in this venture. And no pride' (148). He realized that by joining 'Gandhi Café' he 'had come home to no clarity of vision' (148).

But Harish-Harry's 'commitment' to his dual/hyphenated identity was terribly shaken by his own daughter. The girl was being Americanized, against the wishes of her parents: 'Nose ring she found compatible with combat boots and clothes in camouflage print from the army-navy surplus' (148). When all his attempts to bring her back from the path of being American failed, he slapped her and asked her to go away. The girl hit back by saying: "I didn't ask to be born. . . . You had me for your own selfish reasons, wanted a servant, didn't you? But in this country, Dad, nobody's going to wipe your ass for free" (149). Shocked by the vehement reaction of his recalcitrant and irreverent daughter, Harish-Harry got drunk and gave vent to his dormant hatred for the white men in the presence of his kitchen staff: "And they think we admire them!" He began to laugh. "Every time one enters my shop I smile"—he showed his skeleton grin—"Hi, how ya doin', but all I want is to break their necks. I can't, but maybe my son will, and that is my great hope. One day Jayant-Jay will smile and get his hands about their sons' necks and he will choke them dead" (149). He broke into tears at the ingratitude of his daughter and the indignity in having to genuflect before the white men. What calmed his troubled conscience was the thought of making money: "Within this thought he found a perfectly reasonable reason for being here, a morality to agree on, a bridge over the split—and this single fact that didn't seem a contradiction between nations he blazoned forth" (149). It was the pleasant thought of earning dollars as well as his hope of possessing a bigger house than his Gujarati rival, Mr. Shah, that sustained Harish-Harry in his undignified existence which was full of contradictions. Mr. Shah had seven rooms in his house which were all empty 'except for TV, couch, and carpeting' and everything was white because 'white symbolized success out of India for the community' (149).

Chapter XXV

With the advent of winter, the cook and Sai took the judge's dog, Mutt, to the deaf tailors in the market to make a blanket coat for her. It did not snow in Kalimpong but there was frost and the high mountains around the town were streaked with white. It was biting cold in Cho Oyu and the cracks and holes of the decayed bungalow gave off 'a sterile smell of winter' (151). With winter came Christmas and Sai, 'Vaselined shiny and supple' (151), joined a party at Mon Ami with Father Booty and Uncle Potty. The gentleman farmer and the Swiss priest sang together and Lola, Noni and Sai joined in the carousal, 'all drunk and wild' (152). The beautiful evening spent in merry-making brought back the memory of bygone days. At the end of dinner, they tasted the celebrated Christmas pudding which was made 'holy with a sanctifying crown of brandy flame' (152). The Anglophile sisters had brought out all their ornaments made in England for the occasion: snowflakes, snowmen icicles, stars (152). They displayed 'little trolls, and elf shoe-makers' which they stored the rest of the year in the attic 'along with the story of the English ghost' (152) to frighten people away. There were also knitted socks from the Tibetan refugee village, coral earrings, bottles of homemade brandy gifted by Father Booty, books with transparent rice paper sheets and ribbed bamboo spines made in Bong Bustic that added an ethnic touch to their collection. After dinner they drank rum. Under the influence of wine, Lola became very nostalgic and she 'drew a pure memory from the depths' of her mind for guests. Kiran Desai uses flashback to describe the life in Kalimpong before the Nepalese insurgency and explore the conflicting cultural identities—Indian and European—of educated and privileged Indians like Lola and Noni and Indianized foreigners like Father Booty. Lola narrated her experience of adventurous trekking to Thumpu, the Bhutanese capital, in the 1950s and 1960s. There were practically no roads at that time and they would travel on horseback 'carrying sacks of peas for the ponies, maps, hip flasks of whiskey' (153). During the rainy season, they would wash their bodies in salt water to keep off leeches that would fall on them from the trees. They trekked through fierce and dense forests and emerged into the tops of picturesque mountains 'where monasteries limpet to the sides of rock, surrounded by chortens and prayer flags, the white facades catching the light of the sunset, all straw gold, the mountains rugged lines of indigo' (153). They would visit a monastery, which was as ancient as Buddhism, and was rumoured to have been built when 'a rainbow connected Kanchenjunga to the crest of the hill' (153). The gompas remained deserted during their visit because the lamas, who were also farmers, would be busy in their fields. It was a long and arduous journey and it took the trekkers nearly two weeks to reach Thimpu. While going through the forests, they would often stay in the 'ship like fortresses called dzongs, built without a single nail,' which were 'completely self-contained, with their own armies, peasants, aristocrats and prisoners in the dungeons' (153-54). The travellers would send a messenger ahead with the news of their arrival and the owners of the dzongs would send back a gift hamper to welcome them midway. When they arrived in the dimly lit halls, they would find sumptuous food ready for them to taste. Father Booty, who had often visited the places in connection with his 'dairy outreach programme,' picked up the thread of Lola's recollection and described the wonderful baths in the dzongs which 'were made of hollowed-out tree trunks' with 'a carved slot underneath for heated rocks to keep the water steaming' (154). If they camped outside, the hosts would 'dig a pit by the river, fill it with water, lower hot stones into it' so that the guests could splash about 'with all the Himalayan snows around and forests of rhododendrons' (154). The description of the trekkings in the picturesque mountainous region adds an exotic charm to the novel and serves to revive the old world in which these wealthy and West-aping Indians, the true inheritors of the colonial baggage, preferred to live, ignoring the incipient trouble in hills. Returning home at night, Sai remembered her recent excursion with Gyan to the Darjeeling museum where they had studied the mountaineering equipments and 'samples of dehydrated food' (154) with which Tenzing Norge had climbed Mount Everest. Gyan, as an ethnic Nepalese, was naturally proud of Tenzing whom he believed to be the 'real hero' (155) of the legendary expedition. He viewed the conquest of the tallest peak in the world as a 'colonial enterprise' which had deprived the Nepali sherpa of his legitimate credit. As he said to Sai, "Tenzing was certainly first, or else he was made to wait with the bags so Hilary could take the first step on behalf of that colonial enterprise of sticking your flag on what was not yours" (155). Sai, however, held a different view of man's desire to conquer pristine and sacred nature. While listening to Gyan giving vent to his postcolonial grievance and sense of injustice, she had pondered: "Should humans conquer the mountain or should they wish for the mountain to possess them? Sherpas went up and down, ten times, fifteen times in some cases, without glory, without claim of ownership, and there were those who said it was sacred and shouldn't be sullied at all" (155). Sai's meditation reflects her wise, humanitarian approach to the abiding relationship between man and nature.

Chapter XXVI

This chapter describes the grievances of the Indian Nepalis that fomented the Gorkhaland movement and Gyan's accidental involvement in the agitation which would stymie his fledgling love with Sai and threaten their private world of fancy-free teenage romance. One day after the new year, while buying rice in the market, Gyan confronted a procession led by a group of young men including some of his college friends—Padam, Jungi, Dawa, Dilip ('Chhang, Bhang, Owl, Donkey' were their nicknames)—whom he had ignored since the beginning of his romance with Sai. The youth held their unsheathed kukris aloft and shouted slogans in support of Gorkhaland: 'Jai Gorkha.' Gyan found himself drawn into the procession of GNLF supporters effortlessly and as he floated through the market before the eyes of shocked Marwari businessmen and Newari silversmiths, who were experiencing the vibrations of the incomprehensible slogans, he had 'a feeling of history being wrought, its wheels churning under him, for the men were behaving as if they were being featured in a documentary of war' (157). He was affected by the enthusiasm of the agitators and could not help looking on the scene 'from the angle of nostalgia, the position of a revolutionary' (157). By participating in the procession and shouting slogans to assert his geo-ethnic identity, Gyan felt 'a relevancy, an affirmation he'd never felt before' (157). But he had doubt about the authenticity of the protesters' feeling and their commitment to the cause: "Were these men entirely committed to the importance of the procession or was there a disconnected quality to what they did? Were they taking their cues from old protest stories or from the hope of telling a new story? . . . was the feeling authentic? Did they see themselves from a perspective beyond this moment, these unleashed Bruce Lee fans in their American T-shirts made-in-China-coming-in-via-Kathmandu?" (157). Gyan, like Biju, had wished to leave the country and go abroad. In fact, he had proposed to Sai to fly away to Australia in order to be 'Free from history. Free from family demands and the built-up debt of centuries' (157). For a moment, as he marched along, he was assailed by the feeling that the 'patriotism' of the agitators might be 'false,' that 'it was just frustration—the leaders harnessing the natural irritations and disdain of adolescence for cynical ends' (157). But looking at the faces of the slogan-shouters, he did not detect any cynicism and realized that they 'meant what they were saying; they felt a lack of justice' (157). He remembered the stories of the glorious and daring struggle of the Indian people against British colonialism and thought: 'If a nation had such a climax in its history, its heart, would it not hunger for it again?' (158). While listening to the provocative harangue of a GNLF leader giving vent to the long-suppressed grievances of the Nepalis of India outside the police station where the procession had stopped, Gyan was shocked out of his selfish romantic involvement with a privileged girl at a time when the people of his community were fighting for freedom and dignity. He remembered his last job interview in Calcutta, the casual manner in which he had been rejected, and found an echo in the collective despair of his people:

> "Here we are eighty percent of the population, ninety tea gardens in the district, but is even one Nepali-owned?" asked the man.
>
> "No."
>
> "Can our children learn our language in school?"
>
> "No."
>
> "Can we compete for jobs when they have already been promised to others?"

> "No."
>
> "In our own country, the country we fight for, we are treated like slaves." (159)

A deep-seated sense of injustice and deprivation and a feeling of being discriminated against led the Nepalis of Darjeeling district to demand for self-determination and for a homeland. As the fire-spewing leader said to his audience: "We must fight, brothers and sisters, to manage our own affairs. We must unite under the banner of the GNLF, Gorkha National Liberation Front. We will build hospitals and schools. We will provide jobs for our sons. We will give dignity to our daughters. . . . We will defend our own homeland. . . . If necessary, we will wash our bloody kukris in the mother waters of the Teesta" (159). Gyan was affected by the fervour as thirty GNLF supporters stepped forward and drew blood from their thumbs with their sharp kukris to write a poster demanding a separate Gorkhaland. Open call was also given, through leaflets, to Gorkha soldiers defending the country to quit the army and join the movement. While drinking alcohol with his college friends in Thapa's canteen after the meeting, Gyan noticed that his earlier doubt, sarcasm and hesitation had vanished. He finally submitted himself 'to the compelling pull of history and found his pulse leaping to something that felt entirely authentic' (160). Thus, Gyan, an educated and unemployed Nepali youth, gravitated to the first available political cause in his search for an authentic identity and a better way of living. He joined the ethnic nationalist movement largely as an opportunity to articulate his dormant postcolonial rage and frustration:

> He told the story of his great grandfather, his great uncles, "And do you think they got the same pension as the English of equal rank? They fought to death, but did they earn the same salary?"
>
> All the other anger in the canteen greeted his, clapped his anger on the back. (160)

The movement provided people like Gyan with an occasion to unburden their age-old hatred and despair. The narrator reminds the readers that 'old hatreds are endlessly retrievable' and that they are 'purer . . . because the grief of the past was gone. Just the fury remained, distilled, liberating' (161). The participation in the procession, thus, brought about a remarkable change in Gyan. Suddenly he found himself in a 'masculine atmosphere' (161) and felt ashamed to remember his intimacy with Sai, 'the small warm space they inhabited together, the nursery talk' (161) which now appeared to him to be an impediment on his way to attain adulthood. He decided to join the GNLF and even 'voiced an adamant opinion that the Gorkha movement take the harshest route possible' (161).

Chapter XXVII

The incident in the market brought about a noticeable change in Gyan's attitude to Sai which resulted from his temporary blurring of vision. Affected by the overwhelming fervour of the Gorkhaland movement, he myopically prioritised his racial identity over his identity as a tutor-cum-lover. The very next day he arrived at Cho Oyu to give lessons to Sai in an unpleasant mood. He was restless and angry. It was, as the narrator remarks, 'a petty anger that pulled him back, curtailed his spirit, made him feel peevish' (162). He felt upset at the thought of having to undertake a long, arduous walk in the terrible cold to give tuition, for a small amount of money, to a rich and westernized girl like Sai who lived affluently in an enormous house, 'taking hot baths, sleeping alone in spacious rooms' (162). He remembered the slighting remark of her grandfather made at the night he had been compelled by rain to stay at his bungalow: "Common sense seems to have evaded you, young man" (162). His annoyance and anger had generated in him 'a self-righteous posturing, a new way of talking' (162) that surprised his student. When, in order to cheer him up, Sai told him about the beautiful Christmas party at Mon Ami, Gyan struck an aggressively nationalistic pose and severely criticized her for her colonial hangover and psychological slavery of the West: "Why do you celebrate Christmas? You're Hindus and you don't celebrate Id or Guru Nanak's birthday or even Durga Puja or Dussehra or Tibetan New Year" (163). Without allowing Sai, who had a deep-seated hatred for convent education and all that it was associated with, to say anything in self-defence, he continued: "You are like slaves, that's what you are, running after the West, embarrassing yourself. It's because of people like you we never get anywhere" (162). Sai was 'stung by his unexpected venom' and she made an attempt to justify her action on the ground of her individual predilection and her democratic right: "If I want to celebrate Christmas, I will, and if I don't want to celebrate Diwali then I won't. Nothing wrong in a bit of fun and Christmas is an Indian holiday as much as any other" (163). But it only made him feel 'anti-secular and anti-Gandhian' and he said emphatically, with the intention of hurting her: "it only shows to the whole world that you are a FOOL" (163). Gyan abused his beloved for her lack of self-respect and condemned her slavish imitation of the West: "It's clear all you want to do is copy. Can't think for yourself. Copycat, copycat. Don't you know, these people you copy like a copycat, THEY DON'T WANT YOU!!!!" (164). When Sai, anguished and angry at his inexplicable hatred (because she was not the cause of what he felt but only its focal point), asked him: "if you're so clever, how come you can't even find a proper job? Fail, fail, fail. Every single interview" (164), he thoughtlessly devolved the responsibility on the educated wealthy and westernized class of Indians to which Sai belonged: 'Because of people like you!' (164). Thus, the bickering over the issue of Christmas celebration cast a sinister shadow on their burgeoning relationship and caused a major rift between them.

Chapter XXVIII

Gyan's outburst of hatred against his beloved reminded the guilt-ridden judge of his own hatred for his wife. In England, Jemubhai's Anglo-philia had resulted in self-hatred and hatred for his own people and culture. On his return to India at the age of twenty five, he found himself despising his uneducated relatives and his apparently unsophisticated wife. His return was celebrated by his people as a 'historic event' since he was 'the first son of the community to join the ICS' (165). He was greeted by the same military band that had seen him off and was smothered with garlands. When Nimi—now nineteen—approached him with a garland, they could not directly look at each other. Jemubhai had forgotten that he had a wife back home. She had become irrelevant to him like everything else in his past. Nimi had spent the intervening period in her father's home, cherishing the memory of their cycle ride together and of her 'levitating heart' (166) and felt happy at the thought that he had 'found her desirable' (166). Now, out of curiosity, and also in the right of a wife, she rummaged in the toilet case of her foreign returned husband to see what he had brought from England. Unable to resist the attraction of his 'new possessions,' she picked the powder puff, powdered her breasts and stuffed it inside her blouse. She did it out of her ignorance of, and intense craving for, foreign cosmetics. As the narrator remarks, "she was too grown up for childish thieving, she knew, but she was filled with greed" (166). Jemu, who felt like a 'foreigner' in his native place ('Only his digestion dissented and told him he was home,' the narrator humorously remarks [167]), soon detected the loss and kicked up a rumpus in the house because the stealth did not coincide with his newly acquired 'ideas of privacy' (167). Anxious relatives rushed in his room with a fusillade:

> "But what is missing?"
> "My puff."
> "What is that?"
> He tried to explain.
> "But what on earth is it for baba?" . . .
> "Pink and white what? That you put on your skin? Why?"
> His mother began to worry. "Is anything wrong with your skin?" she asked concerned.
> But, "Ha ha," laughed a sister who was listening carefully, "we sent you abroad to become a gentleman, and instead you have become a lady!" (167)

The embarrassment gave rise in his mind to an inexplicable hatred for his ignorant kin who could not even properly pronounce the thing he had lost: "Pauvdar Paaf," they said in Gujarati accent, which rankled the Cambridge-educated civil servant. An embittered Jemubhai finally accosted Nimi and demanded an explanation. So thoroughly Anglicized he had become that he did not like his beautiful wife's face, which he had once found a terribly 'beckoning thing': 'He did not like his wife's face, searched for his hatred, found beauty, dismissed it. . . . An Indian girl could never be as beautiful as an English one" (168). Nimi denied any knowledge of the stealth and as he turned to go away, he found his precious possession sticking out of her blouse. Filled with an indefinable rage he confronted her: '"You filth!" he shouted and, from between her sad breasts, pulled forth, like a ridiculous flower, or else a bursting ruined heart—his dandy puff' (168). Jemubhai could not forgive the 'illiterate village girl' who had thieved and made him a laughing stock of his family. With a murderous look he chased her down on the floor and, in blind fury, raped her: "Ghoulishly sugared in sweet candy pigment, he clamped down on her, tussled her to the floor, and . . . in a dense frustration of lust and fury—penis uncoiling, mottled purple—black as if with rage . . . he stuffed his way ungracefully into her" (169). His civilized mask completely fell away and he resorted to this 'gutter act' (170) again and again to 'teach her the same lessons of loneliness and shame he had learned himself' (170). He did not speak to her or look in her direction in public. The only genuine feeling he had for her was hatred and so 'any cruelty to her became irresistible' (170) to him. The description of Jemubhai's mechanical, loveless, almost brutish sex with his inert wife also betrays a subtle psychological atrocity he perpetrated on her: "She grew accustomed to his detached expression as he pushed into her, that gaze off into middle distance, entirely involved with itself, the same blank look of a dog or monkey humping in the bazaar; until all of a sudden he seemed to skid from control and his expression slid right off his face. A moment later . . . he withdrew to spend a long fiddly time in the bathroom with soap, hot water, and Dettol. He followed his ablutions with a clinical measure of whiskey, as if consuming a disinfectant" (170). This hatred, cruelty, and impersonal detachment in his dealing with Nimi slowly destroyed her personality and turned her into a living corpse.

When Jemubhai was posted in the district of Bonda in Uttar Pradesh, he took Nimi along with him. He rented a bungalow and hired a female companion, Miss Enid Pott, to teach her English language and manners. But Nimi, who no longer felt any love and respect for her husband, stubbornly refused to learn English and resisted his attempt to Anglicize her. He lost his patience with his wife and found her 'rudely contradicting his ambition' (172). So ashamed was he of the illiterate and unsophisticated girl that he did not take her anywhere. Unlike the wives of other officials, she did not play her part in her husband's career and accompany him on tours. Neglected by her husband, who relinquished his duty, and insulted by his servants, who 'thumped their own leftovers on the table for her to eat' (172), Nimi led a lonely existence within the confines of the bungalow and gradually fell out of life altogether. He found her a 'disruptive presence' (172) in his career and when his irritation became too much to bear, he resorted to physical violence. Once, when she inadvertently soiled the toilet seat due to her ignorance of how to use it, he 'could barely contain his outrage, took her head and pushed it into the toilet bowl' (173). Made psychologically invalid by continuous torture and neglect, Nimi lost her once commended beauty and felt completely disoriented: 'She peered out at the world but could not focus on it' (173). Before long, they began to dread each other so severely 'as if they had tapped into a limitless bitterness carrying them beyond the parameters of what any individual is normally capable of feeling' (173).

Chapter XXIX

This chapter delineates the disastrous fallout of the bickering of Gyan and Sai over the issue of celebrating Christmas. Gyan had hastily left the reading table after harshly calling her 'a little fool' for joining the Christmas party at Mon Ami. Sai began to sob at the vehemence of her lover's criticism and shouted through her weeping: 'You dirty bastard.' He was alarmed by the sight of the terrible wreck he had made of his love and his uncontrolled anger began to frighten him when he saw 'her face through the bars of distorting emotion' (174). He realized that Sai was not the cause of his anger but only its focal point. He had never been bothered about Christmas. She was only 'defining' his newly found racial hatred and he was trying to sharpen it through her. An avid supporter of Nepalese nationalism, he became aggressively postcolonial and denounced Sai for her shameless colonial slavery and mimicry of the West: "Don't you have any pride? Trying to be Westernized. They don't want you!!! Go there and see if they will welcome you with open arms. You will be trying to clean their toilets and even then they won't want you" (174). His anger at 'westernized' Indians like Sai became so fierce that he slammed the gate shut as he left their house. But he could not remain angry for long and felt sorry for his misbehaviour with his beloved. When he returned to Cho Oyu next time he begged unconditional apology to her for his rudeness. After some coaxing, she relented and accepted his apology. A brief reconciliation followed, in spite of her realization that 'she was not the centre of their romance' but only 'a small player playing her part in someone else's life' (175). She submitted herself to the kisses of Gyan, who called her a 'temptress' and admitted her irresistible attraction to him. But the truce did not last long and within moments, Gyan's apology turned insincere and he felt angry with himself for yielding to her charms. Worried about purity for his political cause, he felt that his romance with Sai had sullied him. He was reminded of the 'centre of the Buddhist wheel of life clasped in a demon's fangs and talons to indicate the hell that traps us: rooster-snake pig; lust-anger-foolishness' (175), and a 'feeling of martyrdom' came over him. With a fierce resolution he decided to dissociate himself from Sai: He would have to sacrifice silly kisses for his adulthood' (175). Sai also contemplated her desire, fury and stupidity in her room at Cho Oyu. She tried to subdue her anger at her irrational lover but it kept surfacing despite herself: "What on earth was wrong with an excuse for a party? After all, one could then logically, continue the argument and make a case against speaking English, as well, or eating a patty at the Hasty Tasty—all matters against which Gyan could hardly defend himself" (175). She retaliated against his venomous insult by saying to the emptiness: "You bastard. . . . My dignity is worth a thousand of you" (175). Thus their fledgling romance suffered a serious setback due to Gyan's myopic vision and his concern with 'narrow purity.' His annoyance with himself for giving in to Sai went to such an extent that he told his GNLF friends, at Thapa's canteen how he had been compelled to tutor her for money and how happy he would be if he could procure a job and 'leave that fussy pair' with their 'fake English accent' and 'powdered faces' (176). He even betrayed Sai and her grandfather by passing on the information of the judge's secret assets, including the guns, and of the 'lack of a phone and there being nobody to call' (177) to his comrades. This led to the gun-robbery at Cho Oyu and the judge's humiliation at the hands of the militants. Gyan even rationalized his shameless act of betrayal by accentuating the unbridgeable socio-cultural difference between him and Sai: "Why should he not betray Sai? She who could speak no language but English and pidgin Hindi, she who could not converse with anyone outside her tiny social stratum" (176). He hated her English upbringing and manners as well as her apparent lack of Indianness, which she displayed as a status symbol. It was this hatred that blinded him temporarily and led him to cause great harm to her family. But when his excitement subsided, Gyan was overcome by a profound sense of guilt. He began to feel frightened by his love, its fluidity or 'wobbliness that lent itself to betrayal' (177).

Chapter XXX

This chapter chronicles the superstitious cook's worries about his son, his attempts to send Biju abroad to pursue the American dream, Biju's accident in Gandhi Café and his increasing frustration for his failure to secure a green card and a proper job. The narrative moves from Kalimpong to New York via Kathmandu. With the eruption of political trouble in the hills, Panna Lal felt worried about Biju. One day, while preparing a stew with buffalo meat for the judge's dog Mutt, he was overwhelmed by an irrational thought that he was holding the flesh of his own son in his hand, and that Biju might be dead. This apprehension was the result of an acute sense of guilt generated in his sub-conscious mind by an awareness of telling lies to his master and his failure to appease the insatiate spirit of his dead wife by offering it a proper sacrifice. The cook's wife had died of an accident years ago. She had been killed falling from a tree while collecting leaves for their goat. Everyone in his village, including the priests, had induced in Panna Lal a fear that the ghost of Biju's mother, who had passed away in a violent manner, remained angry and threatened to take Biju with her. They insisted that the ghost had to be appeased with a bali (sacrifice) of a chicken. Frightened by their telegram and goaded by the fellow servants in the judge's household, he wanted to go home immediately. When the judge, angry at this blind superstition, refused to grant him leave, Panna Lal cheated his master with a concocted 'story of the roof of his village hut having blown off again in the latest storm' (179). Years later, his apprehension about his son's safety gripped him afresh: "He become worried now, all these years later, that the sacrifice hadn't really worked, that its effect had been undone by the lie he told the judge" (179). Panna Lal, who embodied the traditional values and superstitions of his own socio-economic class, was thus dogged by his own sense of guilt that induced illogical misgivings about his son, now living in an alien land.

The cook's first attempt to send Biju to America four years ago had proved abortive. A recruiting agent for a cruiser ship line had come to Kalimpong to seek applications for 'basic drudge staff' with the promise of procuring 'legal employment in the USA' (179). Panna Lal had summoned his son from their village home in Utter Pradesh for the interview, defying the objection of his master who wanted Biju to work in his house after the cook's retirement. He managed 'fake recommendations' for Biju and certificates regarding his moral character and cooking skills from Father Booty and Uncle Potty. After the successful interview, they submitted a medical form, which was filled in free by the sympathetic doctor in the market who had her son in America, and a bank draft of eight thousand rupees that covered the processing fee and the cost of the training camp which was scheduled to be held in the agency's main office in Kathmandu. Biju travelled to Nepal's capital two weeks later only to find that he had been cheated. There was no such office and the address given by the recruiting agent was fake. He made his second attempt at migrating to America through a direct application for a tourist visa at the US embassy. One notices certain sympathy in the narrator's tone as she recounts the desperation experienced by Biju and people like him as they stood in the queue for a visa. The sympathy is born out of the novelist's personal experience. Kiran Desai has admitted in an interview: "I have stood in line myself at the American embassy many times over and witnessed the scene unfold." ['Human warmth is such an innate part of India']. This is how she describes the people waiting for a visa outside the embassy: "Outside, a crowd of shabby people had been camping, it appeared, for days on end. Whole families that had travelled, from distant villages, eating food packed and brought with them: some individuals with no shoes, some with cracked plastic ones; all smelling already of the ancient sweat of a never-ending journey" (182). She depicts how a section of Indians demean themselves for a chance to escape to America. They falsify documents and behave like beggars to get a tourist visa: "Sometimes every single paper the applicants brought with them was false: birth certificates, vaccination records from doctors, offers of monetary support" (183). The chapter shows the Indian prejudice against black people ("Black people, living like monkeys in the trees, not like us, so civilized" [185]) and their failure to distinguish between Africans and black Americans (185). It highlights the discrimination made between the privileged and the poor applicants for visa by the embassy officials and their 'impatience with all Indians . . . with their lies and crazy stories, and their desire to stay barely concealed under fervent promises to return' (184). But nothing is more disturbing than the scene in which Biju joined the long line of Indians scrambling to reach the visa counter first:

> Stink and spit and scream and charge; they jumped toward the window, tried to splat themselves against it hard enough that they would just stick and not scrape off; young mowing through, tossing aside toothless grannies, trampling babies underfoot. This was no place for manners and this is how the line was formed: wolf-faced single men first, men with families second, women on their own and Biju, and last, the decrepit, Biggest pushers, first place; how self-contented and smiling he was; he dusted himself off, presenting himself with the exquisite manners of a cat. I'm civilized, sir, ready for the U.S, I'm civilized, mam. Biju noticed that his eyes, so alive to the foreigners, looked back at his own countrymen and women, immediately glazed over, and went dead. (183)

The uncivilized behaviour of the Indian applicants and their willingness to degrade themselves for an American visa led Biju to contemplate: "In this room it was a fact accepted by all that Indians were willing to undergo any kind of humiliation to get into the States. You could heap rubbish on their heads and yet they would be begging to come crawling in" (184). He, however, passed the test and was granted a tourist visa for fifteen days. Biju became, in the words of an applicant he had known in the queue, 'the luckiest boy in the whole world' (187) and he went to a park to celebrate his great luck: 'Raw sewage was being used to water a patch of grass that was lush and stinking, grinning brilliantly in the dusk. Out of the sewage Biju chased a line of pigs with black watermarks across their bellies, ran after them in jubilation. "Hup hup," he shouted' (187). The very next day, he sent his father a telegram to inform him of his success. The news was received with much enthusiasm by Sai, who shouted "Hip

hip hooray" in joy, although she felt sad at the 'realization that the cook had his own family and thought of them first. . . . She was just the alternative, the one to whom he gave his affection if he could not have Biju, the real thing" (187).

Biju stayed in America a little more than three years. While working in his last employer Harish-Harry's kitchen at Gandhi Café, one day he skidded on some rotten spinach and broke his knee. When he requested the Gujarati businessmen to call a doctor for him, the latter became furious. Instead of owning up any responsibility and arranging for his treatment, he began to shout: "My responsibility! . . . You slip in the kitchen. If you slip on the road, then who would you ask, hm? . . . I take you in. I hire you with no papers, treat you like my own son and now this is how you repay me! Living here rent-free. In India would they pay you? . . . Is it my fault you don't even clean the floor? YOU should have to pay ME for not cleaning, living like a pig. Am I telling YOU to live like a pig?" (188). Biju vehemently protested, thus exposing Harish-Harry's shameless exploitation of helpless compatriots who crowded the American cities, often illegally, in search of jobs: "Without us living like pigs, what business would you have? This is how you make your money, paying us nothing because you know we can't do anything, making us work day and night because we are illegal. Why don't you sponsor us for our green cards?" (188). But even after this 'volcanic explosion' (188), Harish-Harry remained unperturbed. Instead of medicines, he brought Biju prasad from a temple. The wry authorial remark that followed unveiled the actual relationship between the master and the servant: "And in that prasad Biju knew not to expect anything else. It was a decoy, an old Indian trick of master to servant, the benevolent patriarch garnering the loyalty of staff; offering slave wages, but now and then a box of sweets, a lavish gift" (189). People from every corner of the globe rushed to America to pursue their dreams of a better and more comfortable living. They were prepared to risk death and suffer all sorts of humiliation to gain an access to that new El Dorado, the land of plenty and wish-fulfilment. But what they really achieved from that painful migration was the loss of human dignity and freedom. The narrator highlights this ambivalence of human migration to the new world when she says, soon after

Biju's quarrel with Harish-Harry: "it WAS so hard and YET there were so many here. It was terribly, terribly hard. Millions risked death, were humiliated, hated, lost their families—YET there were so many here" (189). While recuperating, Biju lay on a mattress in the kitchen and watched through the grate the movement of the sun on a row of buildings opposite Gandhi Café: "From every angle that you looked at this city without a horizon, you saw more buildings going up like jungle creepers, starved for light, holding a perpetual half-darkness congealed at the bottom, the day shafting through the maze, slivering into apartments at precise and fleeting times" (189). It is this darkness at the bottom of prosperity and development in the age of globalization that Kiran Desai illuminates in her novel.

Biju's growing sense of frustration caused by the failure to find a satisfactory job and the continuing green card problem made him ill so much so that he began to lose his temper: "The green card, green card, *machoot sala oloo ka patha chaar sau bees* green card that was not even green. It roosted heavily, clumsily, pinkishly on his brain day and night; he could think of nothing else" (190). The gut annoyance at the green card combined with the irritation, caused by his father's endless letters requesting him to find jobs for other people's sons, and made him 'violently angry' (190). Lacking the confidence of Saeed Saeed, who had once told him: "Anything you want, you try and you can do" (190), Biju was filled with self-pity and the thought of going back to India crossed his mind: "Maybe . . . maybe he would return. Why not? To spite himself, spite his fate, give joy to his enemies, those who wanted him gone from here and those who would gloat to see him back—maybe he *would* go home" (191). As he stayed back to lead a miserable and undignified life, his father in Kalimpong drew a solid satisfaction from his son's misunderstood position in America. While he wanted to return, his father advised him to stay and make money as long as he could.

Chapter XXXI

As winter turned to spring, the political trouble on the hillside began to get worse. The GNLF announced its newly drawn plan of action to achieve its goal, a separate homeland. Strikes and roadblocks to paralyse economic activities in the hills were followed by non-participation in national celebrations, boycott of elections, non-payment of taxes, and the burning of the Indo-Nepal treaty of 1950 that had legalized the inclusion of Darjeeling and Kalimpong into West Bengal. Everybody, Nepali or not, was forced to contribute to the GNLF funds and purchase cassettes of fiery speeches made by Subhas Ghising, the chief leader of the organization, and Pradhan, its top man in Kalimpong. Every family was asked to send a male member to witness the consignment of the Indo-Nepal treaty to flames. In March, Sai and her Anglicized neighbours—Uncle Potty, Father Booty, Lola and Noni—made a trip to Darjeeling Gymkhana to exchange their library books before the political turmoil intensified further. The vehicle in which they travelled was a 'rough jeep' of the Swiss Dairy. Apart from the passengers and the books, it carried several wheels of cheese which Father Booty was taking to deliver to a hotel and a convent. The Swiss priest was hopeful that he would be able to persuade others to switch from Amul to his product. The jeep whizzed through teeming nature in buoyant spring when every creature and every flower flung forth pheromones to attract their mates. As they drove by the garden of St. Joseph's convent, which was 'abuzz with . . . fecundity,' Sai wondered whether 'it discomfited the nuns' (194-95). Amorous butterflies flew past the jeep windows into the deep valley below and the 'delicacy' and 'courtliness' of their love reminded Sai, as a contrast, of her own ugly fight with Gyan over the Christmas party. Lola and Noni waved to various people they met on the way, not to everybody but to those only whom they liked. They greeted Mrs. Thondup, an 'elegant lady' who came from an aristocratic Tibetan family, and her young daughters, Pem Pem and Doma who read in Loreto convent. The girls were of Sai's age and thus supposed to make friends with her. But they avoided the judge's granddaughter because of her 'oddness' (194). The narrator explains the class-conscious Bengali sisters' predilections and dislike thus: 'they liked aristocrats and they liked peasants; it was just what lay between that was distasteful: the middle class bounding over the horizon in an endless phalanx' (194). Thus, they did not wave to Mrs. Sen, who was emerging from the post office, because of her middle class background and her rivalry with Lola over their daughters. But they waved to the Afghan princesses sitting on cane chairs in their garden amidst flowering white azaleas that looked 'virginal yet provocative' (195), and to the 'angelically beautiful' (195) orphans in the Graham's School playground. As they passed by the army jogging along the road, Lola informed her co-passengers of the 'rumours of increasing vegetarianism' among the soldiers. She also voiced one of her pet theories that 'to be in the army [one] should eat fish at least' (195). When Sai asked her why a man in the army should be a non-vegetarian, she offered a post-Darwinian naturalistic view: "To kill you must be carnivorous or otherwise you're the hunted. Just look at nature—the deer, the cow. We are animals after all and to triumph you must taste blood" (195). Lola's words trace the reason behind the manifestation of violence and aggression in man, both at the individual and the racial levels, to his basic animal instincts which he has inherited through the long process of evolution. As the jeep stopped for a few seconds to allow a pair of young and handsome Buddhist monks to cross the road to the gates of a mansion, Uncle Potty remembered the first time he had met Father Booty, 'their admiring eyes on the same monk in the market,' which had started 'a grand friendship' (196) between them. The vehicle hurtled through the forests abounding in *sal* and *pani saaj* trees, descended into the Teesta valley, with its 'tropical density of air' and 'greater concentrations of butterflies,' and rose up again into the hills full of pine and ether 'amid little snips of gold rain' (196). Father Booty told others that it was called '*metok-chharp'* or 'blossom rain' i.e. simultaneous rain and sunshine, which was regarded as something 'very auspicious in Tibet' (196). As they approached Darjeeling, they were dismayed by the degradation of the town that 'looked like a garbage heap rearing above and sliding below' (197). Lola was about to make a disapproving remark about its decline when suddenly, before their awe-struck eyes, 'the clouds broke and Kanchenjunga came looming . . . close enough to lick' (197). At the Gymkhana, Uncle Potty parted company. He did not come to Darjeeling to change books but 'to procure enough alcohol to last him through civil unrest' (197). Reading was not his cup of tea, even though he had studied at Oxford. Uncle Potty had hailed from a renowned family in Lucknow. He had had an Anglicized upbringing and called his parents Pater and Mater. His mother had been a 'notorious flirt' in her youth and after enjoying as much fun as she could, she married a diplomat. They celebrated their marriage by purchasing two fabulous racehorses who once made a front-page story in the *Times of India.* In course of time, vanquished by bad luck, the couple sold the horses along with their expensive home in London and returned to India to take shelter in an ashram where they howled to God to save their souls. After making a plan with his neighbours to meet for the lunch, Uncle Potty proceeded to the wine shop 'with the dregs of his family fortune in his pocket' (198) while the others went to the library. The Gymkhana library was housed in a 'dim morgue-like room' that was suffused with the smell of 'aging books' (198). There were old and bound copies of newspapers (like the *Himalayan Times* and the *Illustrated Weekly*) and raj fiction like *The Far Pavilions* and *The Raj Quartet*. But neither the Westernized Indians—Lola, Noni and Sai—nor the Indianized Swiss national Father Booty liked English authors writing about India, because such works with their exoticism and bizarre incidents, 'perverse romance, spilled blood, and miscarriage' (198), turned their stomach. They unanimously agreed that Anglo-Indian writings did not 'correspond to the truth' (198). They preferred writers like P.G. Woodhouse and Agatha Christie who wrote about English countryside. Lola and Noni, in particular, were enamoured of the manor house novels because reading them they felt 'as if [they] were watching those movies in the air-conditioned British council in Calcutta' (198-99). While Father Booty went to search books in the mysticism stacks, Sai began to examine the 'endless accounts of travel in India' (199) She found in book after book the identical 'scene of late arrival at a dak bungalow, the cook cooking in a black kitchen' (199). Browsing through the bookshelves, she not only 'located' herself but also understood the historical factors, like centuries of subjugation by the economic and cultural powers of the West, which had shaped all those characters and impelled their journeys: "Sai realized that her own delivery to Kalimpong in such a manner was merely part of the monotony, not the original. The repetition had willed her, anticipated her, cursed her, and certain moves made long ago had produced all of them: Sai, judge, Mutt cook, and even the mashed-potato car" (199). While books like *My Vanishing Tribe* revealed to her how little she knew about the original inhabitants of the hills, the Lepchas and the Rong pa, works such as *The Indian Gentleman's Guide to Etiquette* by supercilious Englishmen like H. Hardless only served to scratch an old wound and filled her mind with postcolonial anger: 'the fury they ignited wasn't old; it was new' (199). Soon she joined Noni and the librarian who were discussing Dostoevsky's *Crime and Punishment* and the 'Christian ideas of confession and forgiveness' that 'seemed to favour the criminal over the righteous,' and 'place the burden of the crime on the victim' (200). The librarian, who happened to be the sister-in-law of the doctor they all visited in Kalimpong, supported the Hindu view of Karma, which, she believed, provided a better system: "You get what you deserve and you cannot escape your deeds" (200). But Noni pointed out its drawbacks by observing: "But we, too, have wriggled out! Not in this lifetime, we say, in others, perhaps" (200). Sai, who had been silently listening to the discussion, vociferously supported her and added: "Worse are those who think the poor should starve because it's their own misdeeds in past lives that are causing problems for them" (200). Sai's anguished remark and the philosophical contemplation that it generated in her mind reveal the novelist's liberal humanism that goes beyond the narrow cultural, national and religious boundaries to embrace the entire mankind. They have a direct bearing on the pervasive atrocity and injustice in the novel and are meaningfully related to the 'loss' in its title: "The fact was that one was left empty-handed. There was no system to soothe the unfairness of things; justice was without scope; it might snag the stealer of chickens, but great evasive crimes would have to be dismissed because, if identified and netted, they would bring down the entire structure of so-called civilization. For crimes that took place in the monstrous dealings between nations, for crimes that took place in those intimate spaces between two people without a witness, for these crimes the guilty would never pay. There was no religion and no government that would relieve the hell." (200)

Their voices were soon drowned out by the sounds of slogans coming from a procession of zealous GNLF supporters in the street. At first, the privileged people like Lola and the librarian, who were ignorant of the grievances of the ethnic Nepalis against the outsiders, tried to dismiss it as a '*tamasha*' of a 'few degenerate people' drumming up the 'illiterates' (201). But they felt the impact of the movement when they went to the dining room of the Gymkhana to eat. The harried looking manager came rushing out of his office to beg apology and to inform them that they had been obliged to close the dining hall due to cash flow problems caused by the dwindling number of visitors. The political turmoil over the Gorkhaland issue had started scaring tourists away from the beautiful hill station.

Chapter XXXII

This chapter describes the judge's visit to the Gymkhana club in Darjeeling and his meeting with his only friend Bose after thirty-three years which only served to unlock the floodgate of unpleasant memories and remind him of some humiliating experiences in the past he had tried hard to forget. It was the last time they met each other and also the last occasion when the reclusive judge had driven his car out of the gates of his walled-in bungalow. It was Bose who had proposed the meeting. The judge was not sure why he had gone, whether 'out of curiosity' or 'out of some vain hope of putting his memories to sleep' (202). But he went to Darjeeling because, otherwise, Bose would come to Cho Oyu. Over glasses of Talisker brought by Bose for them to share, they reminisced about the bygone days of glamour and adventure that sharply contrasted with the present decline of the Gymkhana. While enjoying heartily Bose's gossips about some of their ICS colleagues and the miserable life each one had been leading, the judge was pained by the scene of decay unfolding before him: "two white haired Fitzbillies in the corner of the club, water-stained *durries*, the grimacing head of a stuffed bear slipping low, half the stuffing fallen out. Wasps lived in the creature's teeth, and moths lived in its fur, which also fooled some ticks that had burrowed in, confident of finding blood, and died of hunger" (203). The portrait of the British king and queen in coronation array above the fireplace had been replaced by one of Gandhi, showing his lean body and thick ribs. The replacement was, the judge thought, 'hardly conducive to appetite or comfort in a club.' (203) They could still imagine what the scene must have been like in the colonial time: "planters in boiled shirts riding for miles through the mist, coattails in their pockets to meet for tomato soup. . . . The playing of tiny tunes with fork and spoon, the dancing against a backdrop that celebrated blood-sports and brutality" (203). They could still find incidents of massacres, fishing expeditions to the Teesta, and tiger hunting recorded in delicate handwriting in the old guest registers of the Gymkhana. But the convivial atmosphere and the spirit of bon-homie that induced pleasant memories were disrupted when Bose reminded the judge how rustic the latter had been during his student life in England: "Remember how I took you to buy the coat in London? Remember that awful bloody thing you had? Looking like a real *Gigowwalla*? Remember how you used to pronounce *Jheelee* as *Giggly*? Remember? Ha ha" (203-4). The reminder was a deliberate attempt on Bose's part to humiliate his friend and it filled the judge's heart with 'a surge of venomous emotion' (204). The narrator skilfully analyses the judge's psychological reaction to Bose's remark and to his perverted attempt to establish his positional superiority over his friend: "how *dare* this man! Is this why he had made the journey, to raise himself up, put the judge down, establish a past position of power so as to be able to respect himself in the present? . . . The judge looked for the waiter. They should order diner, get this over with, make it an early night. He thought of Mutt waiting for him" (204). So enraged was he that he tried to ignore his Bengali batch-mate in the ICS from whom the earlier brilliance had gone out. But, instead of relenting, Bose 'hysterically . . . accelerated the pace and tone of his invasiveness' (204). The judge sought to psychologically counter the attempt to humiliate him by remembering how Bose had lost the court case which he, along with some other Indian civil servants, had filed against the British Government to win a pension equal to that of a white ICS man. They had approached the judge to join them but he had refused to get involved. Because by that time he learned his cynicism, unlike Bose who still remained naïve. His son had also inherited this naiveté and lost a similar case against his white employers. Bose lashed out at the discrimination made in the payment of salary between Indians and the Westerners which he found unbearable. He became a spokesman of the third world and screamed against the continuing Western hegemony in the age of economic globalization and against the injustice meted out to the people of the underdeveloped countries: "profit could only be harvested in the gap between nations, working one against the other. They were damning the third world to being third world. They were forcing Bose—and his son into an inferior position—thus far and no further—and he couldn't take it" (206). What rankled him most was the attitude of the Indian civil servants who, unable to rid themselves of the colonial legacy, did not support his cause: "He thought of how the English government and its civil servants had sailed away throwing their *topis* overboard, leaving behind only those ridiculous Indians who couldn't rid themselves of what they had broken their souls to learn" (205). With his 'unshakable belief in the system of justice' (205) he had gone to the court again and again and had lost his case every time. His repeated losses evinced how he was humiliated by the British legal system in which the white judge would bring down his hammer 'always against the native, in a world that was still colonial' (205). Bose's only antidote against this injustice and insult was a secretly nurtured hatred against the British whom he repeatedly called "Bastards!," "*Goras*," "*Bloody white people*" and whom he held 'responsible for all the crimes of the century' (206). The judge silently listened to Bose giving unrestrained vent to his anti-British sentiments, and clenched and unclenched his hands and jaw to suppress his mounting rage until, finally, he burst out in spite of himself: "YES! YES! YES! They were bad. They were part of it. And we were part of the problem, Bose, exactly as much as you could argue that we were part of the solution" (206). He angrily left the table and walked into the kitchen to ask for dinner only to be slighted by a waiter who, 'functioning like a communist employee,' existed 'comfortably away from horrible capitalist ideas of serving monied people politely' (207). The following conversation between the judge and the waiter gave the former a shocking idea of how the social hierarchy was overturned and discarded in the wake of the political turmoil in the hills:

> "Roast mutton with mint sauce. Is the mutton tender?" asked the judge imperiously. The waiter remained unintimidated: "Who can get tender mutton?" he said scornfully.
>
> "Tomato soup?" . . .
>
> "Oh no," the waiter said, shaking his head and smiling insolently.

(207)

During dinner Bose made a last and valiant attempt to retract and effect reconciliation. He wanted to be assured by the judge that nothing had changed and that they were still friends:

> He now pleaded directly with the judge: "We're friends, aren't we?"
>
> "Aren't we? Aren't we friends?"
>
> "Time passes, things change," said the judge, feeling claustrophobia and embarrassment.
>
> "But what is in the past remains unchanged, doesn't it?"
>
> "I think it does change. The present changes the past. Looking back you do not find what you left behind, Bose." (208)

The judge resolved never to meet Bose again. He wanted neither to pretend, like other Indian civil servants, that he had been the English men's friend nor to allow himself to be dragged into dirt by indulging, like Bose, in Britogynism and self-pity. He had carefully maintained an immaculate silence about his past and he would not allow Bose to destroy it. He would not let his pride sink into melodrama at the end of his life by blurting out his guilt because he was aware of the 'danger of confession—it would cancel any hope of dignity forever' (208). They paid the bill, shook hands with each other and hastily said their goodbyes in English because, as the authorial voice puts it ironically, 'the self-consciousness of it, the effort of it, the grammar of it, pulled you up; a new language provided distance and kept the heart intact' (208).

On his way back to Kalimpong, the embittered judge was assailed by the disconcerting memory of two incidents of racist violence that had happened during his Cambridge days. In one incident, he had been terribly insulted by a group of taunting British boys who threw stones, and made monkey faces, at him near a bus stop. In another, and worse, incident, the future judge had run away cowardly when an Indian boy, whom he did not know but who looked 'just like himself, just like Bose' (209), was mercilessly kicked and beaten and pissed on by 'a crowd of jeering red-faced men' (209) behind a pub. The recollection of these incidents evinced not only his sense of guilt for having selfishly escaped without protesting against the inhuman barbarity but also his angst and helplessness to witness the crude manifestation of racial violence.

Greatly disturbed by the memory, he stopped thinking and, by making some 'calibrated gestures' (209), drove the car back to Kalimpong. Close to Cho-Oyu, he saw an army car parked in the darkness from which the cook and some soldiers were hiding boxes of liquor in the roadside bushes. The judge knew about the cook's illicit liquor business. So he ignored it and continued on. His grim expression softened the moment he saw Mutt waiting for him at the gate. His heart 'grew young with pleasure' (209) when the dog jumped into the seat next to her master and rode with him to the garage with 'a regal air' (209). Entering the house he found a telegram from St. Augustine's convent requesting him to take back his orphaned granddaughter, Sai Mistry. Initially he felt disturbed by the telegram and was 'worried that she would incite a dormant hatred in his nature, that he would wish to rid himself of her or treat her as he had her mother, her grandmother' (210). But ultimately he accepted her because he felt that the girl, in whom something of his past had 'survived,' might 'redeem' his life which had been built up on 'certain artificial constructs' (210) and lies.

Sai, after her arrival at Cho Oyu for shelter, turned out to be 'more his kin than he had thought imaginable' (210). He discovered something familiar about her. In more ways than one, the granddaughter continued the journey which had been started by him so long ago. She was, like him 'a westernized Indian brought up by English nuns, an estranged Indian living in India' (210). She had the identical accent, manners and preference for European food. The judge realized that he had committed a serious mistake by disowning his daughter. Deep in the 'backwaters of his consciousness' he felt that 'an imbalance in his deeds [was] balancing itself out' (210). It struck him that this teenage girl, whom he did not—surprisingly—hate, might be 'the only miracle fate had thrown his way' (210).

Chapter XXXIII

The Nepalese insurgency assumed a grim dimension; it became increasingly violent and threatened the lives of the people in the hills. Six months after Sai and her Anglicized neighbours made the library trip to Darjeeling, the Gymkhana club was forcibly taken over by armed GNLF cadres who camped out in its spacious and expensively decorated rooms and spoilt its colonial accoutrements, thus 'ridiculing even further whatever pretensions the club might still harbour despite having already been brought low by the staff' (211). They not only drank up the entire liquor in the bar but also stockpiled guns, drew maps of strategic areas, plotted the bombing of bridges, and hatched daring plans to intimidate and extort money from the managers of the tea gardens who fled for fear of life from the plantations stretching all over the Singalila mountains. When the seditious insurrection was over, the GNLF signed a peace treaty, under the supervision of the Centre, with the Marxist government of West Bengal that granted limited autonomy to the Indian Nepalis through the formation of Darjeeling Gorkha Hill Council. A public surrender of arms was staged in the Gymkhana Club on October 2, 1988. Thousands of Ghising's men surrendered their guns that included the judge's rifles looted from Cho Oyu, ammunition and explosives. But when Sai and her neighbours were turned away from the deserted dining hall of the Gymkhana, they could not imagine things to go down in the club so quickly. After considering various alternatives, they decided to lunch at Glenary's. As they trooped into the hotel, Father Booty was greeted elegantly by some dining Christian priests who addressed him as '*Monsignor*,' thus 'bringing a whiff of Europe to them' (212). The room was full of boarding school children who were jovially enjoying their lunch out. The elderly children were celebrating their birthdays on their own while the younger ones were accompanied by their parents who had arrived from Calcutta and the neighbouring countries and from the surrounding tea plantations to visit their progeny. 'Taking swift advantage of parents' melting eyes—almost time to say goodbye' (213), some children insisted on having more of their favourite ice-creams and the parents yielded to the emotional blackmailing: "Please, Ma, please, Ammi, please, Mummy," mother's eyes turned toward father, "Priti, no, it is quite enough, don't spoil him now," then giving in, knowing Ma, Ammi, or Mummy would be weeping all the lonely road back to the plantation or airport or train station' (213). While watching the small family dramas enacted in the room, Sai 'felt suddenly bereft and jealous of these children' (213). She wistfully thought: 'Had her mother been like this? And her father?,' and asked herself: "Why couldn't she be part of that family? Rent a room in someone else's life?" (213). As the group waited for their food, they heard 'the noise of the parading [GNLF] boys going by again' (214). When they were leaving the restaurant, they encountered the same procession coming back up the road and shouting slogans in support of their political demand: "Gorkhaland for Gorkhas." As they stood back to let the procession pass, Sai suddenly found Gyan in a tomato red sweater, 'rallying on behalf of independence of Nepali-Indians,' and 'yelling lustily in a way she couldn't recognize' (214). To her surprise, Gyan refused to acknowledge her: "She opened her mouth to shout to him, but at that moment he caught sight of her, too, and the dismay on his face was followed by a slight ferocious gesture of his head and a cold narrow look in his eye that was a warning not to approach. She shut her mouth like a fish, and astonishment flooded over her gills' (215). She felt so insulted at his rejection that in reply to Noni's question: "Isn't that your mathematics tutor?," she told a lie ("I don't think so") and began to scrabble for dignity and sense. Sai felt so ill that on the way back to Kalimpong she began to retch, vomiting up the food she had eaten at Glenary's. Their vehicle was stopped and detained near the Teesta bridge by security guards for inspection. The eruption of violence in the hills had made the guards extra careful. While the other passengers waited impassively in the car, Father Booty got out to stretch his limbs and spotted a remarkably beautiful butterfly fluttering beguilingly on a cable of the bridge. In great enthusiasm, he snapped a photograph of the colourful insect. It was out of his knowledge that photography was strictly prohibited, for reasons of security, on the bridge which was an important link of the country with her north-eastern states bordering China. Nor did it help that he was a foreigner. The harmless photograph of a butterfly was regarded by the checkpoint guards as an irrefutable proof of espionage. They confiscated Father Booty's camera and began to search the jeep in which they found the Swiss priest's unsold cheese and the pile of books he and his neighbours had borrowed from the Gymkhana library. In reply to the officer's question: "Why are you reading it?," Lola arrogantly said, "To take my mind off all of this," gesturing 'vaguely and rudely at the scene in general and the guard himself'

(217). Angry at her insolence, he ordered his subordinates to take the books and the camera to the police station for thorough examination. He paid no heed to Noni's persuasion and Lola's threat to take up the issue with higher authorities. Even Uncle Potty's attempt to bribe them with bottles of liquor he had purchased in Darjeeling did not work. In the midst of all these, Sai remained unfazed and silent: 'she was still thinking about Gyan ignoring her, and she didn't care the books were gone' (219). She found it hard to believe that Gyan, who had admitted her irresistible charm ("I can't resist you. . . . I have to keep coming back" [219]), could refuse to recognize her so heartlessly. Terribly upset by the insult, she returned home in an embittered mood and went straight to bed without eating her dinner. This greatly offended the aged cook who had been waiting for her.

Chapter XXXIV

Father Booty found himself in serious trouble because of his innocuous photograph of a beautiful butterfly. A week after the incident on the Teesta bridge, the authorities returned the confiscated books, declaring them 'harmless.' But they took a stern view of the Swiss Priest's photograph which showed the sentry post at the highly sensitive and strategically important bridge. His attempt at self-justification ("I was in a hurry. I forgot to focus properly' [220]) was ignored. The police ransacked his home and took away everything (from a radio to a bottle of Black Cat rum) they found there. Further investigation revealed that Father Booty was a foreigner who had been living in India illegally without renewing his permit: 'he had allowed his residence permit to lapse in the back of a mouldy drawer for to renew the permit was such bureaucratic hell' (220). He did not deny that 'he was a foreigner' but unfortunately, he 'had lost the notion that he was anything but an *Indian* foreigner' (220). In the end, this amiable philanthropist, who had lived in Kalimpong for forty-five years, loved the place as his own home, and contributed to its economic upliftment through his model dairy, was summarily ordered to leave. He went from pillar to post—the SDO and the police chief, the army Major Aloo and the forest department officials—for help but in vain. He found these influential people, who had, in peaceful times, enjoyed his company as well as the products of his dairy and talked about mushrooms and bamboo clumps growing on his property, either too busy or too scared to help him. Some of them even bluntly said, "We can not allow a threat to our national security" (221). When he spoke about his home, his dairy and the cows, he was rudely reminded that they were as illegal as their owner and that a foreign national could not own property in the country. Technically, however, Father Booty was not the owner of the dairy; it was in the name of Uncle Potty. The priest had signed the ownership papers on behalf of his friend because Kalimpong had been declared long ago as 'an area of high sensitivity' and the law permitted the army to appropriate any unoccupied property. As he imagined his cows being driven out by army tanks, his heart sank. The thought of leaving the 'solidly constructed' house he had affectionately named *Suktara* which had been built on a craggy mountainside full of 'violet bamboo orchids and pale ginger lilies spicing the air' (222), and which allowed a glimpse of the Teesta flowing on to join her spouse, the Brahmaputra, filled him with profound sadness. He had loved this home 'fiercely, intensely' since 'such wilderness could not incite a gentle love' (221). But the people of Kalimpong had no time and taste to appreciate and honour the noble sentiments of a foreign national. Within two days, he was compelled to sell the house at a throwaway price to a Nepali doctor who intended to start a private nursing home there. He was helpless because the sly doctor took advantage of his precarious condition and arranged it in such a way that he had no choice but to sell the house to him. Uncle Potty tried to console his friend by saying: "I will look after the cows, Booty. . . . No worries. And when the trouble is over, you return and take up where you left off" (222). The three of them—Uncle Potty, Father Booty and Sai—sat one evening in Booty's house, drinking Old Monk and listening disconsolately to the tape-borne voice of Abida Parveen, singing "*Allah hoo, Allah hoo, Allah, hoo . . . Mujhe jaaaane do.*" It was their valedictory get-together. Uncle Potty's assurance could not comfort Father Booty because he knew his friend to be an inveterate alcoholic and, therefore, unreliable. He held himself and his failure to renew the permit responsible for his present plight: 'He felt a lack in himself, despised his conformity to the ideas of the world even as he disagreed with them' (223). The forceful and inhuman eviction of the benevolent priest incensed Sai who held Gyan accountable for the whole thing: "This was as Gyan's doing, she thought. This is what he had done and what people like him were doing in the name of decency and education, in the name of hospitals for Nepalis and management positions. In the end, Father Booty, lovable Father Booty, who, frankly, had done much more for development of the hills than any of the locals, and without screaming or waving kukris, Father Booty was to be sacrificed" (223). Thus, the militant nationalism of the Nepali Indians led to the partitioning of people and put an end to 'a grand civilization' (223) that had been created through the confluence of music, alcohol and friendship over the years, defying the shadow lines of race, religion, language and culture. It was a great loss that dejected Father Booty's friends and acquaintances including Sai and Potty. While watching the fast expanding darkness that crept up from the valleys far below to envelop their faces and 'climbed over the tops of their heads and on to extinguish Kanchenjunga glowing a last brazen pornographic pink' (223), Sai ruminated over the inheritance of this irredeemable loss:

> There were concert halls in Europe to which Father Booty would soon return, opera houses where music moulded entire audiences into a single grieving or celebrating heart, and where the applause rang like a downpour. . . . .
>
> But could they feel as they did here? Hanging over the mountain, hearts half empty—half full, longing for beauty, for innocence that now knows. With passion for the beloved or for the wide world or for worlds beyond this one. (223)

She thought of her own indefinable longing for love and companionship in the early days at Kalimpong and her mind went back to the day of the gun robbery at Cho Oyu when everything started crumbling around her.

Chapter XXXV

Sai was indirectly responsible for the gun-robbery at Cho Oyu because it was she who had told Gyan about her grandfather's hunting rifles in order to impress him. Nobody in the house paid any attention to the guns which had been left mounted on the wall, gathering dust. To them, the rifles were 'retired artifacts relegated to history, seen too often to notice or think about (224). Gyan was the last person to bring them down from the wall and examine them out of curiosity. It had never occurred to her that those rusty weapons 'might be resurrected into use' or they could be used in committing crimes 'that would, when dot was linked to dot, be traced to their doorstep' (224). She told Gyan stories of her grandfather's hunting expeditions which she herself had heard from the cook in her early days at Cho Oyu: "A great shikari he was, Saibaby. He was very handsome, and he looked very brave and stylish on his horse. The villagers would call him if there was ever a man-eater around" (224). The old man had made up such marvellous stories of his master's lost glory in order to enhance his own feeling of self-respect. Over the years he had grown to believe and enjoy his pieces of fiction, and the more he repeated them, 'the more they became truer than the truth' (225). But the loot of the guns was taken very seriously by the police who came to investigate the crime and ransacked the cook's quarter in search of a clue. The seriousness of the incident, which coincided with the eruption of insurgency in the hills, was proved again when one morning, soon after Father Booty's expulsion from Kalimpong, the SDO visited the judge with some armed guards to apprise him of the development in the investigation: "The perpetrators are still absconding . . . but please don't worry, sir. We will nip this in the bud. Crack down on anti-social elements" (225). He gave the official version of the new threat to national security: "They are using the problems of Bhutan, Assam as an excuse to make trouble here. This country of ours is always being torn apart and it's sad for people like us, brought up with national feeling, and worst for you, sir, who struggled for our freedom. . . . These anti-nationals have no respect for anything or anyone, not even for themselves. . . . The whole economy is under threat" (225). He added for Sai's information that the economy of the Darjeeling district depended on three Ts: "Tea! Timber! Tourism!" When his ebullience and flattery of the Anglophile judge as a freedom fighter met with silence, the loquacious SDO tried to ingratiate himself with the retired ICS officer by telling shikar stories of his own father and referring to his hobby of gardening and love of flowers. Before leaving the bungalow, he requested the judge to inform him if they faced any more trouble. The narrator gives an ironic description of this pompous braggart's departure: "He did up his shawl like a nationalist—Flap! Wrap! Things to do! No time to waste! Nation calls! And he got back into his jeep. The driver backed out of the gate, roared away" (226). The cook became hopeful after the officer's assurance to nab the culprits but the experienced judge remained cynical: "They never find anyone" (226). Sai remained silent 'because she couldn't stop returning to the thought of Gyan avoiding her' (226). The SDO, however, kept his word and the police swung into immediate action. The concluding section of the chapter describes the ineptitude and brutality of the state police who picked up a miserable drunk, who was 'a customary sight lying oblivious to the world in a ditch by the side of the market road' (226), in connection with the gun robbery at Cho Oyu and tortured him mercilessly to wring out a confession from him: "The more he screamed the harder they beat him; they reduced him to a pulp, bashed his head until blood streamed down his face, knocked out his teeth, kicked him until his ribs broke" (226). The man begged for mercy and screamed to claim his innocence: "I didn't steal guns from anybody, I didn't go to anyone's house, nothing, nothing, some mistake" (226). His piteous screams, the narrator comments, 'heralded the end of normal life on the hillside' (226). But the police paid no heed to his desperate shrieks that tore up the air because they were 'just practising their torture techniques, getting ready for what was coming' (226-27). By the time he was released from police custody, the man had been turned into a pathetic wreck. He had lost his power to stand on his feet and the light had been permanently extinguished from his eyes: "They would heal into horizonless, flat blanks that would forever cause others to recoil in fear and disgust" (227).

Chapter XXXVI

It was at this stage Biju learnt about the political turmoil in Darjeeling through an Indian newsagent in New York, Mr. Iype, and felt worried about his father. The trouble was made by the Nepalis and it had been going on for some months. The entire hillside had been virtually cut off from the rest of the country by violent agitations, strikes and road blockades. Biju had not received any letters from his father for a long time and he had held the usual disruptions, like bad weather and incompetence of the postal department, responsible for the break in correspondence. Mr. Iype was angry at the sinister attempt to destabilize India by the ethnic Nepalis whom he called 'very troublesome people' (228). He forgot the syncretic culture of the country and gave vent to his narrow nationalistic feelings: "They should kick the bastards back to Nepal. . . . Bangladeshis to Bangladesh, Afghans to Afghanistan, all Muslims to Pakistan, Tibetans, Bhutanese. Why are they sitting in our country?" (228). When Biju, who had inherited the traditional logo-centric humane values from his father, asked Iype: "Why are we sitting here?," he shamelessly answered: "This country is different. . . . Without us what would they do?" (228). The news made Biju apprehensive and, 'with gradually building momentum, he became convinced his father was dead' (229). Unable to bear the tightening unease, he slipped out of Gandhi Café imperceptively and booked a twenty-five dollar call to Kalimpong from a public telephone booth. As there was no telephone in the judge's bungalow, he rang the number for the Metal Box guesthouse and requested the watchman to call his father. Thus, a few weeks before 'the phone lines were cut . . . the roads and bridges were bombed' by the violent GNLF cadres and the people of the hills 'descended into total madness' (229), Biju established contact with his aged father. The Metal Box watchman rushed to Cho Oyu, rattled its iron gate and informed the cook, who had been preparing a broth for the judge's pet: "La! Phone! La Telephone! Telephone call from your son. La! From America. He will phone again in one hour. Come quick!" (229). The cook went out immediately, leaving the broth to Sai's care. The narrator provides a hilarious interlude in which the Metal Box watchman's entire family came running from their hut outside, gathered in the drawing room of the guesthouse to listen to and give running commentary on the telephonic conversation between the cook and his son. She humorously remarks, "Every time the phone rang, they ran with committed loyalty. Upkeepers of modern novelties, they would not, *would not,* let it fall to ordinariness' (229-30). The private conversation between the father and the son, disrupted by the poor telephone service in the conflict-torn district was enthusiastically heard by them. They giggled in anticipation as the cook shouted into the receiver:

> "HELLO?"
> "HELLO? HELLO?"
> . . . .
> "HELLO?"
> "HELLO? PITAJI??
> "BIJU?" By natural logic he raised his voice to cover the distance between them, sending his voice all the way to America. (230)

The family watched not only for the change in the cook's expressions but also 'for hints as to what was being said at the other end, wishing to insinuate themselves deeply into the conversation, to become it, in fact' (230). The novelist brilliantly depicts their indirect but avid participation in the dialogue between Biju and his father:

> '"HELLO HELLO????"
> "???? HAH? I CAN'T HEAR. YOUR VOICE IS VERY FAR."
> "I CAN'T HEAR. CAN YOU HEAR?"
> "He can't hear."
> "WHAT?"
> "Still can't hear?" They asked the cook. (230)

Biju could not hear what his father was saying at the other end due to the disturbance in the line but he could feel the atmosphere of Kalimpong through the telephone: "The atmosphere of Kalimpong reached Biju all the way in New York; it swelled densely on the line and he could feel the pulse of the forest, smell the humid air, the green-black lushness" (230). The noise in the room made it difficult for the cook to listen to his son. Angry at the loss of precious seconds bought by Biju in America, he waved them away. The family withdrew for a moment but, growing accustomed to his dismissive gestures, they returned again. The father and the son bootlessly shouted into the telephone receivers to reach each other because the 'shadow of their words was bigger than the substance' and the 'echo of their own voices gulped the reply from across the world' (231). The wife of the watchman went out to examine the fragile telephone connection 'trembling over ravines and over mountains, over Kanchenjunga smoking like a volcano or a cigar' (231) and reported that the disturbance was caused by the wind blowing outside. The children went up

relieved at the respite it offered. He even tried to rationalize his conduct and believed that no serious harm had been done: 'Let the world carry on outside for a bit, and then when it was safe, he'd visit Sai and cajole her into being friends again' (272). In the relative safety of home, he evaluated his own character and arrived at the conclusion that his trouble had started when he tried to be part of politics and submitted himself to the pulls of history: "He wasn't a bad person. He didn't want to fight. The trouble was that he'd tried to be part of the larger questions, tried to become part of politics and history" (272). But after his failure to find a sense of purpose and direction in history and politics, he realized that 'happiness had a smaller location' and that tiny joys could be found only by 'turning the wheels of a simple life' (273). In fact, Gyan, who had joined the movement for Gorkhaland, was remarkably different from the one who felt disillusioned in the end, when he realized his folly to give priority to his ethno-racial identity above all other considerations. But his rationalization of his uncivilized behaviour with Sai only proved his own hypocrisy and cowardice which he sought to camouflage as a longing for an 'ordinary existence situated between meek contours' (272). This is evident from the narrator's analysis of his despicable conduct during his internment in the house: 'He had a lot of time to think, and as the hours went by, he unearthed the grout from his belly button, the wax from his ears with a blunt lead pencil, listened to the radio and tested the cleanliness of the orifices against the music, tilting right, left: "chaandni raate, pyaar ki baate." (273). But soon he was overpowered by a strong sense of guilt and he realized that he could never be happy and innocent again after what he had done to Sai and her family: 'how could he have told the boys about the guns? How? How could he have put Sai in such danger? His skin began to crawl and burn. He couldn't lie on the bed any longer. He got up and paced up and down' (273). The guilt hung heavy on his heart and made him think seriously about a rapprochement with his estranged and seriously wronged beloved. Thus, as Gyan and Sai remained confined in their rooms, suffering from remorse and pain of unrequited love respectively, they missed the defining moment of the Gorkhaland movement—the burning of the Indo-Nepal treaty of 1950, which led to a terrible eruption of violence and turned the picturesque hill town into a veritable inferno.

Chapter XLIII

27 July 1986 was a black day in the history of the Gorkhaland movement. It had rained throughout the previous night and the cook, who was to represent the judge's family in the GNLF march, had prayed he would not have to go. But in the morning the rain stopped and the sky became partly clear. The cook was compelled, against his wishes, to leave the house for participating in the demonstration. On the way, he met his friend, the Metal Box watchman, and together they went to the Mela Ground. The entrance gate to the ground was mounted with a statue of Mahatma Gandhi, apostle of non-violence, to commemorate Indian Independence. Several thousands of people had arrived there, not only from Kalimpong but also from the surrounding villages and towns. When all the participants had collected, they would ceremonially march to the police station to set the Indo-Nepal Treaty on fire. The cook appreciated the organizational skills and discipline of the GNLF. It was not an easy matter to make such a huge gathering at a short notice. The cook and the watchman stood and waited like thousands of other participants until a leader blew a whistle and ordered them to move forward. Everything was going according to plan and the two friends, who hoped that the programme would be over in an hour, began to anticipate their lunch. But suddenly, as the procession reached the junction, something unexpected happened: "A volley of rocks and stones came pelting down from behind the post office, where the cook had waited for his letters from Biju and which, he noticed sadly, was barred and shut. The stones hit the rooftops, BANG BANG BANG BANG, then they came flying with greater momentum, bounced down, and injured some of the people, who went reeling back. Bruises. Blood" (275). Although it would never be known who the miscreants were, it was rumoured that they had been hired by the police 'so that the marchers might be goaded into returning the insult, throwing rocks back, thus giving the police an excuse to react' (275). The police, however, denied this allegation. They claimed that the GNLF supporters had brought stones with them 'to throw in the face of law and order' (275).

Kiran Desai presents the apogee of violence when a gruesome battle ensued between the protesters and the defenders of law, the policemen. The cook, who was separated from his friend in the midst of the skirmish, watched a bizarre scene unfolding before his awe-struck eyes: "And then, BAM BABAM, the air was full of stones and bottles and brickbats and screaming. The crowd began to collect rocks, raided a building site for more; the police began to chase the crowd; the stones came down; everyone was being hit, people, police; they jumped on one another, beating with sticks, bashing with rocks; began to slash with their sickles—a hand, a face, a nose, an ear" (275).

Finally, the police, who could not control the unruly mob and bear the tension any more, opened fire, killing thirteen local boys. And the protesters retaliated by knifing some policemen to death: "One jawan was knifed to death, the arms of another were chopped off, a third was stabbed, and the heads of policemen came up on stakes before the station. . . . A beheaded body ran briefly down the street, blood fountaining from the neck, and they all saw the truth about living creatures—that after death, in final humiliation, the body defecates on itself" (276). Helpless before the explosion of mob fury, the policemen 'ran backward like a film in reverse' (276). Some got into the police station and locked the door while others ran into private homes. Three constables took shelter in Mon Ami, thus providing Lola with an opportunity to ridicule them: "Pathetic . . . you are the police?!" Because now they were at her mercy and she wasn't at theirs. "Didn't help us all this time, and now see, need our help!" (276).

Meanwhile, the GNLF men continued rioting in the bazaar. They pushed police jeeps into the ravine and set buses on fire. The flame from the burning vehicles 'reflected garishly on the settling mist of evening, and the fire spread to the jungles of bamboo' (277). The ghastly battle between an ethno-racial group fighting for the right to self-determination and the custodians of law elicits a wry comment from the narrator: "This was how history moved, the slow build, the quick burn, and in an incoherence, the leaping both backward and forward, swallowing the young into old hate. The space between life and death, in the end, too small to measure" (276). The scene, describing one of the most abominable eruptions of hatred and violence that human civilization has witnessed in recent times, largely justifies Pankaj Mishra's observation in the *New York Times* that 'despite being set in the mid-1980s, [*The Inheritance of Loss*] seems the best kind of post-9/11 novels."

As the cook, like everyone else, ran away from the blood-soaked streets of the burning bazaar, he was amazed by a view of the snow-white peaks of the Kanchenjunga presenting a stark contrast to the scene of inhuman barbarity below: "Above was Kanchenjunga, solid, extraordinary, a sight that for centuries had delivered men their freedom and thinned clogged human hearts to joy" (277). But, as he crawled his way back to Cho Oyu, crying inconsolably, with his heart being clawed by panic, like a 'scrabbling rodent creature' (277), he felt that the mountain would never be the same to him again. The cook, who had already observed how the insurgency had overturned and discarded social hierarchy in the hills, now found his own life descending into chaos as the nation prepared, ironically, to fight itself: "army tanks rolling down from the cantonment area into the town. Instead of foreign enemies, instead of the Chinese they had been preparing for, building their hatred against, they must fight their own people." (278). Suddenly Kalimpong, an indivisible part of India, turned into an area where non-Nepalis like the cook felt they did not belong. They became unwanted foreigners in their own country. He found the civilized place disintegrating and became apprehensive about his own son.

Chapter XLIV

The incidents of horror continued unabated through the cyclical change of seasons, 'through winter and a flowery spring, summer, then rain and winter again' (279). Kalimpong, 'trapped in its own madness' (279), remained completely cut off from the outside world due to continuous roadblocks and imposition of curfew. People were compelled to stay locked in and barricaded. Those, who refused to support the movement, were harassed and beaten by the GNLF men. The Bengali-speaking people became the obvious target of popular hatred. They were put on the other side of the argument and delineated as enemies. They were excluded from the society of the Tibetans, Lepchas, Sikkimese and the Nepalis. Nobody acknowledged them publicly. Shopkeepers refused to sell them goods for fear of GNLF backlash. Even children were affected by this communal hatred: 'Little children lined up in rows to spit at Lola and Noni as they walked by' (280). The land grab went on and a good portion of the Mon Ami estate was forcibly occupied by the trespassers.

As political negotiations failed to work out a solution, violence escalated, turning Kalimpong, a civilized and peaceful hill resort, into a 'ghost town': "The circuit house was burned, and the house of the chief minister's niece. Detonators set off landslides as negotiations went nowhere. Kalimpong was transformed into a ghost town, the wind tumbling around the melancholy streets, garbage flying by unhindered. Whatever point the GNLF might have had, it was severely out of hand; even one man's anger, in those days, seemed enough to set the hillside alight" (281). Only the women came out on the roads. The men remained confined within home, trembling 'for fear of being picked up, being tortured on any kind of flimsy excuse, the GNLF accusing them of being police informers, the police accusing them of being militants' (281).

Unnerved by the explosion of collective violence that betrayed the aberrational psychology of both the mutinous mob and the insensitive police, the cook, who embodied the traditional humane values of his own class, at first tried to seek consolation in the hope that it "will be all right, everything goes through a bad time, the world goes in a cycle, bad things happen, pass, and things are once again good" (281). But after realizing the frailty of his own life as a non-Nepali in Kalimpong, he lost his conviction and felt that his hope was devoid of wisdom. Suffering from acute scarcity of food, the judge's family survived on *dalda saag, bhutiya dhaniya, ningro* fiddleheads, *churbi* cheese and bamboo shoots—things they could never imagine before.

It was during this period of crisis that the father and the wife of the drunkard, who had been tortured and blinded by the police, came back to the judge to seek his help and ask for some food so that they did not die of starvation. But he treated them again with inhuman apathy that amounted to cruelty and ordered the cook not to give them anything but to herd them out. The judge's cruel indifference was his way of avenging his own humiliation at the hands of the

Nepali hooligans during the gun robbery, an incident which had shaken the very foundation of his smug socio-cultural superiority. A few days later, the desperate pair returned again to Cho Oyu and when its residents were busy—the judge having his bucket bath, the cook churning butter in the kitchen, and Sai smarting from the pain inflicted by her inconsiderate and estranged lover—and did not see them or hear their approach, they stole the judge's pet dog, Mutt, and went away.

Chapter XLV

Biju returned to India in the Gulf Air plane that looked like 'a failing bus labouring through the sky' (285). The loaded aircraft provided little comfort but the passengers felt comfortable. They were 'sweat-gluey, fate-resigned, but happy' (285) because they were going home. At Heathrow airport, the plane docked 'at the far end that hadn't been renovated for the new days of globalization but lingered back in the old age of colonization' (285). Biju noticed the North-South divide and the glaring discrimination made by the airport authority and the airlines between the passengers of the third-world and those from the first: "All the third world flights docked here, families waiting days for their connections, squatting on the floor in big bacterial clumps, and it was a long trek to where the European-North American travellers came and went, making those brisk no-nonsense flights with extra leg-room and private TV, whizzing over for a single meeting in such a manner that it was truly hard to imagine they were shitting peeing, bleeding-weeping humans at all" (285).

At Frankfurt also, Biju underwent a similar experience: "The planeload spent the night in a similar quarantined zone, a thousand souls stretched out as if occupying a morgue, even their faces covered to block the buzzing tubelights" (285). The plane stopped briefly at the gulf countries—Abu Dhabi, Dubai and Bahrain to allow men to clamber on. The passengers were given cheap lunch packets. The atmosphere inside the plane became suffocating: "Added to the smell of sweat, there was now the thick odour of food and cigarettes, the recycled breathing of an entire plane, the growing fetor of the bathroom' (286). Biju was least concerned with all these. He went to the overflowing bathroom and saluted himself in the mirror. He did not come back to India with any dejection; nor did he suffer from any sense of failure. He returned home with a feeling of triumph because he had been saved from having to compromise his basic human dignity. He was going back to be re-united with his father and to relish the taste of figurative homecoming as a release from the bondage of spiritual slavery to the West which had earlier psychologically crippled Jemubhai Patel. He was not at all burdened by the memory of his stay in America. As the narrator puts it, "Here he was, on his way home, without name or knowledge of the American president, without the name of the river on whose bank he had lingered, without even hearing about any of the tourist sights—no Statue of Liberty, Macy's, Little Italy, Brooklyn Bridge, Museum of Immigration . . . no gospel churches of Harlem tour" (286). Instead, he began to make plans for the future. He would buy a taxi and drive up and down the hills on market days. The ground beneath his feet in America had proved to be shaky and unstable. Biju, therefore, dreamt of rebuilding his home in India in a securer way: 'And he'd build a house with solid walls, a roof that wouldn't fly off every monsoon season' (286). As the plane flew towards India, he played in his mind, again and again, the scene of meeting his father and wept 'at thought of so much happiness and emotion' (286). He would sit with his father in their own home, drink *chhang* together, and tell him the crude jokes he had overheard being cracked by some drunken passengers on the plane.

Chapter XLVI

The loss of Mutt was detected in the afternoon. It was her stew time. The cook had boiled soy Nutrinuggets with pumpkin and Maggi soup cube because meat was unavailable in the market. The judge was worried that his beloved pet should have to eat like this but she had already eaten the last of the meat. He shouted for the dog to come but she did not answer:

> "Mutty, Mutt, stew. . . ." The judge walked around the garden, out of the gate, and walked up and down the road.
>
> "Stew stew—"
>
> "Mutty Mutt? MUTT?" His voice became anxious.
>
> The afternoon turned into evening, the mist swept down, but Mutt

didn't appear. (288)

The dog did not return even when the darkness settled in. Worried about Mutt, he went out with the biggest flashlight in the house and began to search for her in the jungle. He waited for her on the veranda all night, listening to the howls of jackals and watching the falling lanterns of the drunkards that plummeted like shooting stars from the mountains. By the time the dawn broke, he grew frantic. The loss of Mutt unhinged Jemubhai because the absence of the dog, whom he loved more than any of his human relatives, from his claustrophobic and guilt-ridden personal world suggested the loss of the last vestige of existential meaning in his life. The crisis compelled him to put an end to his self-imposed isolation within the boundary of the crumbling colonial edifice and venture out to the small *busti* houses in search of the expensive redsetter. The judge, who had carefully avoided human company, now asked the milkman and the baker, people belonging to much lower social ranks, if they had seen his dog anywhere. They denied any knowledge and referred to Mutt as 'kutti' which angered the judge very much. He went to the market and asked the plumber, the electrician and the deaf tailors about Mutt. He received 'blank faces' everywhere and 'some angry laughter': '"*Saala, Machoot* . . . what does he think? We're going to look for his dog?" People were insulted. "At a time like this. We can't even eat!"' (289) He knocked on the doors of his neighbours with whom he had not talked for years—Mrs. Thondup, Lola and Noni, Uncle Potty and the Afghan princesses, and inquired after Mutt, a dog of very high pedigree whom he had collected from a reputed Calcutta kennel. Most of them narrated to the solicitous judge their own experience of having lost a dog earlier. Uncle Potty suspected the local thief Gobbo who had poisoned his Kutta Sahib years ago. Anglophile Lola took this opportunity to give the harried judge a sermon: "The trouble with us Indians is that we have no love of animals. A dog, a cat is there just to kick. We can't resist . . . we feel satisfaction in this" (290). Almost everyone he met 'responded with immediate doom. . . . They were already reconciled to Mutt's fate, and the judge wished to strangle them as they spoke' (289).

His anguished search for Mutt ended in failure as he was not helped by any one. Even the SDO snubbed him: "A dog! Justice, just listen to yourself. People are being killed. What can I do? Of course I have such high regard. . . . I have made time despite worry of being accused of favouritism . . . but we are in an emergency situation. In Calcutta, in Delhi, there is great concern about this severe deterioration of law and order, and in the end that's what we must think of, isn't it so?" (291) The officer even fixed the judge with 'a gluey look' which convinced him that he meant to be rude. The policemen, who used to feel awed in his presence only a few months ago, behaved with him insolently and began to snigger when he sought their help: "Ha, ha, ha. Come about his dog! Dog? He, ha ha ha ha . . . Madman!" (291). They rudely asked him to get out of the station.

Convinced of the fact that the old world was disintegrating around him, that he had lost his earlier clout and his authority as well as privileged position had gone, 'frittered away in years of misanthropy and cynicism' (292), he broke down and began to shout pathetically 'all the language that was between Mutt and himself, sending nursery words of love flying over the Himalayas' (292). The loss of the dog, which had so far defined and justified the judge's existence as a master, created an acute sense of crisis about his identity which, in turn, led to his self-humiliation.

Chapter XLVII

In the aftermath of the Mela Ground massacre, the administrative backlash began. The police were reinforced and they hunted down the GNLF men and combed the remote villages in order to weed out Gorkhaland supporters from the Marxists and the Congressmen. The police also raided the tea gardens which were closed down in the wake of insurgency and their managers, taking lessons from Assam, fled to Calcutta. People wanted by the police were always on the run, taking shelter in the houses of wealthy and privileged people of the town whose homes, they knew, would never be searched. Reports of border crossing between India and Nepal and of retired army personnel offering training to the militants and saboteurs appeared in the press. But the movement was apparently spearheaded by young boys who took 'their style from Rambo, heads full up with kung fu and karate chops, roaring around on stolen motor cycles, stolen jeeps, having a fantastic time. Money and guns in their packets. They were living the movies' (294).

The atrocity and infernal carnage unleashed by the ideologically uncommitted boys seemed to be an expression of their newly discovered belligerent identities as well as their repressed cruelty and barbarity. Absolute anarchy prevailed on the hillside as the GNLF men 'arrived with masks in the night, climbed over gates, ransacked houses' (295). They made no distinction between Nepali and non-Nepali-speaking people and looted the poor and the privileged alike: 'Seeing a woman walking home bundled in a shawl, they made her unwrap it and took the rice and the bit of sugar she'd concealed' (295). The state-sponsored terrorism was rivalled by the macabre atrocities perpetrated by the riotous insurgents:

> On the road to the market, the trees were hung with the limbs of enemies—which side and whose enemy? This was the time to make anyone you didn't like disappear, to avenge ancient family vendettas. Screams continued from the police station though a bottle of Black Label could save your life. Injured men, their spilling guts wrapped in chicken skins to keep them fresh, were rushed on bamboo stretchers to the doctor to be stitched up; a man was found buried in the sewage tank, every inch of his body slashed with a knife, his eyes gouged out. (295)

The inhuman barbarity let loose by the political insurgency thus turned the civilized place into 'a darkling plane' where, 'swept with confused alarms of struggle and flight / . . . ignorant armies clash[ed] by night' (Matthew Arnold, 'Dover Beach'). They failed to distinguish between friends and foes and killed each other indiscriminately.

The ordinary residents of Kalimpong were no doubt shocked by the heinous and persistent brutality, but they were also surprised by the mundaneness of the violence. They grew gradually bored as they discovered the extent of the perversity of the human heart and faced 'the stench of unimaginable evil' (295). Confronted with 'the larger-than-life questions,' 'caught up in the mythic battles of past vs. present, justice vs. injustice' and 'swept up in extraordinary hatred' (295), these most ordinary people found themselves strangely absorbed by the most commonplace of daily problems.

Chapter XLVIII

As the Gulf Air flight landed in Calcutta, Biju smelled once again the strong and familiar odour of phenyl with which a sweeper woman was disinfecting the floor. The woman was 'both destitute and with a talent for being exceedingly irritating' and she presented a 'potent mixture of intense sympathy and intense annoyance' (296). Several planes had arrived at the same time and there was a motley and unruly crowd of diasporic Indians collecting their luggage at the conveyor belts. Biju found 'more varieties of Indians than the ones showcased on Gulf Air . . . back in the common soup after deliberate evolution into available niches abroad' (296). There were the yuppie and the hippie Indians, the 'funky Bhangra boy,' Indians who still maintained their culture and went to the temples abroad, the poor taxi drivers and toilet cleaners as well as rich computer boys and young 'straight-laced businessmen' (297). There were 'Indians who lived abroad, Indians who travelled abroad, richest and poorest, the back-and-forth ones maintaining green cards' (297).

An Indian student had brought back a fair blonde American. He pretended to be normal and tried to be easy but his 'every molecule [was] tense and self-conscious' (297). Behind the student stood two Indian girls who 'made vomity faces' at him. One of them remarked, "Must have got off the plane and run for an American dame so he could get his green card and didn't care if she looked like a horse or no. *Which she does!!!!*" (297). As one man said sympathetically to the Indian girls but sounded 'as if he were trying to console himself': "Our ladies are the most beautiful in the world," a woman retorted, "Yes, our women are the best in the world . . . and our men are the absolute worst *gadhas* in the whole wide world" (297).

Two Indians who had come in the Air France flight, stood at a distance with disdain on their faces. One of them was from Ohio and the other was from South Dakota. Both were affluent and non-resident Indians. They were waiting for their luggage and criticizing the incompetence of the people of their country. "Just look at this," the Ohio man said, "each time you come back you think something must have changed, but it's always the same" (297). The South Dakota man agreed with him and added: "That's right . . . you don't like to say it, but you have to. Some countries don't get ahead for a reason" (297). But their luggage did not arrive and Biju overheard a fracas at the Air France counter where passengers with lost luggage had to fill out forms for compensation. The Airline made indecent discrimination in the distribution of compensation. As an aggrieved Indian passenger, whose suitcase had been lost, screamed in protest against the preferential policy, "They are only giving compensation to non-resident Indians and foreigners, not to Indian nationals. Why? . . . Unfair unfair UNFAIR UNFAIR. . . . Treating people from a rich country well and people from a poor country badly. It's a disgrace. Why this lopsided policy against your own people?" (298) The non-resident Indians holding green cards and passports remained cool and 'looked complacent and civilized' (298). Their manners showed they were taken care of well in both India and abroad. The narrator delineates the attitudes of these people very realistically: "That's just how it was, wasn't it? Fortune piled on more good fortune. They had more money and because they had more money they would get more money. It was easy for them to stand in line, and they stood patiently, displaying how they didn't have to fight anymore" (298). And if they found any 'resentful or nationalist kind of employee' at the immigration or security check, who 'would take pains to slow-torture them under any excuse' (299), they would disregard it as 'jealousy' of their success.

The Ohio man, who had criticized 'incompetent India' for the loss of his luggage in Air France, even thought that his own father was jealous of him. Unlike Mr. Kakkar, who had given a simplistic explanation of American affluence and hegemony to Biju before the latter's departure, the Ohio man's father examined the craze of the people of poor countries for the American dream from a humanitarian perspective. America, according to this gentleman, not only lured people, brought up in the lap of abject poverty and superstitious backwardness, with its material opulence but also provided shelter to those like his son who wanted to run away from the fear of having to suffer from qualms of conscience which were their ineluctable experience when they lived amidst appalling poverty in their native countries: "immigration, so often presented as a heroic act, could just as easily be the opposite; that it was cowardice that led many to America; fear marked the journey, not bravery; a cockroachy desire to scuttle to where you never saw poverty, not really, never had to suffer a tug to your conscience; where you never heard the demands of servants, beggars, bankrupt relatives, and where your generosity would never be openly claimed; where by merely looking after your own wife-child-dog-yard you could feel virtuous. Experience the relief of being an unknown transplant to the locals and hide the perspective granted by journey" (299). Although the Ohio man shrugged this disconcerting insight into the process of migration as simple jealousy and 'third world chip on the shoulder' (200), it adds an extra perspective to the novel and marks it out from the general run of immigrant literature.

After returning to Calcutta Biju felt like returning to his mother's lap. It was a real homecoming for him as he happened to discover his true identity after his prolonged humiliation and indignity of having to live as an illegal immigrant on the American soil: "Biju stepped out of the airport into the Calcutta night, warm, mammalian. His feet sank into dust winnowed to softness at his feet, and he felt an unbearable feeling, sad and tender, old and sweet like the memory of falling asleep, a baby on his mother's lap" (300). He felt relieved of 'the enormous anxiety of being a foreigner,' of the 'unbearable arrogance and shame of the immigrant' (300), and realized that he had regained the clarity of vision: "He looked about and for the first time in God knows how long, his vision unblurred and he found that he could see clearly" (300).

Chapter XLIX

The loss of Mutt mentally unbalanced the judge so much that he indulged in self-humiliation. Undoing his education and the well-nurtured façade of his intellectual, rational and agnostic self, the Cambridge-returned member of the ICS, 'who had made a long hard journey to jettison his family's prayers' (301), gambled with fate and made strange bargains with God: "If you return Mutt, I will acknowledge you in public. I will never deny you again, I will tell the world that I believe in you—you—if you return Mutt" (301).

The judge's words are reminiscent of the prayer of Sarah Miles, the saint-sinner-adulteress in Graham Greene's novel *The End of the Affair*. Sarah prayed to God for the life of her lover, Maurice Bendrix, who had apparently been killed in an air-raid: "Let him be alive, and I will believe." By night a disquieting thought struck Jemubhai's mind: 'Was this faith that he had turned away, was it paying him back?" (301). He was overcome with remorse and a strong sense of guilt. The loss of Mutt, he felt, might be a divine retribution for 'sins he had committed that no court in the world could take on" (301). But then doubt entered his mind: "But who could be paying him back? He didn't believe in angered divinity, in a scale of balance. Of course not. The universe wasn't in the business of justice. That had simply been his own human conceit—until he learned better" (302). He now regretted that he had abandoned his family, insulted his father and returned his wife: "Yet he thought of his family that he had abandoned. He thought of his father, whose strength and hope and love he had fed on, only to turn around to spit in his face. Then he thought of how he had returned his wife, Nimi" (302).

He bitterly remembered the incident which had led him to send Nimi home. One morning, when the judge was away from Bonda on an official tour, Nimi, the obedient wife of a loyal servant of the Raj, participated half-heartedly in a rally of the Congress Party organized to welcome Nehru at the railway station. She was taken there by a group of ladies led by a passionate Congresswoman, Mrs. Mohan. But it was regarded by the authority as an act of insubordination which seriously compromised the judge's career. When Jemubhai returned from the tour, he was given the disconcerting news by the district commissioner who warned him against repetition of such incidents and said, "I trust that no member of your family will do anything to compromise your career again. I'm warning you, Patel" (303). Jemubhai was enraged at his wife's independence which had put him on the wrong side of history. He returned home, fixed himself a drink and confronted Nimi with the irrefutable evidence of her misdeed. He asked her a series of questions but Nimi, 'summoning up the same spirit of the powder-puff night' (304), defied him and remained silent. When, angry at her disobedience, the judge called her 'bloody stupid,' she broke her prolonged silence and, to 'his amazed ears and her own shocked ears, as if waking up to a moment of clarity before death, she said: "You are the one who is stupid"' (304). This resulted in an amazing act of violence and in a merciless physical torture by her male-chauvinist and Cambridge-educated husband:

> For the first time he hit her, although he had wanted to before and fought the urge for some time. He emptied his glass on her head, sent a jug of water swinging into the face he no longer found beautiful, filled her ears with leaping soda water. Then, when this wasn't enough to assuage his rage, he hammered down with his fists, raising his arms to bring them down on her again and again, rhythmically, until his own hands were exhausted and his shoulders next day were strained sore as if from chopping wood. He even limped a bit, his leg hurting from kicking her. "Stupid bitch, dirty bitch!" The more he swore, the harder he found he could hit. (304-5)

Then she bought her a ticket and returned her to her family in Piphit because he realized that he could not bear her any longer and that if things went on like that, he would 'skid from control and jeopardize his career to commit a final violent act' (305). Six months later, a telegram came from Nimi's uncle (her father Bomanbhai had passed away in the meantime) to announce the arrival of a baby. Her family hoped that the baby 'would bring the father back to their community' (306) and, influential as he was now, he would help them. But Jemubhai did not go to see his daughter, nor did he take Nimi back when she was ready to return. Even the pleadings of his aggrieved father, who went to Bonda to persuade his son to take Nimi back, failed to change his mind. He said to his son: "Our family honour is gone. We are lucky Bomanbhai is dead, thank God. It's the scandal of the town" (306). The reply the Cambridge-returned judge gave his father only exposed the hollowness of his education as a means of civilizing and humanizing an individual: "Why are you talking like this?" he said to his father. "You're following the script of a village idiot. She is unsuitable to be my wife" (306).

Jemu, the best bet of his family, thus let down his father whose love and strength he had constantly fed on. He abandoned his family and betrayed it 'for the sake of false ideals' (308): "He had been recruited to bring his countrymen into the modern age, but he could only make it himself by cutting them off entirely, or they would show up reproachful, pointing out to him the lie he had become" (306). He had shamed his family, shamed the family of his wife, stolen her dignity, turned her into a human wreck—a very embodiment of her family's humiliation, and then abandoned her with the child he had begotten. Nimi's uncle, who had usurped Bomanbhai's property, turned her out of his house and she spent the rest of her life miserably with a sister. A few months after independence, when Jemu, like other Indian members of the ICS, rose to a very high position, he received a second telegram informing him of the death of his wife (who had caught fire over a stove). Jemubhai chose to believe that it was an accident and so he did not suffer from any guilt. As the narrator puts it movingly: "Ashes have no weight, they tell no secrets, they rise too lightly for guilt; too lightly for gravity, they float upward and, thankfully, disappear" (308). The touchingly poetic words evince the total degeneration of Jemubhai and his criminal dereliction of duty as a responsible human being towards his wife whom he had liked only once in his life: "He was twenty, she fourteen. The place was Piphit and they were on a bicycle, traversing gloriously down a slope through cow pats" (308).

He did not accept his parental responsibility of the girl whom he had accidentally begotten while engaging in one of those beastly sexual acts with his abhorred wife. He condemned her to convent boarding schools and never enquired after her whereabouts when as a college student she fell in love with and married an air force pilot who was a Zoroastrian and had grown up in an orphanage. When many years later her daughter Sai arrived at his doorsteps for shelter, he 'hoped an unacknowledged system of justice was beginning to erase his debts' (308).

The loss of Mutt, whom he loved much more than any one of his human relatives, might be, he now felt, a punishment for all those accumulated sins. Overcome with an indelible sense of guilt, the judge went out searching for his pet canine over the mountains, his voice splintered as he sent out funny words of love to the lost bitch: "Mutt. . . . My funny love. My naughty love. My funny naughty love" (308). He was joined in this bootless search by Sai and the cook whom the occasion provided an opportunity to disguise their individual worries and loss.

a tree to hold the swaying telephone line steady and 'a gale of static inflicted itself on the space between father and son' (231). The conversation resumed and Biju and the cook exchanged a few brief, clipped sentences hurriedly. Each learnt that the other was alive and everything was all right with him. Panna Lal advised his son not to worry about him or anything at Kalimpong but to mind his own health. Soon they found that despite their emotion they had nothing more to say and fell abruptly into silence. When the cook, prompted by the watchman, asked his son when he would come, Biju almost burst into tears because he could not say that he 'hadn't even attained the decency of being granted a holiday now and then. He could not go home to see his father' (232). The telephone suddenly went dead and the father and the son were left stranded in the unbridgeable distance that lay between them. The cook made a desperate attempt to shake the phone back into life, for he wanted to say 'good-bye' to Biju. But the electronic gadget remained mute and he put it down, trembling. The watchman consoled his distraught friend by saying that Biju would ring again and that he would come back fat from America. The unfinished conversation only served to intensify the unbearable feeling of emptiness that Biju had hoped to dispel by making the phone call: 'He could not talk to his father; there was nothing left between them but emergency sentences, clipped telegram lines shouted out as if in the midst of a war' (232). He was over-whelmed by an ominous apprehension that he might never see his father again if he continued to stay in New York. He knew that such things always happened: 'ten years passed, fifteen, the telegram arrived, or the phone call, the parent was gone and the child was too late. Or they returned and found they'd missed the entire last quarter of a lifetime, their parents like photograph negatives' (233). Even worse tragedies were known to have taken place. The children returned home from abroad only to find that the love between them and their parents had vanished. Only the façade remained while the emotion itself 'had been eaten from inside, like Cho Oyu being gouged by termites from within' (233). Biju remembered how his father had once written to him out of ignorance: "Are you growing fat, beta, like everyone in America?" (233) And he had written back untruthfully: "Yes, growing fat . . . when you see me next, I will be myself times ten" (233). Both he and his father had enjoyed the joke at that time. But he was shocked by his mendacity when he went to a cheap store and found that he had to buy shirts of children's size. The shopkeeper, a Pakistani from Lahore who watched from a ladder in the centre to make sure nobody stole anything from the racks, regarded him with suspicion for his guilt-stricken look. Biju, suffering from 'a feeling of culpability,' missed Saeed Saeed terribly because he wished to look at America, even if briefly, 'through the sanguine lens of his eyes' (233).

Chapter XXXVII

Despite the SDO's claim to the contrary, the situation in Kalimpong deteriorated very fast. A series of strikes called by the GNLF disrupted normal life. The police had begun to arrest and torture random people all over the town. There was acute scarcity of food in the market and even privileged people like Lola fought with their neighbours for the last jars and cans. Curfew was imposed by the authority to prevent violence and the inhabitants, who were obliged to remain confined within their houses, had 'a feeling of being stifled in a place that was . . . generous with space if nothing else' (235). A reign of terror was unleashed by the GNLF. The shops and offices remained closed. Everyone was terrorized to keep their shutters down and not to look out of their windows. Roadblocks completely cut off Kalimpong from the rest of the country and prevented tea, timber and stones from being transported from the hills. The GNLF cadres demanded huge sums of money from those whom they allowed to go through and compelled people to buy GNLF speeches and Gorkhaland calendars. Truckfulls of Gorkha volunteers arrived from Tindharia and Mahanadi to attack the police station, and even tear gas and lathi-change failed to scatter them away. They resorted to increasing violence to attain their political objective, formation of a separate Gorkhaland that would include the three subdivisions of Darjeeling, Kalimpong and Kurseong and parts of Jalpaiguri and Cooch Behar districts. Lola was shocked by the nefarious plot to disintegrate the country and destroy peace in the hills. India was an idea or a concept to her and the separatist movement was an attempt to attack and crumble this idea. The narrator analyses her thoughts in the following words: "What was a country but the idea of it? She thought of India as a concept, a hope, or a desire. How often could you attack it before it crumbled? To undo something took practice; it was a dark art and they were perfecting it. With each argument the next would be easier, would become a compulsive act, and like wrecking a marriage, it would be impossible to keep away, to stop picking at wounds even if the wounds were your own" (236). They were getting bored by the forceful confinement in their house. They could not go out and meet people. They were done with the library books but they could not think of returning them because the Gymkhana club had been forcibly occupied by the GNLF men who had herded out the librarian and the desk clerks in order to enjoy the space and privacy of the place themselves. Tourists stopped coming from Calcutta in view of the political disturbances in the hills and consequently the hotels and company guesthouses were closed down. Children were 'plucked from boarding schools as parents opened the papers to read with horror of the salubrious climate of the hills being disturbed by separatist rebels and guerilla tactics' (237). There was no fuel in the town—either gas or kerosene, and people were compelled to cook on wood. There was no water and, as the power stations had been gutted down to protest against the arrests of GNLF men at roadblocks, there was no electricity either. As the fridge went silent, Lola and Noni were forced to cook all the perishable food at once. The poignant smell of mutton cooking drew a group of passing GNLF boys, who were looking for shelter, into Mon Ami. They climbed through the kitchen window and intruded into the house. The sisters had moved two enormous locks from the tin trunks that contained valuables to the front and back doors of the house as extra precautionary measures. Several 'objects of worth' were left vulnerable in the attic above their heads—family puja silver, Bond street baby cups, an expensive telescope made in Germany, their grandmother's pearly earrings, and bat eyeglasses, articles which the narrator describes as 'Magpie things gleaned from a romantic version of the West and a fanciful version of the East that contained power enough to maintain dignity across the rotten offences between nations' (238). In reply to Lola's question why they had trespassed on their house, the boys, who were disconcertingly polite despite their forced entry and rebel camouflage dress, said that they had come to sell calendars and cassettes for the GNLF movement and collect 'contribution to the effort for Gorkhaland' (238). Lola, angry at their audacity and presumptuousness, was unwilling to make any contribution. But Noni with her practical sense and hidden sympathy for the Gorkhas' cause, advised caution because any recklessness would lead them into further trouble. They bought three calendars and two cassettes. Still, the boys did not leave the house. They ate all the food cooked by the sisters and slept on the floor. They were sure that police would never search for them in the house of the privileged people. The sisters, like their pet cat Mustafa, felt their 'self-respect assaulted' (239) and spent the night awake, having barricaded their bedroom door with a heavy chest of drawers. They hoped that Budhoo would come and scare the boys with his gun. But the Nepali watchman surprisingly did not appear that night and Lola suspected his complicity in the crime. She rebuked Noni for giving in to the boys' demand and mimicked her softness towards the militants: "You're the one who is naïve: 'They have a point, they have poiiiintt, three fourths of their point if not the whole poiiint,' now look . . . you stupid woman!' (239) Before leaving the house next morning, the boys threatened the sisters with dire consequences if they informed the police. As they 'left with the rice and the soap, the oil, and the garden's annual output of five jars of tomato chutney' (240), they noticed the huge empty space in the property that stretched into a lawn and that could 'accommodate a thin line of huts' (240). Even before a month had passed, the Bengali sisters woke up one morning to find that their property had been illegally occupied under the cover of night and a hut had been built up at the bottom of the garden's vegetable patch. They rushed out of their rooms to protest against this forceful encroachment. But the intruders arrogantly brushed aside their accusation:

> They rushed out: "This is our land!"
>
> "It is not your land. It is free land," they countered, putting down the sentence, flatly, rudely.
>
> "It is our land."
>
> "It is unoccupied land." (240)

When the sisters threatened to call the police, the intruders simply shrugged, turned back and went on working. Thus Anglophile Lola and Noni were shocked out of their genteel retirement and forced to take note of what was happening around them.

Chapter XXXVIII

The intruders' defiance of the owners of Mon Ami originated from an old feeling of anger that could not be separated from Kalimpong. As the narrator remarks, 'It was part of every breath. It was in the eyes that waited, attached themselves to you as you approached, rode on your back as you walked on, with a muttered remark you couldn't catch in the moment of passing' (241). The rising militancy, a violent expression of the long-suppressed anger and despair of the ethnic Nepalis, shocked the rich and privileged people like Lola and Noni who had never paid any serious attention to the sons of the soil and their problems. But trouble on their doorstep made them alert to the socio-political ferment which was born of a desperation to settle the historical ledger: "Only before, the sisters had never paid much attention for the simple reason that they didn't have to. It was natural they would incite envy, they supposed, and the laws of probability favoured their slipping through life without anything more than muttered comments, but every now and then, somebody suffered the rotten luck of being in the exact wrong place at the exact wrong time when it all caught up—and generations worth of trouble settled on them" (241). To Anglophile people like Lola and Noni, who, with their colonial baggage, were a *de trop* anachronism in postcolonial India, this came as a profound shock: "Just when Lola had thought it would continue, a hundred years like the one past—Trollope, BBC, a burst of hilarity at Christmas—all of a sudden, all that they had claimed innocent, fun, funny, not really to matter, was proven wrong" (241-42). Compelled by circumstances to look at the world around them, they realized that it really mattered to partake of tinned ham roll in a country where people mostly lived on rice and dal, to live in a big comfortable house and 'to fly to London and return with chocolates filled with kirsch' (242). Their very wealth which had so far protected them from trouble, now made them vulnerable. As the narrator aptly remarks: "The wealth that seemed to protect them like a blanket was the very thing that left them exposed. They, amid extreme poverty, were baldly richer, and the statistics of difference were being broadcast over loudspeakers, written loudly across the walls. The anger had solidified into slogans and guns, and it turned out that they, *they*, Lola and Noni, were the unlucky ones who wouldn't slip through, who would pay the debt that should be shared with others over many generations" (242). Lola, the widow, went to Pradhan, the flamboyant chief of the GNLF's Kalimpong wing, to complain about the illegal encroachment on their property by his followers. Pradhan, who 'looked like a bandit teddy bear, with a great beard and a bandana around his head' (243), controlled his wing 'like a king his kingdom, a robber his band' (243). He was rumoured to be wilder and angrier than Subhas Ghising, the leader of GNLF's Darjeeling wing, who was a better politician and possessed literary talent. But her mission proved abortive. Instead of doing any justice by way of arranging for the retrieval of her property from the possession of his followers, Pradhan grossly insulted the helpless and elderly woman. He rakishly said to Lola: "I am the raja of Kalimpong. A raja must have many queens. . . . I have four, but would you, . . . dear Aunty, would you like to be the fifth? . . . And you know, you won't be bearing me any sons at your age so I will expect a big dowry. And you're not much to look at, nothing up . . . nothing down" (243). As Lola—ridiculed, detested, the butt of the crudest joke—left his house, she could hear Pradhan and his men laughing behind her. And, strangely enough, she shifted the oppressive burden of her humiliation on to her dead husband and his old-fashioned, gentleman's notion of retirement in the hilly resort: "Joydeep . . . look at what you've done, you bloody fool!!! . . . Look at what you've left me to! Do you know how I have suffered . . . where are you?! You and your piddling little life, and look what I have to deal with, just look, I don't even have my decency" (245). She even called him a 'bastard' for his foolish ideas of countryside living which had embroiled her and her sister in such trouble and threatened them with forcible ejection from their own house. But, in a moment, she remembered the romantic Joydeep, who read Yeats and Rilke and used to kiss her glistening eyes before leaving for work, and became weak: "Your eyes are lovely, dark and deep./ But I have promises to keep,/ And miles to go before I sleep—/ And miles to go before you sleep" (246). She was so upset by the insult that she did not talk to Nani, who had been anxiously waiting for her to return. She went straight into the bathroom, shut it from inside and sat trembling on the closed lid of the toilet. She did not respond to Noni's importunate requests to come out of the toilet and talk to her. Lola was angry with her sister who sympathized with the Nepalis and believed that the GNLF's cause was partially justified. The ensuing quarrel between the two sisters brought to the fore their attitudinal differences over the Gorkhaland issue:

> Noni at the door: "Are you all right?"
>
> Loudly, Lola said: "No, I'm not all right. Why don't you go away?"
>
> "Why don't you open the door?"
>
> "Go away I tell you, go join the boys in the street whom you are always defending."
>
> "Lola, open the door."
>
> "No."
>
> . . .
>
> "Well, sister, in any such situation atrocities are committed under cover of a legitimate cause—"
>
> "Bosh."
>
> "But if we forget there is some truth to what they are saying the problems will keep coming, Gorkhas have been used—"
>
> "Cock and bull," she said crudely. "These people aren't good people. Gorkhas are mercenaries, that's what they are. Pay them and they are loyal to whatever. There's no principle involved, Noni. And what is this with the GOrkha? It was always Gurkha." (246-47)

As their world crumbled before them, the westernized sisters shockingly realized that they had been fools living in a realm of make-believe: "they had been wrong. The real place had evaded them. The two of them had been fools feeling they were doing something exciting just by occupying this picturesque cottage, by seducing themselves with those old travel books in the library, searching for a certain angled light with which to romance themselves" (247). They indulged themselves in the pretension of keeping up civilization in that backward 'place of towering, flickering green' (247) while the local people, like their watchman Budhoo and maidservant Kesang, who led parallel lives of poverty and deprivation, did not suffer from any such self-consciousness or illusion. The sisters carefully maintained various objects of modernity, like radio, T.V., hot water bottle, Swiss knife, mosquito net etc., which were to them, 'talismans imbued with the task of transforming reality into something otherwise, supplies manufactured by a world that equated them with courage' (247-48). But, in reality, these objects were synonymous with cowardice. Faced with the existential crisis, the sisters recognized that there was a certain depth to their lives and emotions beyond their own significance.

Chapter XXXIX

As the ethno-racial insurgency grew in strength, all the gentle lives were upended and those who had enjoyed power and privilege were compelled to taste life without them. While Kalimpong was rocked by sporadic fits of violence, Sai continued to smart from the insult caused by Gyan's refusal to acknowledge her in Darjeeling. She remembered his ferocious look that had warned her to stay away from him. He had come to Cho Oyu one last time after the library trip to Gymkhana club and 'sat at the table as if in chains' (249). Sai felt ashamed of his disgraceful behaviour: "A few months ago the ardent pursuit and now he behaved as if she had chased and trapped him, tail between his legs, into a cage!" (249) The sudden change in him surprised her and she began to abhor Gyan for she 'could not believe she had loved something so despicable. Her kiss had not turned him into a prince; he had morphed into a bloody frog' (249). In reply to her question: "What kind of man are you? . . . Is this any way to behave?," Gyan admitted his mental confusion and said: "I'm only human and sometimes I'm weak. Sorry" (249). The casual expression of sorrow only served to unleash a 'demoness of rage' in her and she sharply reacted to his admission of human weakness by saying: "At whose expense are you weak and human! You'll never get anywhere in life, my friend, . . . if this is what you think makes an excuse. A murderer could say the same and you think he would be let off the hook to hop in the spring?" (249-50) Gyan's racial bias came in sharp and fierce conflict with Sai's unprejudiced sanity in their mutually virulent verbal encounter: 'He began to feel irritated, for, really who was she to lecture him? "Gorkhaland for Gorkhas. We are the liberation army." He was a martyr, a man; a man, in fact, of ambition, principle' (250). Angry with himself and with Sai, he stormed off by saying: "I don't have to listen to this" (250). Yet, she could not forget her relation with Gyan and desperately hoped that he would come back. The intensity of her desire almost drove her mad, and 'sick with the desire to be desired' (250), she waited for his return. She seemed to have lost her former skill at solitude.

Marooned at home during the curfew, she waited for her lover and read Emily Bronte's bleak novel *Wuthering Heights* with its passionate love, strong hatred and stormy feelings that imparted 'a wild animal feeling to her gut' (250), and still Gyan did not return to her. The instincts of violence and hatred that estranged the lovers from one another were shown to operate in the world of animals and insects also. Sai noticed the sight of a 'dead scorpion being dismantled by ants—first its popeye arm went by, carried by a line of ant coolies, then the sting and, separately the eye' (250).

Sick with futile waiting, she visited Uncle Potty and in response to his hearty welcome, she smiled only out of politeness. Looking at Sai's lovelorn condition, Potty 'felt a flash of jealousy as do friends when they lose another to love, especially those who have understood that friendship is enough, steadier, healthier, easier on the heart. Something that always added and never took away' (250). He was scared to find her subtracted by love. Uncle Potty, who had himself been a great lover of love in his youth, had anticipated this long ago and had tried to indicate to her that she must look at love intelligently: 'it was tapestry and art, the sorrow of it, the loss of it, should be part of the intelligence, and even a sad romance would be worth more than any simple bovine happiness' (251). When Sai visited Mon Ami, Lola and Noni were amused by her condition which provided them with 'a bit of fun in the midst of trouble' (251). They guessed about the lover and asked her his name. But fortunately she caught a common cold that 'shrouded [the] fall of her dignity . . . muddled the origin of her streaming eyes and . . . shuffled the symptoms of virus and disgraceful fall from the tightrope of splendorous love' (251). She suffered terribly: 'Her eyes were red and raw, spilling over. Pressure weighed downward like a gestapo boot on her brain' (252). But she could not forget Gyan for a moment. Suffering from 'the perpetual gnawing urgency and intensity of waiting,' she wondered: "Was her affection for Gyan just a habit? How on earth could she think of someone so much?" (252) Sai tried to console herself and accept the loss of love gracefully: 'There was grace in forgetting and giving up . . . it was childish not to—everyone had to accept imperfection and loss in life' (252). But her attempt failed and uselessly she tried to combat her restlessness until she realized that it was she who had to relent and take the initiative for effecting a reconciliation. So, as the curfew was lifted, she 'started out on the undignified mission of searching for Gyan' (252) in order to restore her broken relationship with him and salvage her own dignity.

Chapter XL

Sai's mission to find out Gyan and effect a reconciliation proved disastrous. She did not find him anywhere in the market and went to the Kalimpong college where he had studied. She walked by the deserted classrooms with their 'chloroformed atmosphere,' and 'blackboard still with its symbols and calculations' (254), and then moved around the other side of the mountains which overlooked the Bong Busti where Gyan lived with his family. It took two hours downhill journey to reach his house situated in the poorest part of Kalimpong which was 'quite foreign to her' (254). Gyan had told her the stories of his ancestors in the British army but remained silent about his present family. Sai had a premonition and she felt that she should not venture forth. But she could not stop herself. She passed by several churches which were dark and closed because 'the missionaries always left in dangerous times to enjoy chocolate chip cookies and increase funds at home, until it was peaceful enough to venture forth again, that they might launch attack, renewed and fortified, against a weakened and desperate populace' (254). Kiran Desai's attitude to the church and the missionaries in north-eastern India evinces her dislike and distrust and shows that she looks at events through the lens of her Indianness. While passing by fields and small clusters of houses, Sai was 'confused in a capillary web of paths that criss-crossed the mountains' (254) and led to huts perched on thick bamboo ledges. Watching the scene of dismal poverty, Sai realized that she had committed a grave mistake by deciding to come to the place: 'Tin roofs promised tetanus; outhouses gestured into the ether so that droppings would fall into the valley . . . in these homes it was cramped and wet, the smoke thick enough to choke you, the inhabitants eating meagrely in the candlelight too dim to see by, rats and snakes in the rafters fighting over insects and birds' eggs . . . all the men drank too much, reality skidding into nightmares, brawls, and beating' (254-55). A woman holding a baby pointed at Gyan's house which looked like 'a small, slime-slicked cube' from which 'cement corrupted by sand . . . came spilling forth from pockmarks as if from a punctured bag' (255). Sai was shocked by the grim picture of poverty, disease and deprivation in Bong Busti where Gyan lived in a cube-like hole: "There were houses like this everywhere . . . common to those who had struggled to the far edge of the middle class—just to the edge, only just, holding on desperately—but were at every moment being undone, the house slipping back, not into the picturesque poverty that tourists liked to photograph but into something truly dismal—modernity proffered in its meanest form, brand-new one day, in ruin the next" (255-56). The house did not go with either Gyan's appearance or his education. Nor did it match his future. Like the judge, he was the chosen son of his family; much was sacrificed for his success. Sai felt ashamed of her lover who 'must have hoped his silence would be construed as dignity' (256), and experienced a distaste for herself for having been connected, unknowingly though, with this indigent enterprise. She stood undecided for some minutes, looking at a harem of chickens that formed 'a grotesque bunch, rape and violence being enacted, hens being hammered and pecked as they screamed and flapped, attempting escape from the rapist rooster (256), the rooster that 'climbed out of [a] pot and began to strut about . . . the only grand thing around, crowned, spurred, crowing like a colonial' (257).

The image of violence in the animal world foreshadows the imminent explosion of hatred and cruelty between the lovers. Gyan was outraged by Sai's presence in his house: 'How dare she seek him out to find her indulgence in pity!' (257). She encountered a stony Gyan who asked her in a refrigerated voice, "What do you want?" (257).

Sai was bitterly angry with her lover for his hypocrisy and pretension ('Pretending one thing, living another. Nothing but lies through and through' [257]). Astounded by the apparent indifference of the man who had ardently pursued her only a few months ago, Sai hid her real intention behind her visit to his house and asked him instead about the expulsion of Father Booty from Kalimpong for which she held him responsible. Evidently outraged at the injustice done to the philanthropic priest, who had been forced on to a police jeep leaving for the Bagdogra airport at Siliguri, 'having lost everything but his memories' (257) and being compelled to leave 'his friend Uncle Potty in mourning, drinking, the world breaking in waves about him,' she accused Gyan: "Look at what you people are doing" (258). She reminded him that the Swiss priest had done much more for the people on the hills than any Nepali would ever will and told him: "You, for one, are better gone than Father Booty" (258). At this, Gyan's ethno-nationalistic feelings were stirred and he responded angrily: "In fact, good thing they kicked him out . . . who needs Swiss people here? For how many thousands of years have we produced our own milk? . . . We don't want any cheese and the last thing we need is chocolate cigars" (258). Gyan's intolerance and uncivilized mode of behaviour so infuriated Sai that she anticipated the taste of blood which she wished to draw by clawing him and plucking out his eyes. But outwardly she remained cool and argued: 'Civilization is important' (258). He scoffed at her argument by saying: "That is not civilization, you fool. Schools and hospitals. That is." Blinded by uncontrollable fury at his audacious attempt to trample upon her human dignity, Sai hit him below the belt: "But you have to set a standard. Or else everything will be brought down to the same low level as you and your family" (258). Gyan counter-attacked her by saying: "I see, Swiss luxury sets a standard, chocolates and watches set the standard. . . . Yes, soothe your guilty conscience, stupid little girl, and hope someone doesn't burn down your house for the simple reason that you are a fool" (258-59). Sai answered back: "If this is what you've been thinking, why didn't you boycott the cheese instead of gobbling it down? Now you attack it? *Hypocrite*!" (259)

The romance between Gyan and Sai thus turned into a fierce battle in which they attacked each other like sworn enemies. Sai accused Gyan of unfairness because he hated her for 'big reasons' which had nothing to do with her and directly accused him of betraying her family to the GNLF hooligans. Gyan, who had been frightened by the violent turn that the Gorkhaland movement was taking and felt worried that he would not be able to live up to his revolutionary proclamations, was nonplussed by her accusations which posed a serious challenge to his racial as well as male-chauvinist identity. His desire for adulthood was kindled by her indisputable allegations ('He needed to be a man. He needed to stand tall and be rough' [259]) and he felt that 'he owed much to his rejection of Sai' (260) who suddenly ceased to be a miraculous and inspiring person and appeared to be 'a mirror that showed him himself far too clearly for comfort' (262).

Unable to swallow the insult to himself and his family, he violently retaliated by throwing her into a lantana bush and beating her mercilessly with a stick before the awe-struck eyes of his sister. He ordered Sai never to come to his place again and she threatened his sister by saying: "Good you saw, good that you heard. Go and tell your parents what your brother has been up to, telling me he loves me, making all kinds of promises and then sending robbers to our house. I'll go to the police and then let's see what happens to your family" (262).

In this way, their love was consumed by violence and hatred and their inter-communal romance was thwarted by reasons beyond their comprehension and control. Sai returned home slowly, squirming in the pain of insult and unrequited love, and felt amazed to find how the history of her family repeated itself in her own life: "Gyan would find adulthood and purity in a quest for a homeland and she would be left forever adolescent, trapped in shameful dramatics. This was the history that sustained her: the family that never cared, the lover who forgot." (265)

But she had an innate strength to rise above her personal sorrow and sympathize with other human beings in distress. Thus, when, after returning home from Bong Busti, she found that the father and the wife of the drunkard arrested and tortured by the police, who had come to the judge, walking half a day from their village across the

Relli river, to beg for mercy and help, had been treated by him with hideous apathy and turned out with inhuman indifference, she was overwhelmed with pity. She enquired of the cook if he had given the helpless creatures any food. When Panna Lal went out with a sack of rice, he found that the pair had disappeared in the darkness of night.

Chapter XLI

The unfinished telephonic conversation with his father had generated an unshakable unease in Biju. He had attempted to telephone his father again on the next day and the day after but to no avail. The phone at the Metal Box guesthouse had completely gone dead. Moreover, Mr. Iype, the news agent, had informed him that there was more trouble in Kalimpong and it would continue for a while because the Nepalis were very violent people.

In order to divert his disturbed mind, Biju went to the riverside park for a walk. While he was watching how the great waves of the Hudson 'were torn up and ripped forward, the wind propelling the gusts upriver' (266), someone told him from behind: "Look at that. It's getting fucking Biblical. . . . Fucking Job. Why? Why?" (266). Looking back, Biju found a mad and intelligent person with fat face and scanty hair who camped out at a bookstore. He asked Biju, "You know what the name of this river really is?" As Biju remained silent, he answered: "Muhheakunnuk, *Muhheakunnuk*—the river that flows both ways . . . *both ways.* That is the real fucking name." (267) It struck Biju: "But what was the false name then?" But he did not say anything, because he could not identify himself with America and its history. He remained a foreigner for ever. As the narrator remarks, "Biju possessed no name at all for this black water. It was not his history' (267). The crazy fellow continued to tell him the story of the river and of the arrival of Moby Dick: 'And then came *fucking Moby Dick.* The river full of *dead fucking whales.* The *fucking carcasses* were hauled up the river, *fucking pulverized* in the factories' (267) to extract oil and prepare corsets. But Biju, burdened as he was with his own anxiety, had no interest in his rambling talk, and walked away from the place saying "No speak English" (267). This is what he always said to crazy people, who started up conversations with him in the city, 'to the irascible ornery bums and Bible folk . . . chasing after infidels' (267).

He had once met a Lithuanian follower of ISKON who had arrived at New York via Vilnius and Vrindavan. The Hare Krishna disciple offered him a brochure with a lurid picture of Lord Krishna in the battlefield of Kurukshetra. But a 'reproachful veggie look accompanied the brochure to the former beef cook' (267). Biju had averted his gaze from the man 'as if from an obscenity. In its own way it was like a prostitute—it showed too much' (267). The incident had shaken him and filled his mind with some unanswered questions: "What was India to these people? How many lived in the fake versions of their countries, in fake versions of other people's countries? Did their lives feel as unreal to them as his own did to him?" (267). Biju was assailed by doubt and self-questioning: 'What was he doing and why?' (268) The questions had not haunted him before he left India. But while walking back to Gandhi Café, he was overwhelmed by the sheer emptiness of his life in America which had not added up to anything: 'he was emptying out. Year by year, his life wasn't amounting to anything at all; in a space that should have included family, friends, he was the only one displacing the air' (268). Although 'another part of him had expanded: his self consciousness, his self-pity' (268), this awareness only made him long to fade into insignificance, to 'return to a life where he might slice his own importance, to 'where he might relinquish this overrated control over his own destiny, and perhaps be subtracted from its determination altogether' (268). With the realization of the purposelessness of his life, the thought of returning home struck his mind again, this time more forcefully. He now wanted to go back to his native place where he might 'experience [the] greatest luxury of not noticing himself at all' (268). Biju was advised by his well-wishers not to go back. Mr. Kakkar, the proprietor of Shangri-la Travel, told him that he would commit a big mistake if he went back: "Going back? . . . don't be completely crazy—all those relatives asking for money! Even strangers are asking for money. . . . I'm telling you, my friend, they will get you; if they won't, the robbers will" (269). It was Mr. Kakkar who told Biju about the American hegemony in the new and discriminatory economic system:

> America is in the process of buying up the world. Go back, you'll find they own the businesses. One day, you'll be working for an American company there or here. Think of your children. If you stay here, your son will earn a hundred thousand dollars for the same company he could be working for in India but making one thousand dollars. How, then, can you send your children to the best international college? You are making a big mistake. Still a world, my friend, where one side travels to be a servant, and the other side travels to be treated like a king. You want your son to be on this side or that side? (269)

Despite his warning, Mr. Kakkar sold him a ticket to India on Gulf Air and Biju went out on a shopping spree. He purchased lots of modern gadgetry for himself and his father. He felt neither dejected nor remorseful at the thought of going back. Once the decision to return home was taken by him, Biju, interestingly, began to resuscitate his happy memory of the country; he did not 'think of any of the things that had made him leave in the first place' (270).

Chapter XLII

Gyan bribed his sister to keep the fight between him and Sai a secret. But the moment he left the house, the girl switched her loyalty and disclosed what had happened to her family. When he returned home, he found that the entire household was aware of his brawl with his fiancée, 'expanded to theatrical dimensions' (271). The reference to guns 'had the astonishing effect of waking his grandmother up out of a stupor' (271). The old woman rolled up a newspaper and smacked Gyan very hard on the head and on his bottom. She angrily said to her grandson: "Take control of yourself. Running around like a fool, paying no attention to your studies! Where is this going to get you? In jail, that's where" (271). She locked Gyan up in his room in order to prevent him from mixing with Sai and participating in the violent movement. When his friends came to look for him and announce the GNLF's edict that every family in the town had to send a male member to represent the household in its rally to be held in the Mela Ground the very next day, she sent them away by telling a lie: "He is sick. . . . Very sick. Can't see you any more" (272).

Although Gyan pretended frustration at this familial ban, he felt

Chapter L

After reaching Siliguri, Biju found no bus to Kalimpong. The situation in the hills had deteriorated. Things were very tense and no vehicle could go to Kalimpong because the roads were completely closed. As the man at Siliguri bus station, who was surprised at Biju's ignorance of what had been happening on the hillside, said: "Can't go. There's no way. There's an emergency situation and they've put up roadblocks, spread Mobil oil and nails all over the streets—roads are completely closed" (310). When he learnt that Biju had come from America and was totally out of touch with the country, the man took pity on him. He showed Biju, who insisted on going to Kalimpong to see his old father, a way out: "Listen," he said, "go to Panitunk and you might find some vehicle from there, but it's very dangerous. You will have to beg the GNLF men" (310).

After four days' waiting Biju found a GNLF jeep leaving for Kalimpong. They rented extra seats for extraordinary amounts. At first they refused to rent any seat to Biju. But when he showed them his wallet, which opened to American dollars, they agreed. He paid some more dollars for his luggage; they piled his cases on to the vehicle's roof and bound them with rope. Biju was so ecstatic, felt so light-hearted at the prospect of returning home and getting re-united with his father that the journey to Kalimpong with the GNLF men did not frighten him. Riding high in the jeep on the road over the insane and unpredictable river Teesta that leapt both forward and backward within each moment, Biju 'looked down over at oblivion, hurried his vision back to the gouged bank. Death was so close—he had forgotten this in his eternal existence in America—this constant proximity of one's nearest destination' (311).

There were nearly a dozen land-slides on the road between Siliguri and Kalimpong, and as the jeep waited for them to be removed, Biju remembered: "This was where his father lived and where he had visited him and where they had hatched the plot to send him to America, and [he] had, in his innocence, done just what his father had, in his own innocence, told him to do" (311). His father did not know the terrible pain of exile he had experienced in America. Biju realized that people like him, who had been compelled to leave their family for work, had always lived a divided life: 'their hearts always in other places, their minds thinking about people elsewhere' (311). They 'could never be in a single existence at one time' (311). And it felt wonderful to be able to have things different again.

Chapter LI

The chapter begins with a terrible dream of the psychologically disturbed judge. Exhausted from unfruitful waiting for Mutt, he fell asleep and dreamed that his beloved dog was dying: 'for a moment she came out of a delirium, gave him a familiar look, wagged with a heroic effort, and then, in a second it was gone, the soul behind the eyes' (312). He cried out her name, desperately looking for a flicker of life. But the cook, who also figured in the dream, said, 'with an air of finality': "she is dead, look" (312). He lifted one of Mutt's legs and let it drop but she did not snap back. Nor did she flinch when he flicked her body with his nails. The judge screamed and warned the cook against touching his pet canine: "Don't touch her! I'll kill you!" (312). Then the dream ended and he woke up from sleep. Convinced by the logic of the dream, he held Panna Lal responsible for Mutt's disappearance and the next day, after his return from another bootless search, he threatened the cook by saying: "If you don't find her RIGHT NOW, I'LL KILL YOU. That's it. I've had enough. It's your fault. It was your responsibility to watch her when I went for my bath" (312).

The insult made the cook feel distraught, because he also loved Mutt very much. The only difference was that, unlike the judge, he had always looked upon her as an animal. The master and the servant had lived together under the same roof for many years but there was practically no meeting ground, 'no understanding,' between the two. The judge's threat filled him with a strong sense of guilt: "The cook wondered if he had done something wrong and his guilt began to grow. Had he indeed been negligent? He had failed in his duty, hadn't he? He hadn't looked hard enough. He hadn't shown respect. He should have been watching the dog the day she went missing" (313). He wept inconsolably and disappeared into the forest in search of Mutt, ignoring Sai's importunate request to come back: "Come home, its all right, he doesn't mean it, he is so sad he's crazy, he doesn't know what he's saying." (313) She went up and down the path, walking under the Milky Way and shouting into the silent trees to bring him back. But he did not return.

The search for Mutt took him to Thapa's canteen where he told a group of drunken men what had happened. It only made them laugh. They ridiculed the cook for raising such a commotion over the loss of a dog in a place where human beings died of starvation and disease without being given the slightest attention: 'Dog died! The hilarity spread. They could barely stop laughing. In a place where people died without being given any attention. They died of TB, hepatitis, leprosy, plain old fever. . . . And no jobs, no work, nothing to eat—this commotion over a dog! Ha ha ha ha ha ha' (314).

The only person who did not laugh at the cook's plight was Gyan, who had been let out of the house again. Sitting in a corner of the canteen he thought remorsefully: "Oh, that awful day when he had told the boys about the judge's guns. What, after all, had Sai done to him? The guilt took over again and he felt dizzy and nauseous" (314) Suffering from an overpowering sense of guilt for his abominable betrayal and maltreatment of Sai, Gyan, who had been a victim of temporary misjudgement and blurring of vision, availed himself of the opportunity to redeem his sins and effect a reconciliation with his estranged beloved. Thus, when the cook left the canteen, he went after him to convey a message for Sai: "Tell her that I will look for Mutt. . . . Tell her that I promise. I will find the dog. Don't worry at all. Be sure and tell her. I will find Mutt and bring her to the house" (314).

Though the cook was not impressed by his assurance and was not sure of his ability to find out Mutt, Gyan was convinced that he would have a present for Sai the next time he met her. The hazards and risks involved in the quest would be an act of penance for the disillusioned Gorkhaland supporter who had attained wisdom ('gyan') through remorse, guilt and consequent emancipation from insularity of vision.

Chapter LII

Having lived the shameful and claustrophobic life of a fugitive in the inhospitable basement kitchens of New York, Biju, who had not seen such vastness for a longtime, was overwhelmed by the enormity of the mountainside and the wilderness and opulence of nature around him: "He felt exhilarated by the immensity of wilderness, by the lunatic creepers, the shooting hooting abundance of green, the great caterwauling vulgarity of frogs that was like the sound of the earth and the air itself" (315). Despite the roadblocks and landslides which constantly impeded and delayed their journey, Biju felt patient, 'in the way one feels before the greatness of nature' (315), and waited to see his father. He watched the hunch-backed men and women, who were painstakingly rebuilding the road washed away by landslides, and remembered how, as a child, he was always told by his father to walk across the newly spread pitch in order to reinforce the soles of his shoes. They went through seven landslides but the jeep failed to manoeuvre the eighth. The engine stalled again and again and the vehicle, mired in the mud, rolled back down. The passengers got down, untied the luggage and piled it on the mud. At the eleventh attempt the driver succeeded in negotiating the ruts and unmade soil and the jeep drove forward again. But before they reached Kalimpong, the GNLF men took a detour and, in the late evening, brought the jeep to a village.

The men took down all their belongings including Biju's luggage. He panicked as he realized what was happening but it was too late. Biju was robbed, at gun point, of everything he had brought from America, including his clothes and shoes. Dressed in a toothless crone's flowery nightgown, supplied by the robbers so that he could cover his nakedness, he ran through the jungle chased by a group of dogs who had 'the air of outlaws' and 'gangster swagger' (317). When he was out of danger, Biju sat, exhausted and unburdened, in the middle of the dark forest path, 'without his baggage, without his savings, worst of all, without his pride. Back from America with far less than he'd ever had' (317), and regretted his foolish decision to come back. He remembered Harish-Harry's advice and Mr. Kakkar's warning. He thought of Saeed Saeed who had married an American woman for a green card but fallen in love with a cute Zanzibari girl. In answer to Biju's question, he had confidently replied: "in four years I get my green card and . . . fsshht . . . out of there. . . . I get divorced and I marry for real" (318).

Biju sat alone in the dark forest, in great fear of what he had done. He could not help thinking of 'all that he'd bought and lost' (318) and felt an old throbbing pain in the knee he had broken in Harish-Harry's kitchen floor. Biju was thus engulfed by the violent eruption of ethnic rage in the Darjeeling hills from where he had been physically removed in New York. He was completely dispossessed, robbed of the last vestige of civilization and made even poorer than when he had left the country to pursue the dream of American affluence. No escape or withdrawal from violence was possible for Biju, and for others like him, in the globalized world. There is no evading the wages of terrorism, either of one's choosing or on account of other people's compulsions, Desai's novel seems to suggest.

Chapter LIII

The two separate, though interlapping, threads of the narrative are triumphantly brought together in the concluding chapter of the novel that depicts a heart-warming re-union between Biju and Panna Lal, the son and the father. The cook, who had been threatened by the judge with the words: "If you don't find [Mutt] RIGHT NOW. . . I'll KILL YOU," entered his master's bedroom at the dead of night, wrapped in a haze of alcohol. He was hounded by a feeling of guilt for having cheated Jemubhai in many different ways over the years. Deep within his guilt-ridden soul he realized that unless he made an atonement through a clean confession of his sins, he might not see his son again. He approached the foot of his master's bed with the words: "I'm a bad man, beat me, sahib, punish me" (319). The judge, who was also drunk, was amazed by the otherwise submissive cook's audacity to disturb his sleep. He left his bed and began to smack Panna Lal with his slipper. The more the cook confessed his varied acts of deception and theft and begged for punishment, the harder the judge kicked and hit him shouting all the while: "You filth, you hypocrite. If you want punishment I'll give it to you!" (320). The 'surge of anger' was familiar to Jemubhai Patel because it was out of a similar rage he had once kicked and beaten his wife mercilessly.

Sai, awakened from sleep by the unusual sounds coming from her grandfather's room, rushed in to witness the bizarre spectacle and asked the angry master and his guilt-crazed servant to stop. But none of them paid any attention to her tearful supplication: '"There's something filthy going on," Sai wept and covered her ears, her eyes. "Don't you know? Can't you tell? Something filthy is going on." But they didn't stop' (321). Helpless and distraught, she ran out of the room and stood alone in the 'humus dark' to feel 'the empty burden of the day, her own small heart, her disgust at the cook, at his pleading, her hatred of the judge, her pitiful selfish sadness, her pitiful selfish pointless love' (321).

While listening to the muffled thuds and insane cries of the inebriated old men inside, she thought about Mutt, her grandfather's lost pet, her neighbours and friends, and about Gyan, the object of her incredibly hopeless love and the cause of her ineffable sorrow. But the noise of human violence was soon drowned by the sound of rain that began to fall from an August sky, accompanied by the loud croaking of 'anthem-singing frogs' (322) exulting in their millions. As she stood in the wet, with 'her heart lying in pieces' (322), Sai's personal suffering was sublimated into a genuine humanitarian concern 'for all the sadness in the world' (323) and she attained an inner illumination: 'Never again could she think there was but one narrative and that this narrative belonged only to herself, that she might create her own tiny happiness and live safely within it' (323). This revelation, born out of profound sadness and mature wisdom, seems to sum up the central message of Kiran Desai's transcontinental romp about the globalized world in the new millennium.

An incarnation of suffering, endurance and sympathy, Sai was no longer concerned about the future of Cho Oyu or about its inhabitants. Nor did she feel depressed by the untiring recurrence of abominable human cruelty and violence which had led to wars, destruction of civilizations, displacement, exile and misery:

> All night it would rain. It would continue, off and on, on and off, with a savagery matched only by the ferocity with which the earth responded to the onslaught. Uncivilized voluptuous green would be unleashed; the town would slide down the hill. Slowly, painstakingly, like ants, men would make their paths and civilization and their wars once again, only to have it wash away again. (323)

And in the midst of all would stand nature—unrestrained, pristine, and unconcerned with men's attempts to build and unbuild civilizations. The truth Sai learnt was that whatever happened life would go on in its own rhythm. She knew that the two tired old men would return to their own rooms and continue their monotonous routine: "The new morning would hatch, black or blue, clear or smothered. Breakfast, lunch. The judge would sit at his chessboard, and at 4.30, without thinking, from mere habit, he would open his mouth and say, as he always said, "Panna Lal, bring the tea" (323).

As she stood there, under the sky, disconsolate but sober, Sai thought of her father and his unfinished space programme, of the separate journeys undertaken by her grandfather, his cook, the cook's son, and found a glimmer of strength within her to resolve that she must also leave the claustrophobic and guilt-ridden atmosphere of the decadent and antiquated colonial relic and embark on her own voyage into the world. With this resolution, a new dawn broke out of the womb of darkness, spreading a 'whisky light' across the rain-drenched sky, even as the 'congress of hopeful frogs' (323) continued to sing.

As she turned to go inside, Sai detected a small, almost indistinguishable, figure labouring up the mountain slope covered in clouds and approaching Cho Oyu. The first thought that struck her mind, now completely cleansed of selfishness and egoism, was that of Gyan whom she had forgiven and continued to love: "Gyan? she thought with a burst of hope. A message: I will love you after all" (324). Realizing her mistake, she went into the kitchen and, out of compassion, offered to make tea for the cook who sat hunched up and covered in slipper marks, his face still gripped by a nightmare.

Just at that moment the gate of the bungalow was rattled persistently and, out of habit, Panna Lal slowly walked out to open it. Moments later, Sai heard the cook's voice yelling dementedly: "Biju!" She looked out and found two shadowy figures leaping at each other as the gate swung open. Biju and Panna Lal—two inheritors of loss who had been separated from each other by the claims of modernity and the blinding desire for a better life that lured them into the trap of globalization, were finally united under strange circumstances. They were completely dispossessed and shorn of all false glitters of civilized life, standing in each other's comforting embrace. At this climactic moment, Kanchenjunga appeared above the parting clouds, as if to witness the heart-warming re-union between the father and the son:

> The five peaks of Kanchenjunga turned golden with the kind of luminous light that made you feel, if briefly, that truth was apparent.
>
> All you needed to do was to reach out and pluck it. (324)

Kiran Desai's *Hullabaloo in the Guava Orchard* as a Satirical Novel

SHUBHA TIWARI
A.P.S. University, Rewa

In the age of television and information explosion, much is said and written about the glory, beauty and spirit of India. We perpetually mention and refer to the Vedic Myths, the incredible Ayurvedic cures and our centuries-old yoga. We tend to get euphoric about India's greatness. We also tend to get oblivious of our weaknesses. The novel, *Hullabaloo in the Guava Orchard* by Kiran Desai, comes as a shock to the reader. It brings the reader down to earth. The novel can best be described as a catechizing process for the Indian reader. It compels us to face the realities of our motherland.

'Like mother, like daughter' would not be appropriate to describe Anita Desai's daughter Kiran Desai and her maiden effort at writing fiction, *Hullabaloo in the Guava Orchard.* Kiran Desai does not write like her mother. While Anita Desai dwells deep in the realms of inner psyche, intuition and the dynamics of relationships, Kiran Desai has written a light ironical novel mocking the common illogical ways of India. The essence of everyday existence in India is caught by the novelist in a satirical vein.

The story and the plot are simple and straightforward. The reader is transported to the town of Shahkot. Shahkot stands for an average Indian town with bazars, schools, a degree college, government-offices, banks and its inhabitants. The protagonist Sampath Chawla is an eccentric youth who works in a post-office. His job is dreary and boring. He fills the monotones hours by reading others' letters and by enjoying afternoon siestas. But then fate has something else in store for this erratic boy. One day, on behaving wildly at the marriage of his boss's daughter, he loses his job at the post-office. Life gets hellish for him. Although in his heart of hearts he is glad to be free from the dull job, he is continuously tortured by his father's cynical remarks.

On way to escape the painful perusal of his father for searching a new job, this suffering soul climbs on top of a tree in a guava orchard in the outskirts of Shahkot. When people come to cajole him, he mischievously leaks out personal details of the lives of some of the visitors. Obviously this knowledge comes from his unethical habit of reading others' letters at his previous workplace i.e. the post-office. But these ill-mannered utterings are taken as the vision of a godman. His cowardly escape is considered his lack of interest in 'maya,' this worldly web. Before anyone can grasp the developments, the whimsical lad transforms into a 'Baba,' a Guru, a 'Sanyasi.' Sampath's father, the practical Mr. Chawla smells a great business opportunity in this. He efficiently advertises the newly-thrust spirituality of his son. He himself is not at all deceived about the reality of Sampath. He knows his son is the same old moron. But Mr. Chawla is more than glad about the change in others' perception regarding his son. His good-for-nothing son has made it as a godman. It is happy time for the Chawla family. There is money. There is fame. There is power. There is respect for them all around. Sampath is called 'Monkey-Baba' as monkeys also dwell in that orchard.

Hullabaloo in the Guava Orchard is an ironical novel satirizing Indian mentality. It openly makes fun of our sense of propriety and logic. The major satire of the novel is the Indian sense of religiosity. Anything sells in the name of religion. One is reminded of Pascal who once said, "Men never do evil so completely and cheerfully as when they do it from religious conviction." Different 'Babas' and their followers are growing each moment like a swelling ocean. Just like population or crime, the Godmen are also on an uncontrollable rise. Every region, city, township or even locality has to its credit some kind of spirituality personified. While going through this novel, what strikes home is the absurdity of blind faith and fanatic beliefs. These godmen have the power. But they are not accountable to anyone. Their authority, therefore, stands unchallenged. They bathe in milk, eat rich food and maintain hefty bank accounts. They can occupy government land and use all official facilities free of cost.

Kiran Desai has skilfully brought out the modus operandi of the making of a saint. There are business tricks involved in the trade. It is just a trade, like any other trade. Production, advertisement and selling are in operation. One feels that spirituality is the most lucrative business in India.

Later on, the monkeys develop a taste for liquor and create havoc in the orchard. Sampath's father, Mr. Chawla wishes to get the orchard, the place of his great business free from monkeys. But then passions run high on all sides. A monkey protection society is formed to save the animals as they are considered sacred in Hindu religion. Indians are shown wasting their time and energy in futile fights.

Sampath answers the questions of his devotees in a moronic fashion. But then he is no more Sampath; he is Monkey-Baba because monkeys have taken abode around him. He has an aura around him. Each word uttered by him is thought to be loaded with deep meaning and suggestions. Whenever anyone asks him a question, Sampath replies symbolically. For example, a lady is worried about the bad company of his son. She asks Sampath the solution. Sampath begins to reply by saying. "Add lemons to milk and it will grow sour." (74) He answers like this following the great Indian tradition of symbolic discourse in religion. He keeps on pronouncing crazy sentences like one mouse is different from the other; or one can digest fish; or moth will go to the lantern etc. Symbolism is a great asset to Sampath as it curtains his mental deficiency in layers of mystery. People spin their heads in getting at the meaning and the Monkey-Baba is regarded as a great mystic.

One character in the novel is an atheist. He is a member of an atheist society. He is sent to Shahkot to make enquiries regarding Monkey-Baba. He is a pathetic, lonely figure in the novel. While the mob is in the trance of spiritual waves, this fleet fellow is portrayed as a ridiculous loner who is trying to gather facts against the fraud. His condition is wretched. He follows Sampath's mother, Kulfi, when she goes to nearby forest to gather herbs and spices. He is convinced that she mixes some intoxicants in Sampath's food. He keeps a vigil at nights. He makes his logical notes. But what happens to him at the end of the novel? His curiosity takes him to a tree just above the huge cooking pot of Kulfi. When there is the final hullabaloo in the guava orchard, he falls inside the boiling cooking pot and the pot is covered by Kulfi. The meaning of this incident is deep. Reason and rational thinking in India are boiled to death in the cauldron of frenzy and fanaticism.

Apart from the above discussed theme of satirizing the Indian sense of religiosity, the novel has innumerable other ironical comments. From endless transfers of Civil Servants to the repetitiveness of Indian schooling environment to frequent illegal arrangements of electricity supply or water supply, nothing eludes the author's eyes. Everything is captured so flowingly, realistically and naturally. Kiran Desai is not hostile. She is not bitter while writing all these details. She only narrates a funny tale recounting the corruption, the mess and the chaos as necessary details. For example, describing the post office where Sampath worked, she writes about the barbed wire fencing: "Naturally the barbed wire fence was not entirely intact" because the people of Shahkot on seeing the wire, were reminded of its need in and around their houses. Slowly but surely, the poor fencing stands broken. Our tendency to scratch names on monuments is also boldly brought to light in this novel.

Similarly when it rains, the electricity supply goes off, "Ammaji placed buckets outside to catch rain water and brought out candles and kerosene lanterns in preparation for the inevitable breakdown of electricity." This is how the novel moves. The minute delineation of common Indian habits forms the bulk of this novel. Government service and afternoon naps are interlinked to each other. Come elections and all the leaders get ready to take the residents of Shahkot to the 21st century. Our patriarchal set up, the edge the boys enjoy in matrimonial settlements, the way the gods are appeased for a male child or the recurrent wrong numbers on Indian phone system are well written. Everything is accepted by the novelist. There is no sermonizing. This is just how things stand in Shahkot.

Indians predict weather in a final tone. If the wind is blowing from west to east, it will rain or if the atmosphere is still, storm is on the cards. Similarly, as soon as a lady gets pregnant, the predicament regarding the sex of the child picks up momentum. Relatives, friends, neighbours, all are engrossed in thinking, 'Boy or girl'? The breath of the mother is "released happy and full of relief if the baby was a boy, released full of disappointment and resentment if it wasn't." (7)

Overpopulation, stink dust, lack of space in Indian homes and the obsession of taking bath with Lifebuoy soap are touched in such a way that one cannot resist laughter. At times, the novelist is very subtle. Our frequent elections, election-promises and slogans have become a laughing stock: "Not one of the street lights worked and they wouldn't work, everyone knew, until the next election. Then there would be flurry of excitement, with five-and ten-point plans . . . to send Shahkot and its residents bounding into the twenty-first century." (16)

Thus India with all her darkness, sweat, heat, congested localities and houses, dirt and drainage is the background of the novel. One may be allowed to say that basically it is a western way of looking at and analyzing India. Although no one can deny the grotesque details, nevertheless the novel appears to be a slice of India served to the egotist West.

Hullabaloo in the Guava Orchard is a welcome change for a reader of novels. A practical novel with pragmatic subjects and characters is refreshing. It makes one think. Loving our own selves is easy. But analyzing, criticizing and accepting our weaknesses is a difficult task. This task is well achieved by Kiran Desai.

NOTE

1. Kiran Desai, *Hullabaloo in the Guava Orchard* (New Delhi: Viking Penguin India, 1998), p. 9.

Kiran Desai's *The Inheritance of Loss*: The Story of a Diverse Diaspora Called India

PRASANTA BHATTACHARYYA
Rabindra Mahavidyalaya, Champadanga

The subject of Kiran Desai's *The Inheritance of Loss*, among many other things, is India. The fates of all the major characters of the novel are incontrovertibly linked to the fate of a nation whose independent journey through history is only sixty years long. But this journey also has its origin in centuries-old pre-independent, colonized past that formed a lasting legacy of knowledge and mistrust, enlightenment and darkness, broader humanity and narrow sectarianism, cultural dependence and nationalistic confidence—and these are all born both of a continuing cohesion and division between the East and the West, our Bharat and their England.

Kiran Desai's novel getting the prestigious Man Booker Prize of the year 2006 is no independent phenomenon occurring through the successful exertion of someone's individual talent but is part of a now well-established tradition that the politico-historical dialectics of colonialism have generated: a good number of Indian writers in English are thus attaining prestige and international recognition. In fact, Salman Rushdie's 1981 novel, *Midnight's Children* created both a cultural and critical buzz that significantly paved the way for more Anglophonic Indians who took seriously to the business of writing in English.

In this post-colonised and globalized world of new politics and economics—when a quarter of a century after Rushdie's scripting of an epic story of partition and trauma has run down the temporal stream—we continue to see how the likes of Arundhati Roy and Rohinton Mistry and Vikram Seth and Amitav Ghosh are laughing their way to the banks after grabbing fat advances paid out by their publishers doing business worldwide. The morale-boosting winning of a Booker or two has also given a fillip to the new standards of writing set by Indian writers in the literary world and who knows whether the Booker does or does not lead the path to the Nobel Prize in literature for any of this new breed of writers?

The story of the East meeting and perhaps 'eating' and 'digesting' the West, for most of the present Indian writers in English are cultural cross-breeds settling halfway between their Indian birth and a Eurocentric or Americanised upbringing, continues as if to give credence to Thor Heyerdahl's theory of human migration. Millions of people have died to wrest independence from the hands of foreign rulers and to stop being maimed daily by a class of exploiters who happened to be the colonial settlers in our land. Lord Mountbatten rewrote the history of the Indian subcontinent by creating the separate nations of Bharat and Pakistan in 1947, and in effecting this rupture and creating a permanent scar he was no less ably assisted by two grand political patriarchs—Nehru and Jinnah—whose nationalism was born out of a hybridism that characterized a colonial native man's search for power and prestige through his acquiring of 'foreign' English education. Both Nehru and Jinnah's pre-eminence in national politics and in the existing power-hierarchy had a lot to do with their distinction of going to England as parts of a privileged small Indian community and then returning with the halo of a martyr, sacrificing apparently in this process their chances of commercial prosperity within the arena of law-courts or any other prestigious profession. Their ideas of Indian history and culture were, no doubt, coloured by the colonisers' interpretations of it. This seems natural for a man like Jinnah who faced considerable trouble while delivering his platform speeches in Urdu and had them re-scripted in English letters, whose immaculately designed suit and pant only betrayed the signs of an English gentleman passing for a national public figure and whose dining preferences were reported to be that of a European wealthy man's choosing of a continental smorgasbord. Nehru's native identity had a more pronounced inclination towards white Englishness in what we know to be his backroom cavorting with the Governor-general's indulgent wife who lent her charm in a considerable way to shape the history of independence the way it did for us. That both these two young turks were tamed by the mystique of the British Crown is shown through their eagerness to eat out of the hand of Mountbatten the seeds of divisive politics. And when we come across the character of the judge in Kiran Desai's *The Inheritance of Loss*, we find known reverberations and rumblings of a subconscious whose allegiance is firmly directed to the old-world authorities of a colonial past and yet whose possessor is made to live out a later, almost defunct, career in the postcolonial era of independence. He is a good example of the scores of human parasites who lived off doles and condescendingly endowed privileges by virtue of passing the Civil Service Examination held in the very political interest of the master class. But the award of a plum post was won at the cost of rooting out everything native from his personal system to become more English than an average Englishman. So, he is like a later day Gulliver migrating towards the British Isle to curry favour with the English counterparts of the original Houyhnhnms and as his acquiescence backfires—as it always does in any such colonial endeavour, collective or individual—he develops a crushing sense of defeat and inferiority resulting into a sado-masochistic violence that left him a hated recluse even in his own community. His chosen isolation, his strained efforts in powdering his face white, his fear and hate of his wife, his sexual-offence within the safe custody of his official home and his abuse of his granddaughter and physical violence against the devoted cook are results of both individual dislocations and historical compulsions. The continual violence he had to engage in to drive out all traces of ethnicity from his persona in an ill-conceived attempt to become 'equal' with the masters left him bereft of vitality and merit that otherwise were his own inheritance begotten through his biological, parental and communal past. All his misdirected efforts to become what he is not and all his grand personal proclamations against his native identity and tradition leave him mentally paralytic, emotionally blocked and spiritually dead. He unloads the Indian legacy from his being and creates a huge, unfilled personal space. Since his endeavour to fill it up with the borrowed English baggage has been a self-defeating experience, his heart becomes an arid desert zone of cactus land to bar entry to any human being having the slightest desire of exploring this inhospitable human terrain. This is, however, his inner space that lies covered from the public gaze. But also outwardly, he is receding from human contact and his present address that he consciously sets up in a crumbling, isolated house in the hilly town of Kalimpong is a physical metaphor of his present state of exile. His withdrawal into the boundary of his house and his rotting car in the outer yard showing signs of age and disuse aptly summarise a solipsistic slump into passive suffering consisting of bygone memories that regularly visit his waking consciousness to remind him of treasures well lost. This inheritance of loss renders him incapacitated to meaningfully come to terms with the changed scenario of the present. The cracks and fissures of the nation also produced a corresponding personal narration that shows all the chaotic disjointedness of a human mind that internalized the pain of cultural uprooting to become an insubstantial and disembodied spirit of the true-born native self. This dehumanization is shown to be so thorough in the case of the judge that he has signally failed to relate himself with any other human being in this vast, wide world. This huge, companionless outer space called the society thus has become a source of genuine fear and this, in a sense, prompts his final retirement at Cho Oyu—a once sprawling bungalow with an elaborate colonial architectural pattern sold to him by a Scotsman leaving for his home after India wins freedom from the yoke of foreign rule. He had violated his innocent Gujarati wife Nimi, never assumed his responsibility as the father of a girl whom he accidentally created while engaging in one of those beastly and abusive sexual acts with his hated wife, never enquired after the whereabouts of that girl when as an educated adult she eloped with one Mr. Mistry who was in the air force—and she eloped since "This romance had allowed her to escape the sadness of her past and the tediousness of her current girlish life" (26)—never thought of the cook as any better than a sub-human species, and only felt very much bothered when the boarding school authorities have dumped his granddaughter, Sai at his door when her parents in Russia died most unfortunately while being part of a joint space programme. The only creature he can relate to is Mutt—a dog of foreign breed and very high pedigree—who follows her master, to use another colonial metaphor, like Friday followed Crusoe in Defoe's novel. The unquestioning submission of the animal to her possessor re-enacts the relational pattern between the white master and his black or brown servant in the colonies. Psychologically speaking, the guilt ridden heart of Jemubhai Popatlal Patel, as the judge is formally called, can read no incipient sign of protest and hatred in the eyes of his dog that he otherwise found in the stiff inaction and rigid refusal of his wife whom he intended to command and treat like a bitch. The white collar slavery that he suffered in the hands of his English employers makes him embittered and his battered ego of a high native official in turn demands the same servitude in terms of unflinching devotion from his kinsmen who, since they have the intrinsic merit of the *homo sapiens*, can never behave like the loyal canine. That the judge could relate himself only with the unresisting dog speaks volumes about his degraded humanity. His rage against the cook, when the dog is finally lost, is to be contextualised within this format of alienation and desertion: the absence of the dog from his claustrophobic personal world means the absence of the last and perhaps the only vestige of existential meaning that he derived through relational interdependence. Perhaps no dose of calmpose can now give him an arranged relief from the seemingly endless series of onslaughts upon his self coming through the train of past thoughts that relentlessly fill his mind up with memories of trauma and unredeemed guilt.

However, it is through the troubled psyche of the judge that we should look for an interconnected historical route that takes us down to a thriving, bustling and unsettling modernity amidst which Sai, as the young female protagonist, is placed. Born of a Hindu mother and a Zoroastrian father she is the true inheritor of a hybrid identity whose secularity is put to the strains of personal tragedy and political vicissitudes in order, as if, to see its chances of survival. Like her grandfather, Sai prefers English language and European diet over native Hindi and the average Indian food of *dal-roti*. But unlike her grandfather, she also speaks pidgin Hindi, shows a marked hatred of artificial, Anglicized culture in her detestation of missionary insemination that still smacks of colonial superiority and prefers an ethnic Nepali boy as her lover instead of experiencing wet dreams about a European Prince Charming. However, we may well imagine her grandfather letting himself suffer the instinctual pangs of wet dreams about a 'beautiful' white maiden when he felt unnecessarily burdened with an Indian wife too uncivilized and uneducated to be taken to official parties. Interestingly, the narrative of Sai is made to belong to the same familial and cultural roots that once created a human failure named Jemubhai Patel. Her mother's story of existential uncertainty and semi-orphanage was caused by a monumental wrong when Jemubhai's wily father, with the able support coming through matrimonial dowry, set him on the deck of *SS Strathnaver* on way to the white Englishmen's country in search of prestigious education and lucrative job. But the cause and consequence of this wrong was created and also set in motion by an ambitious imperial power whose dynastic designs aimed at creating a spineless class of yesmen whose complicity with the colonial order would only ensure the perpetuation of the exploitative foreign rule. Rootless and directionless, Jemubhai's daughter submits herself to the dictates of a new fate that took her to Russia along with her husband. Sai was left at the care of a missionary boarding school for the all too palpable reason of ensuring for her the best available Indian 'English' education, and had she been there at the side of her parents even an Indo-Russian bonhomie would not buy for her such an education which is internationally acclaimed. The confinement of the missionary schooling walled in more violence than giving protection against it and Sai remained within a moody, sullen girl with certain bad habits like picking her nose in public. The migration of her parents to a relatively unknown country, during a time of sharp polarization in global politics, resulted into their sad demise. And their exit from life forced open an apparently closed route of return to her original home front thus letting the time-present meet with time-past and making an individual journey of a hapless girl to Kalimpong look like a historical meeting point between hybrid modernity with discredited coloniality. This circular revisiting of the present of its past is also done in the manner of an honest search for tradition and identity which, however, seem almost impossible to get hold of in times of tremendous flux and great political turmoil which in the present case is caused by the Nepalese insurgency of the 1980s. With her obvious difference as an individual from her psychologically troubled grandfather, Sai may go on detesting and revolting against him inwardly, and yet the authorial insight continually points to the linkage existing as part of a larger historical time-frame between an individual present and its ancestral past. The difference actually comes out of a similarity that vitally links up an old man apparently arbitrarily with his estranged granddaughter. For example, despite their situational differences in life, Sai's occasional self-absorptions and brooding and pensive self-introspections uncannily resemble the reclusive tendencies and melancholy moodiness of Jemubhai. But whereas Sai endeavours earnestly to get over her personal crises by trying to come to terms with the trials and tribulations that modernity set on her way, the retired judge seems resigned to his present lot. Time does not expand futuristically for him and the only spatial growth his mind can experience is in terms of repetitive retrospections of the past incidents that increase his sense of terrible guilt.

The different tales of Sai and the judge, the cook and his son Biju eking out a paltry living in the busy city of New York, the Nepali tutor of Sai named Gyan and the small neighbourhood community round Cho Oyu consisting of Uncle Potty and Father Booty, Mrs. Sen with her daughter working in America for the CNN and her rivals Noni and Lola whose daughter works in the BBC in UK constitute different strands of a composite story about displacement and disillusion. The mapping of an Indian diaspora is well charted out by Kiran Desai with her focus continually shifting between the sleepy, wetty and icy hill-station of Kalimpong with its mouldering colonial heritage and the international, ever-busy, ever-awake metropolis of New York which happens to be one of the power-centres of a global superpower bent upon expanding its postcolonial bases in as many parts of the world as possible. Interestingly, Sai is placed among a group of old people who swear by and continue to live for old-world charms: therefore Noni and Lola still take their Jane Austen very seriously and while the Swiss Indian foreigner Father Booty can still manage a successful and happy living by going for local sales of his domestically procured dairy products, his friend Uncle Potty can remain a habitual drinker without ever jeopardizing his chances of smooth survival in one peaceful corner of the globe. In contrast, the cook's son, Biju is cast in a world where there seems to exist no settled convention, where native rootedness is seen as backwardness and any observance of communal customs and rituals is dismissed as superstition. So, it does not seem strange when with his 'poor adaptability' and his inhibition intact against eating the flesh of the "holy cow" (135) he has continued his search for an elusive home while living the wretched life of an illegal immigrant in the precarious anonymity of skyscrapers or restaurant-basements like a beast continually driven by its attackers. This modernity chokes his native humanity and so he clings more to his traditional, communal, Indian identity as a defence against a reality that tends to efface his inherited culture for a globalized and homogenized flatness of urban existence which seems to be the fated destiny of hundreds and thousands like him who throng the American cities and suburbs in search of unfulfilled dreams nurtured in the lap of poverty and superstitious backwardness. His slipping a whistle into the window of Indian girls whose ordered food-items he carried to their doorsteps is quite like an Indian boy whose repressed instincts let him taunt the other sex and then flee along the busy Broadway while loudly mouthing a popular Hindi tune from a successful Bollywood movie of the 1980s—Rajendra Kumar's 'Love Story' and Biju satisfies his depressed male ego by wistfully singing about Indian girls: "O, yeh ladki zara si deewani lagti hai" and the tailpiece coming from the authorial wisdom of Kiran Desai is unfailing both in its intended irony and as plainspeak—"Old songs, best songs" (51).

However, the narrative of Sai, who happens to be the chief protagonist of this wonderfully told tale of Kiran Desai, is embedded within a larger, outer and less palpable narrative of authorial diaspora and displacement: there runs a parallel thread between the stories of Sai and Kiran [De]sai. Just after getting the Booker in October, 2006, Kiran gave an interview to the correspondent of *India Today* and has talked in brief about her famous mother who is described as "half-German and her father was from Bangladesh."[1] In this interview, she also talks of her father as "my closest link to India." The marriage between a half-German and half-Bangladeshi mother and a Gujarati Indian father creates a uniquely mixed parental lineage for Kiran Desai. The Zoroastrian father and Hindu mother of Sai only slightly alter this inheritance of mixed culture. The connections and parallels continue even in the narrative of Biju whose forced floating on the international, mixed sea of humanity called New York is definitely charted from the first-hand experience of a writer whose growing consciousness as an adult has been overlaid by the bitter-sweet understanding of diasporic culture. *The Inheritance of Loss* is of course not an autobiography but the book seems a fictionalized version of it. Kiran being born in September 1971 and spending the first fifteen years of her life in her mother country (and she made brief sojourns during this time to Kalimpong at the home of her aunt) before heading for the West for education and career is taking, as if, a literary route to re-visit her past life. But this search for personal history is inevitably linked up with the larger issues of Indian history which is a history of many thousands of diasporas crossing borders over many thousands of years. Several researches now-a-days show how a hitherto staunch identification with one piece of land in one part of India is easily shattered by a farther gaze into the past and a recognition of the constant movements that have characterized the subcontinent over the centuries. In this sense, the small and apparently insignificant township of Kalimpong becomes, in the pages of Desai's novel, a diasporic hub—the Gujarati judge and his cook from Uttar Pradesh, Noni and Lola as two aged siblings, the uncommonly friendly Uncle Potty and his highly Indianised Swiss friend, Father Booty, the garrulous Mrs. Sen, they all show trends of a mostly internal diaspora, the travelling from kingdom to kingdom and state to state in a unique history of human flux, displacement and further settlement. In this sense, Kalimpong becomes a logical extension of New York where the Indian diaspora is manifesting itself in terms of a highly modern and mercantile global culture. Kiran Desai acknowledges her inheritance as something of an advantage: "The Indian diaspora is a wonderful place to write from and I am lucky to be part of it."[2] But the confidence with which she can now talk about it was conspicuously missing in the colonial era. When asked about the larger question of human migration, Kiran Desai's succinct answer gives a real insight into this international issue which is both a problem and an advantage:

> It is something that has been going on forever. I did not realise it at

> first. There are so many interlinked patterns that it becomes important to examine it. It is quite a pertinent issue. Politicians are still talking of taking non-westerners to western countries, people from poor countries to rich ones. It has a darker side. There is a reverse journey happening too, like in my grandfather's time, when they went abroad to study and then returned.[3]

Sai's grandfather, another Gujarati to remind the readers, 'went abroad to study and then returned' to show the 'darker side' of this early trend of colonial Indian migration. Biju is a modern counterpart of the judge who for a change does not end up in Cambridge but in New York which is the new haven of global fortune-hunters. While the judge struggled with his educational endeavours, Biju is struggling with his half-baked cooking skills for who knows he may not one day become the envied owner of a food-chain in America or if possible in this vast wide world for in this era of democracy and globalized economy any obscure but genuine talent making perfect advertisement for itself is up for sale. The usage of a human tool—the judge becoming a stooge in the hands of the colonial government—is only possible in this postcolonial era when it shows considerable commercial potential. The judge tried to forget his Indian identity whereas Biju tries desperately to stay as much as possible within his cultural moorings of an Indian birth. His 'Indianness' fails him miserably in America whereas Saeed Saeed, the African man from Zanzibar whom Biju "admired most in the United States of America" (53) forges a perfect compromise between ethnicity and the demands of American urban modernity. The very Gujarati Harish-Harry, who happens to be the owner of one Gandhi restaurant and who also is the last employer of Biju in New York makes a carefully angled presentation of his halfway identity that wishes to make the best use of the twin worlds of East and West. His Harish-half is perfectly serviceable in a cut-throat, demand-and-supply market economy with the other Harry-half looking duly Anglicized and customized for a large western clientele who will not feel inhibited in such hybrid naming by their general fear of crude Asian and African violence erupting into the streets of America. In comparison with this, the early episode of the gravy boat with the monogram of an English family, JPP, gave the judge a rather crude thrill of borrowed superiority when he bought it from the secondhand market. Thus he continued to impersonate in the mask of a supposedly English name. The acute problem of identity that he suffered from was borne through this self-deluded game of proxy where he secretly engaged himself in an act of colonial cross-dressing: "He had bought it secretly and hidden it within another bag, so his painful pretension and his thrift would not be detected. *James Peter Peterson* or *Jemubhai Popatlal Patel*. IF you please" (171). This seems now tactless and foolhardy compared to the canny survival instincts of a Harish-Harry and many like him who are going to America or other countries and also making it good for themselves.

So, for Indians in the West, the changing trends in living are all parts of a tremendous diaspora which has been too diverse to be defined in a single essence. The first great wave was that of the indentured labourers in the nineteenth century. After independence, many left to take advantage of Britain and America's need to re-build the economy after World War II. This is one historical reason why there is an Indian, a Pakistani or a Bangladeshi living next to an Englishman in Great Britain or an American in the US. In this context, Biju's illegal sojourn into the American territory seems perfectly natural. Though his story harks back to a time at least twenty or so years old, young, less educated and yet aspiring men like Biju are found in hordes by the side of techno-savvy computer professionals and medics and also teachers in today's America and England and Canada who are going there simply in search of more money and fame. But when President George W. Bush warns American schoolchildren of a possible flooding of the professional market by Asians unless they study hard, when the British Government take policy-decisions which are highly discriminatory and loaded heavily against coloured, particularly Asian immigrants of the Indian subcontinent, [4] we feel how these technocrats, despite their handsome contribution to the development of the Western economies and industries, are kept floating like so many Bijus who are the human disposables of new multinational economic systems which would conveniently use them or dump them according to the changing rules and patterns of global commerce and politics. Kiran Desai's novel tries to get away from painting the picture of a homogenous diasporic community. In fact, she gets far away from it. But as an imaginative and sensitive mind that stays alert to any development affecting, impacting this huge diaspora, she tries, being herself a part of it, with increasing sophistication to come to terms with it. For the Indian diaspora—spread out, settled and now very successful—this novel of Kiran Desai reflects back a story of continuous digging out of roots and their re-planting. This seems no mean achievement for a people whose ancestors crossed the 'kala-pani' as porters, unskilled workers and indentured labourers. Indians living abroad are now administrative or professional heads, or they are leaders in the fields of culture including music and literature, not to speak of the academia where they threaten to outnumber even their western counterparts. And since the queues for visas continue to swell from the time of Biju, who in the novel manages to get a permission of some days' travel from the American embassy, it shows a healthy trend of crossing one's national skin in a bid to get under that of the other. Wanderlust can satisfy other kinds of lust—for money, for fame. But sadly for Biju, borders become barriers in his case. And as he stays back in the miserable pattern of his life, his father draws a solid satisfaction out of his son's misunderstood position in life. As he feels threatened under the rule of a temperamental master, Biju feels anxious with the uncertainty of his professional life. While he wants to get back, his father wants him to stay. That he ultimately returns to India amidst political unrest and gets cruelly robbed of his last possessions including his shoes and shirt and pant is a different story. But in America, an Indian software professional and an indentured labourer face almost similar issues in different contexts. And on some important counts like making the economic trajectory, reconstructing an ambience of South Asian domesticity, creating a religious and cultural place at home and finally, relating the politics of migration to the new world, they also tend to behave similarly. No surprise that the western world is in great fear of getting outnumbered by the power of the Asian people who, unlike them, do not use contraceptives and thus go on increasing their human stock in a show of nauseating fecundity! In one striking vignette of the reductive western attitude shown in the manner of a couple who own a restaurant where Biju works for sometime, we read the same fear that has prompted the

American President to be wary of a possible inundation of 'American' society by a flood called the ubiquitous Asian, or the 'Other' populace:

> In the morning, as Biju and the rest of the staff began bustling about, the owners, Odessa and Baz, drank Tailors of Harrowgate Darjeeling at a corner table. Colonial India, free India—the tea was the same, but the romance was gone, and it was best sold on the word of the past. They drank tea and diligently they read the *New York Times*, together, including the international news. It was *overwhelming* (italics mine).
>
> Former slaves and natives. Eskimos and Hiroshima people, Amazonian Indians and Chiapas Indians and Chilean Indians and American Indians and Indian Indians. Australian aborigines, Guatemalans and Colombians and Brazilians and Argentineans, Nigerians, Burmese, Angolans, Peruvians, Ecuadorians, Bolivians, Afghans, Cambodians, Rwandans, Filipinos, Indonesians, Liberians, Borneoans, Papua New Guineans, South Africans, Iraqis, Iranians, Turks, Armenians, Palestinians, French Guyanese, Dutch Guyanese, Surinamese, Sierra Leonese, Malagasys, Senegalese, Maldivians, Sri Lankas, Malaysians, Kenyans, Panamanians, Mexicans, Haitians, Dominicans, Costa Ricans, Congoans, Mauritanians, Marshall Islanders, Tahitians, Gabonese, Beninese, Malians, Jamaicans, Botswanans, Burundians, Sudanese, Eritreans, Uruguayans, Nicaraguans, Ugandans, Ivory Coastians, Zambians, Guinea-Bissauans, Cameroonians, Laotians, Zaireans coming at you screaming colonialism, screaming slavery, screaming mining companies screaming banana companies oil companies screaming CIA spy among the missionaries screaming it was Kissinger who killed their father and why don't you forgive third-world debt; Lumumba, they shouted, and Allende; on the other side, Pinochet, they said, Mobutu; contaminated milk from Nestlé, they said; Agent Orange; dirty dealings by Xerox. World Bank, UN, IMF, everything run by white people. Every day in the papers another thing! (133-34)

But as we talk of the universality of the human diaspora and its inbred level of tolerance, there emerges in different parts of the world its very opposite sectarian tendencies which often take shapes of sustained insurgencies and demand a recognition of racial identities in narrow linguistic, ethnic or regional terms. While we acknowledge the need for internationalism and world humanism, we come across the ugly face of the sons-of-the-soil movements that myopically—

and sometimes not so myopically—ignore the interchanges that took place years and years before they see the efficacy of waging wars, in the name of regionalism or racism. The readily available historical perspective for a diasporic Indian living abroad makes him or her feel not simply like an American, British, Australian or Canadian of Indian origin. Contrarily, a narrow historical view of regionalists living with their families and within their communities which suffer from backwardness and other social ills for years encourage them to think of themselves in terms of wounded pride, unrecognized talent and parochial identities. So, if Sai can think of her existence as fluid and flexible and if the Swissman Father Booty can feel himself to be free in India, Gyan, despite his strong attraction for a girl named Sai Mistry who speaks pidgin Hindi, is gradually but surely drawn into the vortex of political turmoil and bloody violence simply because the agenda of the GNLF directly concerns his Nepalese identity. For Noni and Lola, feeding as they were on the fruits of blissful retirement in their comfortable hilly den, this movement with an ugly, violent face may look like an irresolvable puzzle—they often describe the Nepalis simply in the stereotype of generically violent and uncivilized "Neps," a term which immediately remind us of the pejorative term "Negro" reserved for the Africans living in America for centuries. Now it has been changed for the term Black or Afro-Americans in a more politically correct manner. Kiran Desai intends to explore two kinds of short-sightedness—that of the GNLF activists as also of people like Lola and Noni; her novel seems to have indicted all forms of physical violence for what it does to separate individuals and to mankind in general. But it appears to be a sad development of events when the reviewer of *Kathmandu Post* calls the novel "the result of 'living a bastardized life inside and out of India that Desai seems unable to acclimatize herself (to) either in the western milieu or her own home.'"[5] The supposed 'exploiters' of the Nepalis are still described by this writer-reviewer, one Mr. D.B. Gurung, as "hungry jackals from the plains of Calcutta." When he accuses Kiran Desai "of viewing Kalimpong's Nepali-majority residents as 'crook, dupe, cheat and lesser humans,'" we see how the Nepalis themselves help perpetuate the reductive racial stereotypes by calling themselves obversely in those hated, negative terms.

Moreover, the portrayal of Biju's existential horrors is cause for another offence since the reviewer has seen "many Indian engineers and executives doing the same sort of job or selling hotdogs in the streets of Los Angeles, New York, Chicago and Washington. . . . They would perhaps make more poignant characters than Biju."[6] Unfortunately enough, this Mr. Gurung completely misses the novelistic point about the subcontinental diaspora which Kiran Desai always accompanies with an inward authorial look that not only tries to trace roots and histories but also exposes the inherent inequalities of early colonial or the present global brand of politics. Biju is only a human symbol of teeming millions who suffer due to the continuation of western hegemony in the present discourse of postcolonial politics and economics. His being a simple village-boy from UP does not increase, or lessen for that matter, the problem of suffering and pain in any form of human migration. Very realistically also, Desai does not show the young couple of Sai and Gyan clinging to their private world of a fancy-free, teenage romance when their hormones are pumping at their best. The outer disturbance shatters their nascent world of private love and peace and if the same hormones make Sai inconsolably melancholic, they compel Gyan to get embroiled, sometimes against his saner judgement, in the horrors of arson, looting, theft and murder and ethnic cleansing. But what emerges from the stories of violence, of trauma, of crossing borders, of exploitation, of pensive love, of brutal sex, of questions of identity is the single story of humanism. Nearly every home in Kalimpong is affected by the political upsurge of the Nepali movement that leaves the hills terror-struck. The preoccupation with imaginary shadowlines leaves such a bloody trail in its wake that it raises pertinent questions of partitioning people, their homes, their land, language, customs, rituals on the lines of ethnic identities. The reality and the unreality of territorial borders, the pain of huge human exodus (a majority of which never reaching their destination) bring us back to the very core of the novel which reopens the wounds of migration and partition in different social and historical contexts to show how misconceptions create terrible hardships for both the ethnic and diasporic groups who resort either to agitational politics or cultural politics in order to assert their collective identity and to strengthen their mass base.

The language of Kiran Desai needs special mentioning since she writes superb un-British and un-American English and manages to tell her story in terms of newly forged idioms created in the crucible of her mixed inheritance and imagination. The quick changes of narrational focus shifting between past and present, personal and public and along vertical or horizontal lines of the story create so many threads of tales that the strategic division of the narrative into so many sub-chapters does not seem all that arbitrary. The quick jump-cuts give it a very cinematic feel as the big canvas breaks down into so many sub-parts and catches the narrational representation of the fractured essence of the human self. But an honest effort on the part of the reader to put the novel in its proper historical perspective makes all the fractured parts re-assemble meaningfully like the different designs of a composite social mosaic. This swirling jigsaw puzzle, when cracked, gives the solution along the line of a known testament—live and let live. The parenthetic lines often allow the writer an opportunity to indulge in ironic observations that lend quirky and irreverent humorous touches to the otherwise solemnly described issue (171; 185; 186; 190; 192; 231, etc.). The compounds like "sand-weathered" (136) to describe the Arabic evocation of the name of Allah amidst Middle East deserts, or the expression "wet diarrheal season" to describe the incessant rain fall of hilly Kalimpong in "This aqueous season" (106) are strikingly fresh. Desai also shows herself to be as much adept in catching the chilling details of domestic, market-place or political violence (169-70; 208; 237; 256; 277-78, etc.), as she is capable in evoking the proverbially romantic charms of seasonal beauties with her magical imagery and mystical nature-symbols (229; 230; 258, etc.). The only bothersome note is sounded through the cleverly camouflaged glossary of *desi*, Hindi words aimed at her English-speaking western readership:

> "Pigs, pigs, sons of pigs, *sooar ka baccha*," Biju shouted.
>
> "*Uloo ka patha*, son of an owl, low-down son-of-a-bitch Indian." (23)

Or "*Angrez ke tarah*, like the English." (105) The book is replete with such jarring examples of translation which does lower the dignity and merit of Indian writing in English. Just eight weeks after

Kiran Desai wins her Booker, the half-Indian and half-British thespian Ranjit Bolt comments that "the ethnic factor in new novels can help you" win the Booker and that creative artists increasingly enjoy the advantage of "wearing the ethnic hat."[7] This observation makes the matter more controverted about the global commercial potential of publishing business that arranges the winning of prizes for authors to create new marketing zones through strategic encouragement of new writings. But India as a character or as a theme remains the clear winner even in this game of wide publicity and commercial hard-selling. For a hard-nosed minority, this country shows all the signs of slackening and aging. But if aging, it has done so gracefully as to woo more investors who are eager to put in their money in India as a cultural or literary phenomenon. For the cognoscenti, it is the time to soak in the nation's new aesthetical bounties. The judge in the novel may still misconstrue this land as a total mess—eaten by insurgency and unrest from all sides, and still worse, cracking up with tension at the centre. However, for Sai, who stands an unnoticed witness to the impossibly happy re-union between the cook and his son Biju, the elusive 'truth' of the disconcerting puzzle called human life seems, if only momentarily, gettable and as the author says, "All you needed to do was to reach out and pluck it" (324). In this continual reaching out for human companionship, for peace and happiness that the essential India, with all the contrary pulls of withdrawal and intolerance and sectarian violence waged against its well-being, lives, nay, even marches ahead. The diaspora increases alongside the ethnic groups which continue to strengthen their mass-base. Meanwhile, India thrives on its age-old, time-tested mantra of plurality, of unity in diversity which holds just fine in this dog-eat-dog globalized world of new economics and new politics.

NOTES

1. Interview of the Week: Kiran Desai, *India Today*, Vol. 1 XXXI, no. 43 (24-30 October 2006), 82.
2. *India Today*, 83.
3. *India Today*, 83.

4. See the news on the front page of *The Times of India, Kolkata edition*, 4 January 2007.
5. See this report from Sudeshna Sarkar in *The Statesman, Kolkata edition*, 5 December 2006.
6. *The Statesman*.
7. See this news item from Rashmee Roshan Lall in *The Times of India, Kolkata edition*, 15 December 2006.

Identity Virus and the Antidote: Reading *The Inheritance of Loss*

SISIR KUMAR CHATTERJEE
Hooghly Mohsin College, Chinsurah

After Conrad's *Heart of Darkness*, Golding's *Lord of the Flies*, and Rushdie's *Fury*, Kiran Desai's *The Inheritance of Loss* is (apparently) a most profoundly disturbing book for those who still retain the sensibility to be disturbed in this globalized and marketised world milieu. Kiran Desai is not only a "terrific writer"[1] but also a terrifying one, who in her second, quite deservedly Man Booker-winning novel, is out to shock us into a jolting awareness of the violence—at individual, communitarian as well as ethno-racial levels—that tends to traumatize human life throughout the world.

The book cannot be called a novel proper if one acknowledges the importance of a substantial plot (packed with events affecting the course of interpersonal relationships that weave its narrative matrix) as an indispensable element of this literary genre. It is true that quite a few sensational and excruciatingly agonising incidents do take place in the book, which are likely to tempt an astute film-maker to choose it for cinematising, a work that would not prove unprofitable. But very few of these *action*-sequences happen in the lives of the major individual characters that people this nearly plotless, postmodernist, semi-documentary-semi-fictional work of art. Not all the happenings in it, startling and even lurid as they are in themselves, proceed from the action of all the major fictional personae, although they indeed affect the course of their lives to a remarkable extent, for they are shown to take place more at the racial or ethnic levels than at the individual planes. But, there are at least two plot-seedlings in it. One strand relates the story of Biju, a Nepali youth, and a veritable embodiment of a form of Indian diasporic entity, who has migrated to America to find there the work of a cook, and whose trajectory is mapped as a continuous process of shifting from one restaurant to another, for he fails to manage to procure a green card. The other thread involves a somewhat un (der)developed love story between Sai, the central female character in the book (daughter of Mr. and Mrs. Mistry, the cosmonauts, who died in an accident in Soviet Union, and sheltered by her maternal grandfather, a Gujarati Chief Justice called Jemubhai Popatlal Patel, who lives a reclusive retired life), and a Nepali youth called Gyan, who is her Mathematics tutor. These two strands are intertwined by Pannalal, Biju's father, who works as the judge's cook. The book is written in the background of a disturbed milieu when India had been badly reeling under the menacing political phenomenon of disintegration and fragmentation: "The country, Sai noted, was coming apart at the seams: police unearthing militants in Assam, Nagaland, and Mizoram; Punjab on fire with Indira Gandhi dead and gone in October of last year; and those Sikhs with their Kanga, Kachha, etc., still wishing to add a sixth K, Khalistan, their own country in which to live with the other five Ks." (108). Set at Kalimpong, a hilly town situated in the lap of the Himalayas in the North Western India, in the last two decades of the previous century, during a time when it was plagued by the GNLF insurgency (under the leadership of Pradhan as the head of the Movement's Kalimpong wing, and of Subhas Ghising as the chief of its Darjeeling branch), this postcolonial and postmodernist novel deals with violence and atrocities to a terribly disturbing and nerve-shattering extent—at individual and ethno-racial levels—perpetrated by man on man.

The tenor of this "globalizd novel for a globalized world"[2] is intermittently interspersed with spurts of violent brutality shaking life in the hillside resort. But, as the two narrative threads of the novel stride across continents in a globalized milieu, eruption of violence is not confined to the territories of Kalimpong and the adjacent GNLF-captured regions alone. Savagery in its most bestial form is seen to operate at a racial level in a so-called civilised country like England too, though at some point of time in the past. And, what is more, barbarity is shown to take complete possession not only of an insurgent mob but also of a highly civilised and educated individual who had obtained the degree of ICS from England. All this tends to persuade the reader to phenomenologically probe the basic reason behind the manifestation of aggression in man, who, it is a simple truism, is as much a product of his politico-socio-cultural and ethnogenetic conditions as of his inscrutable archetypal 'feeling universals' inherited through a long, long history of evolution. This observation finds support in Lola's post-Darwinist naturalistic comment made in response to Sai's question as to why, as Lola claims, should a man in the army be a non-vegetarian: "To kill you must be carnivorous or otherwise you're the hunted. Just look at nature—the deer, the cow. We are animals after all and to triumph you must taste blood." (195)

The novel depicts a world in which almost all the characters are shown to betray a bestial instinct that is utterly unbecoming of humans, and this is metaphorically represented through a telling posture of an actual sub-human animal, the judge's dog: "Mutt, catching sight of the shadow of her own tail, leapt and caught it, began to whiz around and around, confused as to whose tail it was. She would not let go, but her eyes expressed confusion and beseeching—how could she stop? What should she do?—she had caught a strange beast and didn't know it was herself." (105) The pervasive violence and atrocity that characterise the world fictionalised in Kiran's book may be constructed as issuing out of the archetypal instinctive drive of man, the greatest of animals, for othering another human or subhuman object, for this act of othering injects into him a sense of power and authority that impel him to nourish a feeling of superiority over someone or something, and thereby help him assert and define his identity. Thus, the novel shows almost every important character both othering and being othered by another character. And this instinctive pull of othering operates in an individual as strongly and aggressively as it does in a race or an ethnic community.

Gyan and Sai, involved in a romantic lock, are portrayed as slighting and humiliating each other. One can, for example, refer to their bitter bickering over the issue of Christmas after the GNLF movement has started. While Gyan was leaving Sai after harshly calling her a "little fool," Sai shouted through her weeping, "You dirty bastard." Gyan countered her invective by reminding her of her colonial slavery: "Don't you have any pride? Trying to be Westernized. They don't want you!!!! Go there and see if they will welcome you with open arms. You will be trying to clean their toilets and even then they won't want you." (174) After his departure, Sai said to the emptiness, "You bastard. . . . My dignity is worth a thousand of you." (175) Gyan's anger at himself for giving in to Sai, the temptress, goes to such an extent that he betrays her and her grandfather by divulging the secret assets of the judge, including the guns, of "the lack of a phone and there being nobody to call for help" (177), to his GNLF friends Chhang and Bhang, Owl and Donkey, at Thapa's Canteen, and even rationalised his act of betrayal. Sai and Gyan are both subclass and are subclassed by each other. They call each other "stupid." After Gyan parts with Sai to join the GNLF movement, the girl one day finds her lover at a GNLF rally in Darjeeling. She wants to shout to him, "but at that moment he caught sight of her. . . and the dismay on his face was followed by a slight ferocious gesture of his head and a cold narrow look in his eye that was a warning [to Sai] not to approach" (215), a "warning [to] her to stay away" (249). And Sai begins to scrabble for dignity and for sense. And she starts to abhor Gyan for she "could not believe she had loved something so despicable. [She realised that her] kiss had not turned him into a prince; he had morphed into a bloody frog." (249). This is how love is othered by violence.

Biju is othered by some of his friends who hold green cards, by the owners of the American restaurants where he worked, and finally, in an extremely pitiable manner, by the GNLF robbers. And Biju, in turn, others the Pakistanis domiciled in America by describing them as "Pigs pigs, sons of pigs, *sooar ka baccha*" (23). Biju's reaction to the group of men, "looking weary as if they'd been traveling several lifetimes," who had come to the restaurant called the Queen of Tarts for seeking some assistance from Saeed Saeed is indeed deplorable. In response to Saeed's question, "What are they doing?," he says, "They are still standing and looking, said Biju, feeling brave and excited by someone else's misfortune. He was almost hopping." (96-97) That Biju nourishes a sense of privileged superiority over those who seek his assistance for migrating to America, and also those acquaintances of his community who could not manage to go to America is evident from the "pride" with which he was returning to Kalimpong, actually after being evicted from that country. Interestingly enough, Biju experienced the same humiliation when he approached Nandu, who lived in Queens, for help. "Nandu had also not answered the phone and had tried to hide when Biju arrived on his doorstep, and then when he [Nandu] thought Biju had left, had opened the door and to his distress found Biju still standing there two hours later" (98), and Nandu advised Biju to go back to India. While working in Harish-Harry's kitchen, one day Biju had skidded on some rotten spinach and broken his knee. When he requested Harish-Harry to call a doctor for him because it was his responsibility, Harish-Harry became terribly enraged, and instead of arranging for the treatment of Biju, he began to shout: "I hire you with no papers. . . . Living here rent-free. . . . What right do you have? Is it my fault you don't even clean the floor? . . . Living like a pig. Am I telling YOU to live like a pig?" (188) And Biju counter-asserts by vehemently rebelling against Harish-Harry's exploitation of people like him: "Without us living like pigs . . . what business would you have? This is how you make your money, paying us nothing because you know we can't do anything, making us work day and night because we are illegal. Why don't you sponsor us for our green cards?" (188)

The judge others his cook, his dog (Mutt), Noni, Sai's first tutor, by abusively describing her as a "Bloody irresponsible woman" (70), his illiterate Gujarati wife named Nimi, Sai, Gyan, and the GNLF activists. He, in turn, is othered indirectly by the British people and directly by the British Government, by his Commissioner friend who "hated" the Gujaratis, and particularly the Patels because he considered them to be cunning self-seekers, by Bose, his only friend while they were in England, by Gyan, by the working class people of Kalimpong, by the Kalimpong SDO, the policemen, and finally by his granddaughter. After Mutt is stolen, Jemubhai, who is more attached to the dog than to his human relatives, asks the plumber, the electrician, the deaf tailors if they have seen the dog anywhere. The people refer to his dog as "*kutti*," which angers him. And, in response to his question, he receives only "blank faces" and "angry laughter." The people insult him in his absence thus: "*Salaa*

Machoot. . . what does he think? We're going to look for his dog?" (289) Then he goes to the SDO, who mildly snubs him by saying: "A dog! Justice, listen, just listen to yourself. People are being killed . . . we are in an emergency situation," and after this the SDO "fixed the judge with a certain gluey look that convinced him he meant to be rude." (291) The policemen, who were waiting in the front room, want to teach the judge a final lesson he will never unlearn. They begin to snigger: "Ha, ha, ha. Come about his dog? Ha, ha ha ha ha. . . Madman! . . . 'Don't waste our time. . . Get out.'" (291)

To cite another instance, during their meeting at Gymkhana at Kalimpong after thirty-three years, Bose reminds the judge of how rustic the latter was: "Remember how I took you to buy the coat in London? Remember that awful bloody thing you had? Looking like a real *gow wallah*? Remember how you used to pronounce *Jheelee* as *Giggly*? Remember? Ha ha." At this, the judge's heart fills with a surge of venomous emotion. And the narrator's analysis of his psychic reaction after this is quite significant: "how dare this man! Is this why he had made the journey, to raise himself up, put the judge down, establish a past position of power so as to be able to respect himself in the present? . . . The judge looked for the waiter. They should order dinner, get this over with, make it an early night. He thought of Mutt waiting for him . . . he tried to ignore Bose." (203-4) And the judge seeks to counter Bose's act of humiliating him by remembering how Bose had lost the case he had filed against the British Government to win a pension equal to that of a white ICS man, and also how Bose's son, too, had inherited this loss. Bose's repeated losses show how he was humiliated by the legal system of Britain, where, every time, the white judge would bring "down his hammer, always against the native, in a world that was still colonial." (205). And Bose's only antidote to his being insulted by the Britons was his secretly nurtured feeling of Britogynism, which is revealed in his repeated act of calling the British people "bastards": "Goras—get away with everything don't they? Bloody white people. They're responsible for all the crimes of the century!" (206)

Lola, one of the widow sisters, constructs a hateful, racial perspective for the GNLF movement. When Noni argues that "They have a point," Lola vehemently protests by saying: "Nonsense. . . .

Those Neps will be after all outsiders now, but especially us Bongs. They've been plotting this a long while. Dream come true. All kinds of atrocities will go on—then they can skip merrily over the border to hide in Nepal. Very convenient." (127) Lola ill-treats the GNLF activists as well as the policemen. She also undermines the Gorkhas when she remarks: "These people aren't good people. Gorkhas are mercenaries, that's what they are. Pay them and they are loyal to whatever. There's no principle involved. . . . And what is this with the GOrkha? It was always GUrkha. AND then there aren't even many Gurkhas here—some of course, and some newly retired ones coming in from Hong Kong, but otherwise they are only sherpas, coolies." (247) She also tries to ignore the GNLF men and the policemen who seek shelter in their house when hunted by each other in turn, and she herself is grossly insulted by Pradhan, when she goes to "the flamboyant head of the Kalimpong wing of the GNLF," to complain about the illegal huts being built by his followers on Mon Ami property. Instead of arranging for the retrieval of her property from the possession of the GNLF boys, Pradhan says to her: "I am the raja of Kalimpong. A raja must have many queens. . . . I have four four, but would you, . . . dear Aunty, would you like to be the fifth? . . . And you know, you won't be bearing me any sons at your age. So I will expect a big dowry. . . . And you're not much to look at, nothing up . . . nothing down." (244) And, interestingly enough, Lola helplessly shifts the oppressive burden of her humiliation on to her dead husband: "Joydeep . . . look at what you've done, you bloody fool!!!. . . Look at what you've left me to! Do you know how I have suffered. . . . Where are you?! . . . Look what I have to deal with, just look. I don't even have my decency." (245)

Pannalal is exploited by the judge, and even the cook slights Gyan, a youth of his own race by remarking to Sai, "It is strange the tutor is Nepali. . . . Nepalis make good soldiers, coolies, but they are not so bright at their studies." (73) He also basks in a feeling of patronising superiority over other fathers. As the narrator writes, "to bolster his son and his own pride, the cook wrote on the blue airmail form: 'Dear *beta*, please see if you can help the Metal Box watchman's son.'" (80) Pannalal displays his positional superiority before the father and the wife of the drunkard who is inhumanly beaten and even blinded by the police (on the charge of being involved in the case of robbery in the judge's house) when they come to pray to the judge for doing something for the release of the hapless man. He also proclaims his superiority over the fruit *wallah*, the deaf tailors, the inept plumber, the tardy baker in the market by insulting them. (278)

At the racial or national level, Indians are hated by every other nation. Saeed Saeed, one of Biju's acquaintances in America, heard from other kitchens "what the world thought of Indians. In Tanzania, if they could, they would throw them out like they did in Uganda. In Madagascar, if they could, they would throw them out. In Nigeria, if they could, they would throw them out. In Fiji, if they could, they would throw them out. In China, they hate them. In Hong Kong. In Germany. In Italy. In Japan. In Guam. In Singapore. Burma. South Africa. They don't like them [Indians]." (77) As Saeed Saeed experienced, Indians "were not allowed to apply" for immigration to America. "Bulgarians, Irish, Malagasys—on and on the list went, but no, no Indians." (81)

The narrator unambiguously depicts the plight of Indian diaspora in the following terms: "It was horrible what happened to Indians abroad and nobody knew but other Indians abroad" (138). This is countered and squared up intellectually and philosophically with an emphatic valorisation of India only a few pages later: "In fact, dear sirs, madams, we were practising a highly evolved form of capitalism long before America was America; yes, you may think it's your success, but all civilization comes from India, yes." (145) Achootan, one of Biju's fellow dishwashers, gives vent to his gut racial hatred before Biju by saying: "These white people! . . . Shit! But at least this country [America] is better than England. . . . At least they have some hypocrisy here. They believe they are good people and you get some relief. There [in England] they shout at you openly on the street, 'Go back to where you came from.'" (134-35) And the narrator shows a pitiably marginalised colonised's helpless way of only verbally othering the colonizers thus: "He [Achootan] had spent eight years in Canterbury, and he had responded by shouting a line Biju was to hear many times over, for he repeated it several times a week: 'your father came to *my* country and took *my* bread and now I have come to *your* country to get *my* bread back.'" (135) Biju's friends settled in America are slighted by the American Governmental policies regarding immigration, and they take revenge by conveniently marrying and divorcing the American women. Indian women are shown to other their male counterparts, who are dehumanised by their craze for a green card, when they comment in Calcutta's Dum Dum airport after the Gulf Air flight by which Biju is coming back home: "Must have got off the plane and run for an American dame so he could get his green card and didn't care if she looked like a horse or no. *Which she does!!!!*" When one man appreciated the Indian girls by saying, "Our ladies are the most beautiful in the world," another woman quipped, "Yes, our women are the best in the world . . . and our men are the absolute worst *gadhas* in the whole wide world." (297) Indian women are marginalisd by the andocentric society and culture. This is poignantly revealed through Nimi's plight. After being terribly tortured and finally driven out by her husband, Nimi goes to her uncle for shelter. But, "The uncle turned his niece from the door. 'You are your husband's responsibility,' he said angrily. 'Go back. Your father gave a dowry when you married—you got your share and it is not for daughters to come claiming anything thereafter. If you have made your husband angry, go ask for forgiveness.'" (306)

The instinct of othering is shown to affect even the children. At a time of violent racism, when the Bengalis are excluded from the society of the Tibetans, Lepchas, Sikkimese and the Nepalis, Lola and Noni are coming back from the shop of Tshering, who refuses to sell eggs to Lola. The shopkeeper tells Lola that he has no eggs. Although Lola sees quite a basketful of eggs in his shop, the shopkeeper tells her that they have been presold. And while coming back to Mon Ami, they see "little children lined up in rows to spit at Lola and Noni as they walked by." (280) The butcher is shown to habitually resort to an extra impetus of a practised violence before he kills a goat: "Before the butcher slit the goat's throat, Biju could hear him working up his disdain, yelling '*Bitch, whore, cunt, Sali*,' at her, dragging her forward then, and killing her." (181)

This instinct of violence and othering is shown to operate in the world of animals and insects too. In course of her journey towards Gyan's residence at Bong Busti, Sai encounters the sights of "Bees noosed by spiders' silk" (254), "rats and snakes in the rafters fighting over insects and birds' eggs," "hens being chased by a randy rooster" (255), and chickens that form "a grotesque bunch, rape and violence being enacted, hens being hammered and pecked as they screamed and flapped, attempting escape from the raping rooster" (256), the rooster that "climbed out of the pot and began to strut about. He was the only grand thing around, crowned, spurred, crowing like a colonial." (257) Sai also notices "a dead scorpion being dismantled by ants—first its Popeye arm went by, carried by a line of ant coolies, then the sting and, separately, the eye." (250) Mutt, the judge's specially-bred bitch (Sai once said to her grandfather, "Your dog is like a film star") too is acutely class-conscious as she slights "all kinds of scurrilous loafers on the hillside, [the] wheedling strays," that is, those that are inferior to her in terms of position and genetic features, although she connives at the amorous advances of the "gentleman dogs" (284). And, interestingly, Mutt too is savagely treated by some creatures more powerful than her, the people who had stolen her, because she disappointed them. When they find that Mutt was merely "a fancy dog," "they tied her to a tree, kicked her." (321)

Othering is shown to operate at a globalized level, when the readers witness the lopsided policy of Air France airline, which, after many passengers discover that they have lost their luggage, gives "compensation to non-resident Indians and foreigners, not to Indian nationals," although the latter are paying as much as all the other passengers. This is indeed a curiously disgraceful situation, where, as one Indian woman points out, "Foreigners get more and Indians get less. Treating people from a rich country well and people from a poor country badly. It's a disgrace." This is a situation where, as the narrator herself remarks, "Fortune [is] piled on more good fortune. They [foreigners] had more money and because they had more money, they would get more money." (298)

It is interesting to note that Kiran Desai's book also presents the people of the third world countries as having their own ways of counter-othering the first world countries like America. This is brought out through the Ohio man's father, who had once been to the States, and had not at all been impressed, even by the size of the house: "What is the point? All that space lying there useless, waste of water, waste of electricity, waste of heating, air-conditioning, not very intelligent is it? And you have to drive half an hour to the market! They call this the first world??? *Ekdum bekaar*!" His comment on the hot dog is interesting too: "The sausage is bad, the bun is bad, the ketchup is bad, even the mustard is bad. And this an American institution! You can get a better sausage in Calcutta!" (300)

The novel thus may be read as showing that othering is an archetypal compulsive instinct required for selfing. This inner, compulsive act of othering, which is man's mode of asserting his power and identity, is most often portrayed in the novel as manifesting itself in the form of a deplorable brutality perpetrated on one individual by another or by a whole racial or ethnic group on another, on one community by another, an act that belies the basic codes of humanity. The judge, during his stay in England, felt vicariously humiliated when he had witnessed the horrible scene of abject insult behind a pub, of an Indian boy, "just like himself, just like Bose, . . . being kicked and beaten. . . One of the boy's attackers had unzipped his pants and was pissing on him, surrounded by a crowd of jeering red-faced men. And the future judge, walking by, on his way home with a pork pie for his dinner—what had he done? He hadn't said anything. He hadn't done anything. He hadn't called for help. He'd turned and fled, run up to his rented room and sat there." (209) When Jemubhai recalls this experience, his candid, conscientious confession of his own sense of guilt for not having protested against this gross racial barbarity but of having selfishly escaped, makes us realise his angst and helplessness to see the spurt of racial violence, and at the same time makes us expect a civilised behaviour from him toward other people. But, our expectation of Jemubhai's manners and pattern of behaviour is frustrated time and again. The way the narrator relates his mechanical and animalish sexual encounter with his wife very subtly betrays the psychic atrocity he perpetrated on her: "She grew accustomed to his detached expression as he pushed into her . . . [and] all of a sudden he seemed to skid from control and his expression slid right off his face. A moment later . . . he withdrew to spend a long fiddly time in the bathroom with soap, hot water, and Dettol. He followed his ablutions with a clinical measure of whiskey, as if consuming a disinfectant." (170) In fact, his act of othering his wife, perhaps because she was illiterate and therefore unfit to be his wife, satisfied the judge so deeply that "any cruelty to her became irresistible" to him. (170) No reader can connive at the outburst of his aggression when she inadvertently dirties the toilet seat due to her ignorance of how to use it. "[When he] found footprints on the toilet seat . . . he could barely contain his outrage, took her head and pushed it into the toilet bowl." (173) No one can forget the barbarity in his treatment of his wife after he came to know that she had attended the Nehru Welcoming Committee Meeting (where Mrs. Mohan had taken her):

> He emptied his glass [of drink] on her head, sent a jug of water swinging into the face he no longer found beautiful, filled her ears with leaping soda water. Then, when this wasn't enough to assuage his rage, he hammered down with his fists, raising his arms to bring them down on her again and again, rhythmically, until his own hands were exhausted and his shoulders next day were strained sore as if from chopping wood. He even limped a bit, his leg hurting from kicking her. 'Stupid bitch, dirty bitch!' The more he swore, the harder he found he could hit. Blotchy bruises showed the next morning in disastrous contrast to the sight of contended civilisation. . . . The bruises didn't fade for weeks. Ten blue and black fingerprints clamped on her arm, a thunder-dark cloud loomed up on her side where he had pushed her into the wall. . . . The quieter she was, the louder he shouted, and if she protested, it was worse. . . . In its purest moments he could imagine himself killing her. (304-5)

The words the Cambridge-educated ICS tells his father, ["You're following the script of a village idiot. She is unsuitable to be my wife."] (306), the father who arranged for his migration to England and who has now come to him to persuade him to take back Nimi, most nakedly expose the hollowness of education and civilisation as a means of humanising an individual. It is the judge who is responsible for the death of his wife, who dies as a consequence of having caught fire over a stove, and the ICS judge "*chose to believe* [italics added] it was an accident." The narrator's touchingly poetic and profoundly empathic comment after this, "Ashes have no weight, they tell no secrets, they rise too lightly for guilt; too lightly for gravity, they float upward and, thankfully, disappear." (308), clearly point to the complete degeneration of Jemubhai. He knows, though others may not, that "he had killed his wife for the sake of false ideals. Stolen her dignity, shamed his family, shamed hers, turned her into the embodiment of their humiliation." (308)

No one would expect him, again, to treat the father and the wife of the drunken but innocent man tortured in the police custody, with such a horrendous apathy and indifference that amount to cruelty, particularly when such behaviour is shown by someone as educated and apparently as civilised as the judge. When the wife (who "looked raped and beaten already") and the father of the drunk came to Jemubhai, "walking half a day from a village across the Relli River," and entreated him to do something, the judge reacted to their appeal thus: "Why come to me? Go to the police. They are the ones who caught your husband, not I. It's not my fault," (263) and then he ordered them to leave the place. His insensitivity becomes extremely crude when he thinks, "he had done his duty as far as it was any citizen's duty to report problems to the police, and it was no longer his responsibility. Give these people a bit and one could find oneself supporting the whole family forever after, a constantly multiplying family, no doubt, because they might have no food, the husband might be blind and with broken legs, and the woman might be anemic and bent, but they'd still pop out an infant every nine months." (264) The Cambridge-educated ICS judge's words here link him with Mrs. Sen, and point to the wastage and misuse of scholarship and education which are thus shown to be only effective enough to dehumanise the humans, to turn humans into humanoids. When these poor and helpless people come to him again and ask for some food so that they do not die of starvation, and the cook is about to give them the atta Sai has brought back, the judge barks, "Don't give them anything," and continues his chess game. They beg with hands folded, heads bent, "Can we live on no food at all? We will be your servants forever. . . . God will repay you. . . . God will reward you." But, the England-educated judge remains unmoved and adamant, and he orders his cook to "Tell them to go." (282) No less brutal is his treatment of Pannalal towards the end of the book. When the cook, as a measure of penance for his sense of guilt confesses how he has deceived and cheated the judge over the years and asks his master to punish and beat him, "The judge was beating him with all the force of his sagging, puckering flesh, flecks of saliva flying from his slack muscled mouth, and his chin wobbled uncontrollably. Yet that arm, from which the flesh hung already dead, came down, bringing the slipper upon the cook's head." (321)

The police, unable to control the GNLF activists, practise their new method of torture on an innocent drunkard: "The more he screamed the harder they beat him; they reduced him to a pulp, bashed his head until blood streamed down his face, knocked out his teeth, kicked him until his ribs broke . . . the police were just practising their torture techniques, getting ready for what was coming. When the man crawled out on his knees, his eyes had been extinguished. They would heal into horizonless, flat blanks that would forever cause others to recoil in fear and disgust." (226-27) *The Inheritance of Loss* presents the climactic form of violence when the GNLF supporters assemble at the Mela Ground of Kalimpong, and very soon a ghastly, barbaric battle ensues between them and the policemen:

> And then, BAM BABAM, the air was full of stones and bottles and brickbats and screaming. The crowd began to collect rocks, raided a building site for more; the police began to chase the crowd; the stones came down; everyone was being hit, people, police; they jumped on one another, beating with sticks, bashing with rocks; began to slash with their sickles—a hand, a face, a nose, an ear. . . . One *jawan* was knifed to death, the arms of another were chopped off, a third was stabbed, . . . a beheaded body ran briefly down the street, blood fountaining from the neck, and they all saw the truth about living creatures—that after death, in final humiliation, the body defecates on itself. . . . The red of blood lay over the market road in slick pools mingled with a yellow spread of dal someone must have brought in anticipation of a picnic after the parade, and there were flies on it, left behind odd slippers, a sad pair of broken spectacles, even a tooth. (275-78)

This scene in which the policemen and the GNLF men are locked in a gruesome battle is the most abominable eruption of violence that human civilisation at the advent of the third millennium could afford to witness.

It is not difficult to explain the reasons behind the outbursts of violence, whether it takes place at the collective, ethno-racial level or at the individual plane. As Amartya Sen, in his latest book *Identity and Violence: The Illusion of Destiny* (published in the same year as Kiran Desai's novel) theorises,[3] terrorism or racial or communal aggression is the result of a philosophic insularity of vision—we indulge in violence when we put obsessive, insistent and overwhelming emphasis on what Sen calls our "unique identity" (Sen 17), that is, only one single aspect (religious, ethnic, regional, and so on) of our identity, when we remain blind and are not "clear-headed" enough to take into cognizance the fact of the multidimensionality or "the plurality of our identities" (Sen 16), what Sen terms our "diverse diversities" (Sen 13). The issue of confusion about identity is clearly suggested in Kiran Desai's book through the narrator's remark on Biju's contemplation on the "deep rift" in the character of Harish-Harry: "He [Biju] . . . tried to be loyal to so many things that he himself couldn't tell which one of his selves was the authentic, if any." (147-48)

Judged from this philosophic perspective about the fact of identity being a multi-layered concept and not a unitary entity, the incidents of violence that take place in Desai's novel both at the individual and at the racial levels can be easily interpreted by placing them within the theoretical framework formulated by Amartya Sen. The Indian boy, who suffered nightmarish humiliation and brutality in the hands of a group of white men in England during Jemubhai's stay there, for instance, was simply a victim of gut racial hatred. The policemen inflict inhuman torture on one innocent drunkard of a man, and this atrocity on innocence, which is indeed a mockery of the crimes of the protectors of law and order, because they instinctively adopt this psychic measure to hide their failure to nab the real culprits involved in the case of robbery in the judge's house, because their identity as the custodian of security and law and order is at stake as they are unable to subdue the GNLF Movement. When they resort to a form of heinous barbarity in an effort to subjugate the mutinous mob, it is indeed an extreme expression of their fear of losing their identity as an armed and politically powered community. The macabre atrocities that the riotous insurgents perpetrate on the fleeing policemen is, similarly, another manifestation of the obsessive stress the rebellious Nepalis have put on their communitarian, geo-ethnic and long-exploited identity, as evident in their slogan "Gorkhaland for Gorkhas" and in the argument with which they legitimise their demand: "We are labourers on the tea plantations, coolies dragging heavy loads, soldiers. And are we allowed to become doctors and government workers, owners of the tea plantations? *No!* We are kept at the level of servants. . . In our own country, the country we fight for, we are treated like slaves. . . . [So] we must unite under the banner of the GNLF, Gorkha National Liberation Front." (158-59) It is not the fact that all the Nepalis or Gorkhas felt the urge to fight for their freedom; and, reversely, nor is it true that the GNLF activists did never go against the interest of the common Nepalis, or that the Movement was at all spontaneous. But everywhere in the world a riotous, mutinous mob is found to resort to violence at the slightest provocation. The eruption of collective violence that the novel portrays in such nauseating, disturbing details only betrays the universal aberrational psychology of the mob that take any insurgency for an opportunity to feed the starved beast in themselves by revelling in anarchy and brutality, as the laws of the civilised society are then suspended by a no-rule state of affairs. The irony of all this is that "Instead of foreign enemies, instead of the Chinese they had been preparing for, building their hatred against, they must fight their own people" (278), which shows that the inevitable result of mob violence in a country for any demand, whether justified or not, is inevitably the devastating disintegration of the country itself, of the whole nation. After the police-mob encounter at the Mela Ground, "Kalimpong was transformed into a ghost town . . . even one man's anger . . . seemed enough to set the hillside alight." Thus, civilisation was put at stake by violence, which affected all, and particularly the innocent commoners: "The men trembled at home for fear of being picked up, being tortured on any kind of flimsy excuse, the GNLF accusing them of being police informers, the police accusing them of being militants" (281), and they have to live "within an imaginary line between the insurgents and the law, between being robbed . . . and being hunted by the police as scapegoats for the crimes of others." (282) The infernal carnage that the book depicts can thus be analysed as an expression of what Amartya Sen describes as the "elementary herd behaviour by which people [are] made to 'discover' their newly detected belligerent identities, without subjecting the process to critical examination." (Sen 10) It is on these utterly anarchic, infernal occasions that the ideologically uncommitted people unleash their repressed cruelty and barbarity and grab the chance "to avenge ancient family vendettas" (295), letting all hell break loose. The GNLF men, the narrator remarks, "arrived with masks in the night, climbed over gates, ransacked houses. Seeing a woman walking home bundled in a shawl, they made her unwrap it and took the rice and the bit of sugar she'd concealed. On the road to the market, the trees were hung with the limbs of enemies—which side and whose enemy? . . . Screams continued from the police station. . . . Injured men, their spilling guts wrapped in chicken skins to keep them fresh, were rushed on bamboo stretchers to the doctor to be stitched up; a man was found buried in the sewage tank, every inch of his body slashed with a knife, his eyes gouged out . . . the [common] residents were shocked by the violence, . . . the extent of perversity that the heart is capable of, . . . faced with the stench of unimaginable evil, . . . quite mismatched with the larger-than-life questions, caught up in the mythic battles of past vs. present, justice vs. injustice—the most ordinary swept up in extraordinary hatred, because extraordinary hatred was, after all, a commonplace event." (295)

The GNLF movement, like any political insurgency in a place does, as Desai presents it, thus pushed Kalimpong into a situation very similar to the one portrayed by Matthew Arnold in the last three lines of his poem "Dover Beach": "And we are here as on a darkling plain/ Swept with confused alarms of struggle and flight,/ Where ignorant armies clash by night." (Arnold 212)

The cause of the outbursts of violence in an individual can also be traced, as mentioned earlier, to the question of identity, which in this case is related to the instinctive compulsion of othering. The judge's cruel indifference to the father and the wife of the drunken Nepali arrested by the Kalimpong police is his way of avenging the robbery in his house committed by a few Nepali hooligans, an incident which has shaken the foundation of his smug socio-positional superiority. The inhuman cruelty to which he subjects his wife is his act of revenge against her for her act of foolishness (because she attended the Nehru welcoming committee meeting at the Cantonment Railway Station, an act which has terribly enraged him because it has blocked his promotion), and for her act of openly defying him by saying to "his amazed ears and her own shocked ears, as if waking up to a moment of clarity before death what she had told him: "You are the one who is stupid" (304), something which at once shatters the long-nourished core of his sophisticated intellectual identity. His act of beating Pannalal is actually an act of vengeance wreaked on a marginalised unit of humanity for the loss of Mutt, the bitch, the othered animal that had so far defined and justified the judge's existence as a master. When the judge's identity defined by the fact of his being the complete master of his pet is faced with a crisis with the loss of Mutt, the judge's intellectual, reason-dominated, agnostic self appears to be simply a well-nurtured façade as it is othered and demeaned by his own archetypal self. As the narrator relates and analyses the situation, "*The judge got down on his knees*, and he prayed to God, he, Jemubhai Popatlal the agnostic, who had made a long hard journey to jettison his family's prayers; he who had refused to throw the coconut into the water," thus prayed like any commoner to God: 'If you return Mutt, I will acknowledge you in public, I will never deny you again, I will tell the world that I believe in you—you—if you return Mutt—' Then he got up. He was undoing his education, retreating to the superstitious man making bargains, offering sacrifices, gambling with fate, cajoling, daring whatever was out there" (301). The judge's self-humiliation, therefore, clearly results from his sense of crisis about his identity. Pradhan subjects Lola to a culturally outrageous insult as a means of establishing his supremacy as a leader of a historic Movement of an ethnic race.

Gyan aligns with the GNLF and parts with Sai, because he seeks, but does not find, the justification of his identity as an educated youth who chooses to prioritise his communitarian adult identity by showing his solidarity to the political stance of his ethno-racial community, and ignores his identity as a tutor-cum-lover of the granddaughter of a privileged and affluent citizen who lives a selfish life in what he thinks is their legitimate territory. As the narrator analyses Gyan's thought-processes after his hearing the exciting and provocative harangue of one of the staunch advocates of the GNLF Movement, that propels him to rebel against his identity as what he takes for an idle, irresponsible romancer: "It was a masculine atmosphere and Gyan felt a moment of shame remembering his tea parties with Sai on the veranda, the cheese toast, queen cakes from the baker, and even worse, the small warm space they inhabited together, the nursery talk—It suddenly seemed against the requirements of his adulthood. He voiced an adamant opinion that the Gorkha movement take the harshest route possible." (161) Gyan becomes so vociferously and aggressively postcolonial and anti-West-aping-people including Sai that he goes to the extent of abusing his beloved. When she tells him of the Christmas party, he sharply retorts: "Why do you celebrate Christmas? You're Hindus and you don't celebrate Id or Guru Nanak's birthday or even Durga Puja or Dussehra or Tibetan New year. . . . You are like slaves . . . running after the West. . . . It's because of people like you we never get anywhere. . . . It only shows to the whole world that you are a FOOL." (163)

After joining the GNLF movement, Gyan betrays not only his beloved and her grandfather, but also an innocent and philanthropic individual like Father Booty, who refuses to renew his residence permit for avoiding the bureaucratic hell, and, therefore, the police ask him to leave India, although he has been working on a model dairy for the economic uplift of the people of Kalimpong, whom he wants to convince "How dairies might create a mini Swiss-style economy in Kalimpong" (257). Sai understands that "This was Gyan's doing. . . . This is what he had done and what people like him were doing in the name of decency and education, in the name of hospitals for Nepalis and management positions. . . . Father Booty had done much more for development in the hills than any of the locals, and without screaming or waving kukris, [but, for an ethnoracial insurgency] Father Booty was to be sacrificed." (223) Gyan's racial bias comes in sharp and fierce conflict with Sai's counteracting, unprejudiced sanity in their mutually virulent verbal encounter over the question of Father Booty's eviction from India. While Sai goes to Bong Busti to effect a reconciliation with Gyan, she tells him: "He's done much more than you ever will for people on this hillside." An angry Gyan responds to this thus: "In fact, good thing they kicked him out . . . who needs Swiss people here? For how many thousands of years have we produced our own milk? . . . We don't want any cheese and the last thing we need is chocolate cigars." Sai grows so angry that she can anticipate the flavour of the taste of blood which she wants to have by plucking out his eyes and kicking him black-and-blue. But outwardly she controls herself and argues, "Civilization is important," to which Gyan counter-argues: "That is not civilization, you fool. Schools and hospitals. That is." "But," Sai, contends, "you have to set a standard. Or else everything will be brought down to the same low level as you and your family." Then they attack and counter-attack quite directly. Gyan says: "I see, Swiss luxury sets a standard, chocolates and watches set the standard. . . . Yes, soothe your guilty conscience, stupid little girl, and hope someone doesn't burn your house for the simple reason that you are a *fool*." Sai answers back: "If this is what you've been thinking, why didn't you boycott the cheese instead of gobbling it down? Now you attack it? *Hypocrite*! But it was very nice to eat the cheese when you got a chance, no? All that cheese toast? Hundreds of pieces of cheese toast you must have eaten. Let alone the chocolate cigars. . . . So greedy, eating them like a fat pig. And tuna fish on toast and peanut butter biscuits!" (258-59)

The love between Gyan and Sai thus turns into a fierce battle for insult and domination over each other when Sai tells Gyan, "You're probably just sitting waiting for your mummy to arrange your marriage. Low-class family, uncultured, arranged-marriage types . . . they'll find you a silly fool to marry and you'll be delighted all your life to have a dummy" (261) and directly charges him of betraying them to the GNLF men. Gyan can not naturally digest Sai's insult to himself and his family for it at once evokes in him a sense of crisis of his socio-cultural identity, and he violently retaliates, throwing her aside into the lantana bushes and beating her about with a stick. Sai threatens Gyan by saying: "I'll go to the police and then let's see what happens to your family. Gyan will get his eyes pulled out, his head cut off, and then let's see when you all come crying to beg." (262) Gyan thus failed to judge or make the appropriate choice as to "what relative importance to attach, in a particular context, to the divergent loyalties and priorities that may compete for precedence."

(Sen 19)[4] His communitarian thinking goads him on "to see community membership as a kind of extension of [his] own self" (Sen 33), to presume that "one's identity with one's community must be the principal or dominant (perhaps even the only significant) identity a person has." (Sen 33) Gyan, in other words, by severing his link with Sai, acts like a rational fool by stressing on his "singular affiliation" (Sen 20).

Kiran Desai's narrative, however, not only disturbs us by holding up the abysmally bleak and irredeemably horrific picture of the bestiality of the animal called man, it also shows some ray of hope still to be cherished even amidst the rampant inhumanity of man. As an antidote to the spasmodic spurts of violence, Desai's book suggests the necessity of inculcating the humane values of love, sympathy, pity, fellow-feeling, mercy, mutual faith, endurance, forgiveness, respect for the traditional mores of Indian culture, in short, to quote Amartya Sen, a sense of the "shared membership of the human race" (Sen. 3). It is interesting to note that in a novel dominated by the people resorting to violence and incidents of savage aggression, there are some characters who, notwithstanding their own little human limitations, stand out to uphold the message that what can save the world from disintegrating into pieces at present is not the capitalistic extension of marketisation but the globalization of the practice of humanitarian virtues. They are Biju, his father, the two widow sisters, Gyan (despite his temporary deviation), and, towering over them all, Sai. It is they, who, like the five peaks of the Himalayas sheltering a terribly trembling and sadly shaken hill town, salvage the world depicted in the book from being miniaturised into a den of wolves and monsters.

Biju, as the son of a cook, has inherited the traditional virtues of a strong sense of rootedness, naivety, innocence and faithfulness. His father has sent him to America so that he can find there a life better than his. Pannalal was sure that "his son was cooking English food, [that] he had a higher position than if he were cooking Indian." He "imagined sofa TV bank account. Eventually," the narrator continues with the cook's dream about his son, "Biju would make enough and the cook would retire. He would receive a daughter-in-law to serve him food, crick-crack his toes, grandchildren to swat like flies." (17)

This dream about his son gives him a sense of mooring. But, America chases Biju away, for he fails to secure a green card, as he refuses to follow the strategy of his acquaintances in that country, those who unconscientiously play the game of marrying and divorcing for a green card which sustains their life of earning dollars.

It would not be impertinent here to ponder in passing on the ironic significance of the title of Kiran Desai's novel. In the context of the globalized world, America with its dollars and material opulence is the most coveted Eldorado for the rest of the world. This is most clearly brought in the unabashed assessment of America by Mr. Kakkar. When Biju thinks of coming back to India to salvage his human dignity, Kakkar, a man thoroughly dehumanised by the craze for dollars, warns him:

> don't be completely crazy—all those relatives asking for money! Even strangers are asking for money . . . maybe you shit and dollars come out. I'm telling you, my friend, they will get you; if they won't, the robbers will; if the robbers won't, some disease will; if not some disease, the heat will; if not the heat, those mad Sardarjis will bring down your plane before you even arrive . . . soft feelings, they will get you nowhere. . . . America is in the process of buying up the world. Go back [to India], you'll find they own the businesses. One day, you'll be working for an American company there or here. Think of your children. If you stay here, your son will earn a hundred thousand dollars for the same company he could be working for in India but making one thousand dollars. How, then, can you send your children to the best international college? You are making a big mistake. Still a world, my friend, where one side travels to be a servant, and the other side travels to be treated like a king. You want your son to be on this side or that side? (269)

If Mr. Kakkar's explanation and assessment of American affluence sounds rather negatively simplistic, the Ohio man's confession of his father's thought regarding this problematises the issue of the craze of the people of the poor countries for American affluence from a positively humanitarian perspective. America, according to the Ohio man's father, not only lures us with its material opulence but also provides a shelter for those who want to escape the fear of having to suffer from perpetual qualms of conscience which are their inevitable experience when they live amidst appalling and pervasive poverty in their own countries: "immigration, so often presented as a heroic act, could just as easily be the opposite; that it was cowardice that led many to America; fear marked the journey, not bravery; a cockroachy desire to scuttle to where you never saw poverty . . . never had to suffer a tug to your conscience; where you never heard the demands of servants, beggars, bankrupt relatives, and where your generosity would never be openly claimed; where by merely looking after your own wife-child-dog-yard you could feel virtuous. Experience the relief of being an unknown transplant to the locals and hide the perspective granted by journey." (299) Mr. Kakkar is, however, not alone to express an ambivalent attitude toward America. All the people of almost all the nations betray an interesting ambivalence to this land of dream-fulfilment—they both hate it and yet desire to be in it. This is brought out in the course of a conversation between Achootan and Odessa. Achootan does not want a green card in the same way as Saeed does. He wants it in the way of revenge. "'Why do you want it if you hate it here?' Odessa had said angrily to Achootan when he asked for sponsorship. And the narrator answers Odessa's question thus: "Well, he wanted it. Everyone wanted it whether you liked it or you hated it. The more you hated it sometimes, the more you wanted it." (135) Biju himself, who is so much humiliated by America, "found that he possessed an awe of white people, who arguably had done India great harm." (77) The narrator succinctly sums up Biju's ambivalence towards America, when she remarks: "Biju couldn't help but feel a flash of anger at his father for sending him alone to this country [America], but he knew he wouldn't have forgiven his father for not trying to send him, either." (82)

Biju's duality of attitude to America and his inner contradiction reach a poignant height when the narrator depicts how, even while wishing to come back to his home in India, and even after developing a gut annoyance at green card ["His papers, his papers. The green card, green card, the *machoot sala oloo ka patha chaar sau bees* green card that was not even green" (190)], he is dying for procuring it: "The green card the green card. . . . Without it he couldn't leave. To leave he wanted a green card. This was the absurdity. How he desired the triumphant After The Green Card Return Home, thirsted for it—to be able to buy a ticket with the air of someone who could return if he wished, or not, if he didn't wish. . . . He watched the legalized foreigners with envy as they shopped at discount baggage stores for the miraculous, expandable third-world suitcase, accordion-pleated, filled with pockets and zippers to unhook further cranies, the whole structure unfolding into a giant space that could fit in enough to set up an entire life in another country," and a little later he wistfully contemplates marrying someone holding a green card, "Even a disabled or mentally retarded green card holder would be fine." (99-100)

This ambivalence of the whole lot of Indians and Pakistanis is clearly betrayed in Omar's assessment of white American women, the instruments for procuring the green card, the globalized symbol of salvation. "White women," Omar says, "look good when they're young, but wait, they fall apart fast, by forty they look so ugly, hair falling out, lines everywhere, and those spots and those veins." Omar makes this comment on the American women while he confides to Biju: "I still have one or two pooky pookies that Thea don't know about." (101) Everybody from every corner of this globalized world seems to rush towards this country to secure a fraction, however small, of its plentiful material resources, its inexhaustible supply of dollars, as a means of living an easier, more comfortable and more dignified life. And they are willing to swallow up all sorts of humiliations for gaining access to America. The narrator harps on this ambivalence by observing soon after Biju's encounter with Harish-Harry: "But it *WAS* so hard and *YET* there were so many here. It was terribly, terribly hard. Millions risked death, were humiliated, hated, lost their families—*YET* there were so many here." (189) This is touchingly represented by Biju's contemplation in the Visa office: "In this room it was a fact accepted by all that Indians were willing to undergo any kind of humiliation to get into the States. You could heap rubbish on their heads and yet they would be begging to come crawling in." (184) But what they *inherit* from this migration is the *loss* of human dignity and of humane values.

Interestingly enough, the title of the novel can be interpreted from another, un-ironic, angle of vision. The word "Inheritance," which is evidently fraught with positive nuances, is privileged over the noun "Loss," which is undoubtedly negatively nuanced, by virtue of being placed first. If one shifts this emphasis on "Inheritance" to apply to the situation of Biju's life, then the title can be construed as suggesting that the loss of the material affluence, of which America is the geo-political and economic symbol, is indeed worth inheriting, if in exchange for this "loss," one can get back one's human dignity and freedom, a state where alone the humane virtues can be exercised to the best of one's desire. Biju's triumph lies in the fact that he transcends his ambivalence towards America. He does not come back to India with dejection. He does not suffer from any sense of failure. On the contrary, he returns with a sense of triumph in that he is saved from having to compromise his basic human dignity, and he has persistently tried to live even in America like "a man full to the brim with a wish to live within a narrow purity." (137) He comes back home to be reunited with his father, and savour the taste of figurative homecoming as a release from the bondage of spiritual slavery, and as "a sense of [regaining his] identity [which] can be a source not merely of pride and joy, but also of strength and confidence." (Sen 1) Biju dreams of rebuilding his home in a securer way. He thinks that "he'd build a house with solid walls, a roof that wouldn't fly off every monsoon season. Biju played the scene of meeting his father again and again like a movie in his head, wept a bit at the thought of so much happiness and emotion." (286) After stepping out of Dum Dum airport, Biju happens to discover his true identity, a space within his own self, as his humiliation of having to stay in America illegally is counterbalanced by his achievement of the clarity of vision, and he feels "the enormous anxiety of being a foreigner ebbing—that unbearable arrogance and shame of the immigrant. . . . He looked about and for the first time in God knows how long, his vision unblurred and he found that he could see clearly." (300)

As the narrator empathically celebrates the end of Biju's demeaned diasporic entity with his homecoming: "This way of leaving your family for work had condemned them over several generations to have their hearts always in other places, their minds thinking about people elsewhere; they could never be in a single existence at one time. How wonderful it was going to be to have things otherwise." (311) The narrator underscores Biju's sense of emancipation from the claustrophobic atmosphere of his perpetually fugitive and therefore undignified existence in America in terms of the Nature images of vastness, wilderness and abundance: "He felt exhilarated by the immensity of wilderness, by the lunatic creepers, the shooting hooting abundance of green, the great caterwauling vulgarity of frogs that was like the sound of the earth and the air itself. . . . So, feeling patient in the way one feels before the greatness of nature, impatient in the way one feels with human details, he waited to see his father." (315) However, while coming back home to Kalimpong from America, Biju had taken along with him quite a few American things ["a TV and VCR, a camera, sunglasses, baseball caps . . . a digital two-time clock and radio and cassette player, waterproof watches, calculators, an electric razor, a toaster oven, a winter coat, nylon sweaters, polyester-cotton-blend shirts, a polyurethane quilt, a rain jacket, a folding umbrella, a Japanese-made heater, a set of sharp knives, a hot water bottle, Fixodent, saffron, cashews and raisins, aftershave, T-shirts . . . whiskey, and . . . a bottle of perfume called Windsong" (270)] bought with the dollars he earned by selling his dignity. But, significantly enough, he cannot take home any of these things, as the GNLF goons rob him of everything, including his belt, his shoes, his jacket, his jeans and his T-shirt, leaving him stark naked but for his underpants, leaving him poorer than when he had left Kalimpong. He is even chased by the dogs set on him by the GNLF men, so that he keeps on running in darkness "without his baggage, without his savings, worst of all, without his pride. Back from America with far less than he'd ever had." (317)

Thus, Biju is completely dispossessed of American affluence in all its forms. He loses all his material possessions. But, the *loss* he suffers, the narrative implies, is worth *inheriting*, for in exchange for this *loss* what he gains is of immeasurable human value—he is finally rewarded with the most desired reunion with his father. Biju's coming back to Kalimpong and to his father reminds us of the homecoming of Langston Hughes, the African American writer, who describes in his autobiography the exhilaration that seized him as he left New York for Africa. He threw his American books into the sea:

"[I]t was like throwing a million bricks out of my heart." He was on his way to his "Africa, Motherland of the negro people!" He basked in visualizing how he would soon experience "the real thing, to be touched and seen, not merely read about in a book." (Hughes 3-10)

Biju's father, Pannalal, the judge's old cook, initially adopts a posture of uppish superiority over those fathers who have failed to send their sons to America, but later on this smug and snug feeling of superiority is sublimated by a genuine philanthropic zeal, as he writes to Biju, "*Biju beta*, you have been fortunate enough to get there, please do something for the others." (95) Undoubtedly at the initial stage, he takes pride in the fact that his son works as a cook in America. But when the political turbulence erupts in Kalimpong, all he yearns is to see his son back home. What is more, he fears that he may not be able to see his son again. This apprehension is the result of his acute consciousness of a sense of guilt for having cheated the judge in many ways. The priests induce in him a fear that the ghost of Biju's mother, who had died violently (she had been killed falling from a tree while gathering leaves for their goat), is threatening to take Biju with her. They insist that the ghost has to be appeased with a *bali* (sacrifice) of a chicken. So he needs to go to his village. But when the judge refuses to grant him leave, Pannalal deceives his master "with a made-up story of the roof of his village hut having blown off again in the latest storm." (179) But after many years, his apprehension about his son's safety grips him afresh: "He became worried now, all these years later, that the sacrifice hadn't really worked, that its effect had been undone by the lie he told the judge." (179)

An embodiment of traditional logocentric humane values of his own socio-cultural class, Pannalal is thus haunted by his own sense of guilt, which becomes all the more pressing after the telephone connection with his son becomes totally snapped so much so that it leads him to feel a compulsion to undergo a process of atonement, which, he believes, is possible to attain only through candid confession of his moral degeneration and through being physically punished by his master. "I'm a bad man," he says to the judge, "I'm a bad man, beat me, sahib, punish me." (319) The judge smacks him over the head with his slipper, beats him hard and kicks him repeatedly. But Pannalal keeps crying: "I've been bad. . . . I've been drinking. I ate the same rice as you, not the servant's rice but the Dehradun rice. I ate the meat and lied. I ate out of the same pot. I stole liquor from the army. I made *chhang*. I did the accounts differently. For years I have cheated you in the accounts each and every day. My money was dirty. It was false. Sometimes I kicked Mutt. I didn't take her for walks, just sat by the side of the road, smoked a bidi and came home. I'm a bad man. I watched out for nobody and nothing but myself—Beat me!" (320) Thus, Pannalal too loses his deceptive veneer of invulnerable honesty and integrity. But, his exposure helps him gain a spiritual freedom after which he becomes united with his son whom he embraces in his untainted arms—two generations, bereft of all false glitters that civilised life tempts us with, standing in each other's pure and purified embrace.

The "two spirited widows of Kalimpong" (131) are an embodiment of human endurance. They have been subjected to hardships and humiliations. But they extend themselves to shelter the hapless and desperate members of distressed humanity, whether they come in the form of GNLF insurgents or of the helpless policemen hounded by the rebels. Lola is shown to hide a soft corner beneath her tough exterior, when she protests against man's cruelty toward the animals: "The trouble with us Indians is that we have no love of animals. A dog, a cat is there just to kick. We can't resist—beat, stone, torment, we don't rest until the creature is dead and then we feel very content." (290) Noni upholds the virtue of unprejudiced sanity. One example can be cited to substantiate this trait of the lady. When Mrs. Sen, who is othered by Lola and Noni who "had always looked down on" her "as a low-calibre person" (131), others the Muslims by commenting on the rapidity with which they are multiplying, "No self-control, those people. Disgusting" (129)], Noni humanely snaps: "Everyone is multiplying. Everywhere. You cannot blame one group over another." (129) Noni even allows the GNLF boys to sleep in their house, and tries to convince Lola that "They have a point." (239)

Gyan was a victim of temporary misjudgement. It is true that he had betrayed Sai and her grandfather in a fit of rage at Thapa's Canteen, after his quarrel with her over the Christmas, over bottles of alcohol, but, the narrator writes, "Next morning, when he woke . . . he felt guilty all over again." (177) The narrator herself evaluates Gyan's character thus: "He wasn't a bad person. He didn't want to fight. The trouble was that he'd tried to be part of the larger questions, tried to become part of politics and history." (272) Certainly, the Gyan who joined the GNLF Movement is vastly different from the one who becomes disillusioned in the end. Indeed, he becomes wise (the word "gyan" in Sanskrit literally means *wisdom*) when he realises his folly and the importance of simultaneously giving priority to "dual loyalty" (Sen 29) or to his multiplicitous and conflicting identities, to human relations above all other considerations. This explains why he suffers from a strong sense of guilt, which is unambiguously revealed in the narrator's analysis of his thoughts: "how could he have told the boys about the guns? How? How could he have put Sai in such danger? His skin began to crawl and burn. He couldn't lie on the bed any longer. He got up and paced up and down. Could he ever be happy and innocent after what he had done?" (273)

It is then that he sincerely longs for reconciliation with Sai, and even takes the initiative toward this end. In Thapa's canteen, where everyone was ridiculing the judge for having raised such a commotion over the loss of his dog at a time when human beings were dying of starvation and for lack of treatment, Gyan, clearly overpowered by his sense of guilt, "wasn't laughing." Instead he thinks: "Oh, that awful day when he had told the boys about the judge's guns. What, after all, had Sai done to him? The guilt took over again and he felt dizzy and nauseous. When the cook left, he went out after him." (314) Thus, ashamed and remorseful for what he has done to Sai and to her grandfather, he tries to effect his reconciliation with her by coming in touch with the old cook and assuring him that he would find out the lost dog of the judge. The hazards and also apparent humiliations involved in this search would perhaps be his act of expiation.

Sai is the only character who is more sinned against than sinning. It is true when Gyan (in the GNLF rally at Darjeeling) casts a fierce, aggressive look at her, she feels like hating Gyan but that is only her act of counter-slighting him to assert her intellectual independence. She also insults him and even threatens his whole family with dire consequences they will face for Gyan's act of manhandling her during their terrible quarrel over the question of Father Booty being forced to leave India at the time when she actually came to meet Gyan for a reconciliation with him, but she does so only when Gyan tramples upon her human dignity by calling her "stupid," "fool" and finally by beating her about with a stick. In fact, she despairs that he is perhaps not worth her, and perhaps she has loved a wrong man. But, she is basically too naïve and immaculate to betray her commitment to her passion, which, once having been, will always be there. More importantly, she can finally appreciate Gyan's folly of prioritising his ethnic, communitarian identity, and the responsibility he believed it involved in the given time of GNLF rebellion over his identity as a lover or simply as a human being, as quite natural. Through suffering she has learnt to appreciate "the variety of motivations that move human beings living in a society" (Sen 21), and can therefore rise to the height of forgiving Gyan his failure to weigh the relative importance of his different obligations. "Sick with the desire to be desired" (250), Sai ultimately realises that "There was grace in forgetting and giving up . . . it was childish not to—everyone had to accept imperfection and loss in life." (252) And so, as "the curfew was lifted, in order to salvage her dignity, Sai started out on the undignified mission of searching for Gyan" (252). This search is thus suggested to be symbolic, if we keep in mind the etymological meaning of the word "Gyan." Sai is suffering and endurance incarnate, a female Jesus. The story of her life bears testimony to this. When the judge treats the father and the wife of the drunken man with inhuman indifference, Sai feels a genuine humanitarian concern for these helpless creatures, and enquires if the cook has given them anything, and that too at a time when she herself has been squirming in the pain of insult and terrible maltreatment from her lover. Even during her phase of emotional despair, she retains her sensibility and her psycho-spiritual capacity to feel grateful "for the greatness of [the mountainous] landscape." (309)

A doyen of sympathy and a representative of archetypal femininity, Sai's heart bleeds for every creature in distress. When the judge threatens his cook by saying "If you don't find her [Mutt] RIGHT NOW . . . I"LL KILL YOU," and Pannalal disappears into the forest in search of the dog, Sai follows him. She "walked up and down the path shouting into the trees for the cook: 'Come home, it's all right, he doesn't mean it, he is so sad he's crazy, he doesn't know what he's saying.'" (313) We witness with reverence the reversal of Sai's role, as she goes to the kitchen to make tea for the cook, "who was covered in slipper marks," and who has spent his life making tea for others. Like the women of Hardy, she shows an exceptional fortitude, for which she is rewarded at the end of the novel with an experience of spiritual deliverance untethered by any prejudices or egotistic inhibitions so that she can declare after seeing Biju whom she had actually mistaken for Gyan: "Gyan? She thought with a burst of hope. A message: I will love you after all." (324) It is her sublimation expressed through her capacity for showing forgiveness that enables her to attain an inner illumination, and helps her to realise at the end of the book the profoundest message of life. With the long protracted reunion of Pannalal and Biju, the father and the son, estranged from each other by the conspiracy and trap of globalization, "The five peaks of Kanchenjunga turned golden with the kind of luminous light that made [Sai] feel . . . that truth [of life] was *apparent* [emphasis added]. All you needed to do was to reach out and pluck it." The truth that Sai realises is that civilisations have been built by men and have been destroyed through their own violence and brutality, and such other negative phenomena, but they have never been able to disprove the verity of humane values and instincts: "All night it would rain. It would continue, off and on, on and off, with a savagery matched only by the ferocity with which the earth responded to the onslaught. Uncivilized voluptuous green would be unleashed; the town would slide down the hill. Slowly, painstakingly, like ants, men would make their paths and civilization and their wars once again, only to have it wash away again." (323) The narrator's comment on the affair of Gyan and Sai, before the former joined the GNLF movement, is quite significant in this context: "Gyan and Sai's romance was flourishing and the political trouble continued to remain in the background for them" (140). This clearly implies that there are some basic humane instincts which can never be smothered by any socio-political upheaval.

Despite all turbulences raging in the background of life, Sai, observes the narrator, "had found freedom and space in love." (143)This postmodernist love story of Gyan and Sai, thus, reminds us of the famous lines from Hardy's poem "In Time of 'The Breaking of Nations'": "War's annals will cloud into night/ Ere their story die." (Hardy 238) In fact, the very existence of violence, aggression or barbarity at the very core of civilisation in all ages all the more necessitates the urgency of inculcating the humanitarian virtues to effect a balance and thereby to contribute to the chastened furtherance or sobered advancement of civilisation. We need to exercise, for example, pity and charity, because there is poverty in the world, just as we need to show mercy and forgiveness because the world is troubled by betrayal, misery and unhappiness. One is reminded of Blake's contention in his poem "The Human Abstract":

> Pity would be no more
> If we did not make somebody poor;
> And Mercy no more could be
> If all were as happy as we. (Blake. 217)

We need, in other words, to keep on craving for attaining global peace and transforming the world into a space for "shared humanity" (Sen 16) by putting in persistent efforts to form what Amartya Sen calls "the global civil society" (Sen xx), by exercising love, pity, charity, mercy, sympathy and such other positive humane emotions as long as the civilisation continues to be plagued by injustice, inequality and violence. Even if we understand the word "apparent" in the framework of the Derridaesque philosophy of relativity of the meaning of signifiers[5], then also we can legitimately argue that Sai's realisation applies equally well to the message the novel purports to convey. What Sai perceives is the simple truth that no truth of life is absolute, and that therefore all truths are only "apparent," that hatred is as much true as love; inequality is as much a reality as man's striving for bringing about equality' injustice is as pervasive as man's craving for justice; suffering is as much actual as the necessity of inculcating fortitude and endurance; antipathy and the instinct of othering are as much tangible as the exercise of sympathy and of the effort to break free of the compulsive control of the ego; violence and barbaric atrocity are as much part of the human race as sanity and civilised behaviour; gain is as much worth inheriting as even *loss*. This truth of life is articulated in a simple but memorable phrasing even by an illiterate Pannalal, who hopes (in times when Kalimpong has turned into a veritable inferno) that "It will be all right, everything goes through a bad time, the world goes in a cycle, bad things happen, pass, and things are once again good." (281) This profound truth of life is succinctly objectified through Father Booty's juxtaposition of the two contrary images: "Very auspicious in Tibet, *rain and sunshine at the same time*" (196, my italics), through the image of the river Muhheakunnuk, "the river [of life] that flows *both ways*" (267), and through the image of the sweeper woman who combines a "potent mixture of intense sympathy and intense annoyance" (296). Through Sai, and Biju and Gyan, and Pannalal, the book upholds the soothing, comforting message that inhuman violence has been the archetypal part of every phase of human civilisation, but it has always been and will always be counteracted by man's capacity for suffering and for extending himself to a superhuman limit through love and pity, that the loss of faith has always been and will always be counterbalanced by its restoration through forgiveness, that the loss of something apparently valuable has always been and will always be counter-adjusted by the attainment or gain of something really invaluable. The truth of life that Sai learns is simply that cruelty, terror and violence in man co-exist with endurance, sympathy, pity, humanity and divinity; and that this truth about the co-existence of contraries in man—the bestiality and the divinity—has to be perceived, assimilated and, above all lived, with the Himalayan stoicism. The image of the peaks of the Himalayas appears in the beginning and at the end of the book, to stay on in the minds of the readers like something permanent in contradistinction to whatever happens in between in the human civilization, the truth of which is only *apparent*. As Blake writes in his poem entitled "A Divine Image," which was intended to thematically counterbalance "The Human Abstract":

> Cruelty has a Human Heart,
> And Jealousy a Human Face;
> Terror the Human Form Divine,

And Secrecy the Human Dress.
The Human Dress is forged Iron,
The Human Form a fiery Forge,
The Human Face a Furnace seal'd,
The Human Heart its hungry Gorge. (Blake 221)

NOTES

1. Salman Rushdie describes Kiran Desai in these terms.
2. See Amit Roy, "Inheritance of Lost Booker," *The Telegraph* (London, Oct.11), 12 October, 2006.
3. The crux of Amartya Sen's thesis is that "Our shared humanity gets savagely challenged when the manifold divisions in the world are unified into one allegedly dominant system of classification—in terms of religion, or community, or culture, or nation, or civilization" (xiii). Sen exposes "the illusion of a singular identity that others must attribute to the person to be demeaned" for "the purpose of denigration (along with descriptive distortions of the ascribed identity)." (8) "Violence," according to Sen, "is promoted by the cultivation of a sense of inevitability about some allegedly unique—often belligerent—identity that we are supposed to have and which apparently makes extensive demands on us (sometimes of a most disagreeable kind). The imposition of an allegedly unique identity is often a crucial component of the 'martial art' of fomenting sectarian confrontation." (Sen xiii)
4. As Amartya Sen contends: "It is not so much that a person has to deny one identity to give priority to another, but rather that a person with plural identities has to decide, in case of a conflict, on the relative importance of the different identities for the particular decision in question." (Sen 29) And Gyan evidently failed to make the right choice. As Sen would have us believe, we should get rid of the illusion of unique identity, of the misunderstanding that identity is a pre-fixed destiny, should recognise our plural identities, and should embrace the truth that identity is a matter not of "discovery" but of "reasoned choice" (Sen 9). "The prospects of peace in the contemporary world," Sen prophetically asserts, "may well lie in the recognition of the plurality of our affiliations and in the use of reasoning as common inhabitants of a wide world, rather than making us into inmates rigidly incarcerated in little containers. What we need, above all, is a clear-headed understanding of the importance of the freedom that we can have in determining our priorities." (Sen xvii) Sen's contention is that we all have to make choices

about which of our loyalties and affiliations we can remain committed to at a given context or about whether we should not maintain a simultaneous allegiance to all or quite a few of our involvements. One can cite the example of the Caribbean poet Derek Walcott who, in his poem "A Far Cry from Africa," condemns the violence of man on man in a tone of scathing satire and biting irony, when he says: "The violence of beast on beast is read/ As natural law, but upright man/ Seeks his divinity by inflicting pain." (Walcott 104) It is in this poem that Walcott gives vent to his sense of psychic impasse issuing out of an inner conflict between his innate pull of his loyalty to his historical African background on the one hand and his irresistible counterpull of his cultural allegiance to the English language and literature on the other:

> Where shall I turn, divided to the vein?
> I who have cursed
> The drunken officer of British rule, how choose
> Between this Africa and the English tongue I love?
> Betray them both, or give back what they give?
> How can I face such slaughter and be cool?
> How can I turn from Africa and live? (Walcott 104-5)

Rabindranath Tagore's Gora, too, was faced with a similar kind of mental pull and counterpull when he had to ask whether he should carry on with his advocacy for Hindu conservatism or explore the possibility of seeing himself in terms of some other identity. Ultimately, however, Gora tided over his intellectual crisis by choosing, with the help of his girlfriend, to prioritise his identity as a human being who was at home in India, not disturbed by the questions of religion or caste or class or complexion. Amartya Sen, therefore, quite justifiably and wisely argues that "Life is not mere destiny" (Sen 39), and that we all have to make choices at crucial junctures about the way we should define our identity at any given point of time in our lives. In fact, *The Inheritance of Loss* implicitly belies Mini Kapoor's observation: "To belong or to unbelong is beyond our choosing," a remark made in her review of Kiran Desai's book under the title "Lives being made over" in *The Indian Express*, 12 October 2006.

5. Within the framework of "Deconstruction," which undermines the notion of "binary opposition" beloved of "Structuralism," complementarity can be one of the meanings of opposition. Deconstructivists argue that it is possible to "detect in each sign . . . traces of the other words which it has excluded in order to be itself." According to them, "one

term of an antithesis secretly inheres within the other" so that "what is outside is also somehow inside, what is alien also intimate" (Eagleton 128-33). Within the Deconstructivist theoretical frame, therefore, the word "apparent" may mean obvious or evident as well as what only appears on the surface, implying thereby something hidden from the common perception or experience.

Works Cited

Arnold, Matthew. *Poetical Works*. Eds. C.B. Tinker and H.F. Lowry. London: Oxford University Press, 1950; Rpt. 1969.

Blake, William. *Complete Writings*. Ed. Geoffrey Keynes. London: Oxford University Press, 1966; Rpt. 1969.

Desai, Kiran. *The Inheritance of Loss*. New Delhi: Penguin, 2006.

Dutt, Ajanta, Ed. *Neruda, Walcott and Atwood: Poets of the Americas*. Delhi: Worldview, 2002; Rpt. 2004. Cited as Walcott.

Eagleton, Terry. *Literary Theory: An Introduction*. Oxford: Basil Blackwell, 1983.

Hardy, Thomas. *Selected Poems*. Ed. Tim Armstrong. London: Longman, 1993.

Hughes, Langston. *The Big Sea: An Autobiography*. New York: Thunder's Mouth Press, 1940; 1986.

Sen, Amartya. *Identity and Violence: The Illusion of Destiny*. London: Penguin, 2006.

Tagore, Rabindranath. *Gora*. Trans. W.W. Pearson. London: Macmillan, 1922.

Kiran Desai's *The Inheritance of Loss:* Looking beyond the Wide Waste

SARITA VEERANGANA
Gaya College, Gaya

Kiran Desai's novel, *The Inheritance of Loss*, for which she was awarded 'Man Booker Prize' in 2007, is a 'tour de force'. This was her second novel, the first being *Hullabaloo in the Guava Orchard*, published in 1998, for which she won 'Betty Trask' award. It was the novel which was highly applauded by Salman Rushdie. By writing *The Inheritance of Loss*, Kiran stole a march on her mother, Anita Desai, the well-known Indian English novelist, who was thrice nominated for 'Man Booker Prize' (*Clear Light of the Day* in 1980, *In Custody* in 1984, and *Fasting, Feasting* in 1999). But the judges missed to see any spark in these works which might have merited the award. There is no denying the fact that Anita Desai has always remained a source of inspiration for her daughter. After toiling for eight years, Kiran got her second novel *The Inheritance of Loss* released in 2006 which was much talked of in the literary circles, arrested the attention of the discerning critics and when it was put to test by a panel of judges consisting of Hermione Lee, Professor of English literature at Oxford University, it came out triumphantly and the judges unanimously declared it to be a masterpiece, a literary product par excellence. Kiran got the much coveted award. She got the award when she was 35. Prior to this, Arundhati Roy got the privilege to get the same award for her novel *The God of Small Things* in 1997, when she was 36.

Kiran dedicated her novel, *The Inheritance of Loss* to her mother: "To my mother with so much love." When asked by Manoj Sharma, the correspondent of *Sahara Times* as to the role played by her mother in shaping the book, Kiran unhesitatingly replied: "When it came to this book, she was the only person who could understand what I was trying to do and what I was going through. She helped with the editing and in the end her opinion was that I had cut a little too much."[1] She records here debt of obligation to her mother for writing this novel: "I wrote this book so much in her company. I owe a debt so profound and so great that this book feels so much hers as it does mine."[2] Even the judges who evaluated the book observed: "I think, her mother would be proud. It is clear to those of us who've read Anita Desai that Kiran has learned from her mother's work."[3]

Born in New Delhi in 1971 to a German mother, Kiran spent her childhood in India and went to England when she was hardly 14 and then moved to United States where she received her education. This enabled her to come in contact with multi-dimensional cultures of different countries and the social milieu which helped her write on a broad canvas.

The Inheritance of Loss has many spectacular features, vivid characterization, well-knit and close-packed plot, bewitching scenic setting, candid and graphic descriptions, unalloyed humour, scintillating and sparkling wit and, above all, a language and style which is her own. The book gives a sombre view of the postcolonial days, when the traditional Indian values were consigned to oblivion. Sometimes the novel has been overpraised and qualities have been assigned to it, just reverse of its literary merit. For example, Pankaj Mishra in a review remarks: "Although, it focuses on the fate of a few powerless individuals, Kiran Desai's extraordinary new novel manages to explore with intimacy and insight, just about every contemporary international issue: globalization, multiculturalism, economic inequality, fundamentalism and terrorist violence."

The reviewer overdoes the fact. What about racial discrimination, colour bias, religious bigotry and fanaticism, secularism and war-mongering? The novel does hint at globalization and terrorist violence. But what has it to do with fundamentalism--maintenance of traditional beliefs in opposition to modern dynamism? The novelist puts her philosophy in the mouth of Noni, which she by way of advice gives to Sai: "Don't go in for a life where time doesn't pass, the way I did. That is the single biggest bit of advice I can give you."[5]

Unquestionably, the novelist is opposed to nostalgia, the wistful longing to go back to the remote past without discrimination, for the past does not always contain everything worth having. The application of fundamentalism in her narrative is, therefore, out of question.

The novelist gives a fine spectacle of Kalimpong but it is not in accord with the changed situation in the 1980s. The novelist speaks of strikes, turmoil, lack of electricity, arrests, Gorkhaland campaign but all this was a worn-out legend in late 1980s. Thus she has presented "a lopsided picture of the locals and the place." (237-38) This was the observation of Bharat Mani Pradhan, a Kalimpong-based social worker."[6] The novel also contains some obscene descriptions, which are not expected of a novelist, initially trained in aesthetic thinking. Two instances will substantiate this point.

The judge recollects his maiden romance with his wife Nimi. He is twenty and his wife is fourteen. "How he had half undressed and hurriedly redressed his wife, of how he had only glimpsed her expression, just bits and pieces of it in the slipping of her pallu over her head . . . pleading but pompous." (38) The other description related to Nimi, who in order to flatter her husband, the judge, shows an unbecoming gesture: "She picked up the judge's powder-puff . . . too grown up for children thieving, she knew, but she was filled with greed." (166) In the first quotation the imagery 'blind sea creature' is patently obscene. Indisputably, it has sexual overtones. And this apart, 'female flesh' in the context of a fourteen year *Kishori* smacks of sexual perversion. The second quotation is equally fatuous. Here Nimi emerges as another Lady Chatterley. The style is reminiscent of Lawrence minus his phallic philosophy.

The loss, the novelist observes in different spheres of Indian life is appalling indeed. It is multifaceted. It concerns love-making, pecuniary implications, social status, self aggrandizement, self respect, righteousness and maintaining of indigenous qualities. Situation has come to such a pass that it has become almost impossible for a westernized Indian to identify himself as an Indian. The situation has gone beyond redemption.

The story of the novel is spread over a period of about four decades from 1943, when Jemubhai Popat Lal Patel was wedded to Bela, who later became Nimi, to 1986, when Biju, the only son of

Jemu's cook came back to his native land India, sentimentally injured, physically harassed, well-nigh a broken man. The plot of the novel is set against the background of Darjeeling and Kalimpong, the Himalayan town, chiefly inhabited by Nepalese, Lepchas, Bhutias and Tibetans. The novel opens with the descriptions of a horrifying scene suggestive of political jingoism. A gang of Nepali teenagers in leather jackets and Khaki pants intrude upon Jemu in his dilapidated house in Kalimpong, terrorize the inmates of the house, intimidate the cook, seek obedience by threats, make the judge and the cook say "Jai Gorkhaland, I am a fool" and finally make off with the trunks, one painted "Mr. J. P. Patel. S.S. Strallnavert" and the other painted "Miss S. Mistry, St. Augustine Convent" leaving behind a trail of smoke emitted by the fire arms. It reminds us of those panicky days when the entire northern India, particularly the hilly tracts, was put in hot water making life insecure.

The most absorbing character of the novel is Jemubhai Popatlal Patel, a Patidar by caste, and ICS officer, who is a retired chief justice living with Sai, his maternal grand-daughter, her pet dog Mutt and his cook in his house named Cho Oyu in Kalimpong. The house was actually built by a Scotsman who went back to Aberdeen. The portrait of the judge has been satirically drawn. He is the worst victim of the loss of inheritance. His loss is irredeemable. The judge is a mixture of opposites. He is a torn soul. He is made a caricature by the novelist. He has completely forsaken his heritage. "He envied the English. He loathed Indians. He worked at being English with the passion of hatred and for what he would become, he would be despised by absolutely everyone. English and Indians, both." (119)

A westernized Indian as he is, he is bound to be doomed not only because he hangs between two cultural traditions but also because he is mentally defunct. The ladies chuckle at him: "But 'Aha' laughed a sister who was listening carefully, 'We sent you abroad to become a gentleman and instead you have become a lady'." (167) Jemu's father breathes a sigh of relief: "Our family honour is gone. We are lucky. Bomanbhai is dead, thank God. It's the scandal of the town." "It was a mistake to send you away. You have become like a stranger to us." (306) The judge does not like his wife although formerly he was madly in love with her. How can he love an unlettered rustic coming from village Piphit? After all, he is raised to the pedestal of an honourable judge. Those days are gone when he was poor and humble and was tagged to a village girl. He warns his wife:

> "Don't show your face outside. People might run from you screaming." By year's end, the dread they had for each other was so severe that it was as if they had tapped into a limitless bitterness carrying them beyond the parameters of what any individual is normally capable of feeling. (173)

"Now Jemubhai wondered if he had killed his wife for the sake of false ideals, stolen her dignity, shamed his family, shamed hers, turned into the embodiment of their humiliation." (308) He recalls the words of his mother. "Didn't his mother think of the inappropriateness of her gesture? Undignified love, Indian love, stinking, unaesthetic love." (38) The judge's pernicious philosophy is: "A human can be transformed into everything. It was possible to forget, and sometimes essential to do so." (308)

Nor is this all. He has been living with his cook for long. But there is no understanding between them. "The judge and his cook lived together for more years than they had been with anyone, practically in the same room, closer to each other than to any human being and nothing, zero, no understanding." (313) While coming back from Cambridge, he brings a jar of green slave, a hair-brush and a comb set in silver, pompom with a loop of silk in a round container of powder. He sips beef tea. He feels flattered when Mrs. Rice addresses him as 'James'. He is obsessed by his power and position. The novelist depicts the metamorphosis in his character with fine artistic strokes. His egotism is described when he makes a monogram of his name with 'JPP' carved on it. His transformation is complete when he becomes completely self-centred in Kalimpong, hates mixing with a commoner. Untrammelled by any consideration, he puts on a weird countenance. He loses touch with his own mother tongue. He reads *How to speak Hindustani*. The perversities his nature is beset with, do not allow him to see things around him distinctly and recognize his own men and prize his own cultural heritage. He is "being mistaken for something he wasn't—a man of dignity." (119) Like other elderly people, "He seemed not to have travelled forward in time but far back." (33) The novelist looks beyond the wide waste and finds every particle of Indianness dwindling into nothingness, Indian values set at naught. The smothered spirit of a westernized Indian of which the judge is a symbol, loving England and English things is well brought out by the novelist.

Though the cook talks tall of his master, the irony is that Jemu was born in 1919 in a humble family of a peasant caste under a palm roof scuffling with rats at Piphit, a small village, which was subsequently owned by Gaekward kings of Baroda and still later by the British. Jemu received his education at Bishop's college on a scholarship. His father earned by procuring false witnesses to give evidence in the court. His father bought a second hand Hercules bicycle for him for Rs. 35. It was just a coincidence that he left for Cambridge and returned from there as a member of ICS. But on his return to India, he completely forgot his humble past days of poverty and deprivation.

Though a large part of the novel is devoted to bringing out the angularities in the character of the judge, the main theme of the novel hinges around Gyan, the principal character of the novel and Sai, the heroine of the novel. Gyan and Sai are introduced relatively late in the story. When the judge finds that Noni is not capable of teaching Math to Sai, he appoints Gyan to guide her in Math and Physics. At that time Sai had just reached the threshold of youth. She was sixteen. Gyan was twenty. Nomita alias Noni and Lolita alias Lola were sisters living in a cottage named Ami. When Lola's husband died of heart attack, Noni shifted with her widow sister. Lola's daughter Pixie was BBC press reporter at that time. Noni was appointed teacher by the judge to teach Sai. But soon it was discovered that she was not well up in Math and so the judge opted for Gyan to teach Math to Sai. When they became close to each other, they narrated their woeful stories before each other. Sai said that around 1961, a Soviet team of an aeronautical and aviation experts came to India to select candidates for the purpose of sending them to space and luckily her father Mr. Mistry was selected and was sent to Moscow, leaving her behind, when she was six years old and was a school girl. But as ill luck would have it, her father died and she became an orphan. Jemu, being her maternal grandfather, maintained her but never called on her. She never met her maternal grandfather till 1957. Her mother was also disowned by the family in Gujarat. She met the cook, when she came to Kalimpong after completing her education in Dehradun seven years back. Though she was an English speaker, while the cook was a Hindi speaker, there was no communication gap between the two. Gyan was moved to listen to the pathetic life history of Sai and said that his plight was no better than hers. In 1880, his ancestors left their village in Nepal and came to Darjeeling in search of work in a tea plantation. The Imperial army selected soldiers over the hills. His great grandfather died in Mesopotamia, where Turkish bullet made a sieve on his heart leaving behind his wife and three sons. After the passing away of his great grandfather, his elder son was appointed in the army, who too was killed in Burma during war operation between the British and the Japanese. Then his brother was taken in, who also lost his life in Italy. He recalled that his father taught in a tea plantation school beyond Darjeeling. In this way, his life is a vale of tears.

As time passes, the reciprocal love of Gyan and Sai begins to blossom. Sai addresses Gyan as 'Kaju' and Gyan addresses Sai as 'Kishmish.' (140) Both miss each other. The novelist describes the passionate love of Sai in the following words: "That night, Sai sat and stared into the mirror. Sitting across from Gyan, she had felt so acutely aware of her self." (74) "Marooned during curfew, sick about Gyan, and sick with the desire to be desired, she still hoped for his return. She was bereft of her former skill of solitude. She waited, read *Wuthering Heights*." (250) "They played the game of courtship, reaching, retreating, teasing, fleeting--how delicious the pretence of objective study, miraculous, how it could eat up the hours." (125)

In a typical Lawrentian style, the novelist describes the delicate moment when they exchanged their kisses.

> "Kiss me!" He pleaded.
>
> "No," she said delighted and terrified. She closed her eyes and felt the terrified measure of his lips on hers-trying to match one's shape with the other. (125)

Despite sincere efforts from both the sides their love does not come to fruition. Gyan likes to possess Sai in her totality. "Gyan and Sai would have melted into each like pats of butter—how difficult it was to cool and compose themselves back into their individual beings." (129)

When Sai puts the baffling question to the cook whether the judge ever loved his wife, the cook replies in affirmative and adds: "There are many ways of showing love, not just the way of the movies-which is all you know. You are a very foolish girl. The greatest love is love that's never shown." (87) The cook's norm of love lends a support to Sai's platonic love. Her ideology is: "Love must surely reside in the gap between desire and fulfillment. Love was the ache, the anticipation, the retreat, everything around it but the emotion itself." (2-3)

Pitted against the anglophile judge, haughty, self-obsessed and submerged in western culture from top to toe is his cook who is every inch Indian though for him western culture and tradition, 'unheard melodies are sweeter.' He is greatly disappointed when Jemu starts living in Kalimpong in an ordinary way. It is a shock for the cook because his father had always served white men only. But by and large, he is a credulous fellow. In the end he is beaten up by the judge, who holds him responsible for the death of his pet dog Mutt.

Biju, the cook's son, goes to United States and becomes a great admirer of the culture of the west. With an infectious zeal, he writes letters to his father praising everything that belongs to America. His friend Saeed's impression is: "Oh, the United States, It's a wonderful country. A wonderful country. And its people are the most delightful in the world." (122) But with the passage of time, he feels the pranks of America. He bleeds. He cries out: "It was horrible what happened to Indians abroad and no body knew but other Indians abroad." (138)

Biju's torments in America are unspeakable. He spends his second year at Pinocchio's Italian restaurant. For some time, he also works at Gandhi café. He wished he were young so that he might have thought of going back to his country. It is too late for him to retreat. In America, Biju finds Indians taking beef. With a heavy and agonized heart, Biju narrated his suffocation to his Muslim friends in

America. Saeed refuses to eat a pig on the ground that he is first a Muslim, then a Zanzibari and then an American. Biju feels that his motherland is beckoning him to come back soon. At last, his ambition is fulfilled. But by that time, Kalimpong is disturbed. There is turmoil, unrest and complete breakdown of administration. No attempt is made by any authority to allay apprehensions, which build up an atmosphere of distrust and disharmony. Nothing, not even Indo-Nepal treaty, gives political leverage to the situation and alleviates the suffering of the innocent local public.

From the pattern and the design of the novel, it is apparent that it is intended to demean the westernized Indians and highlight their wounds. Apart from the judge and Biju, even Sai, the heroine of the novel has been described as a ruined character because she is a westernized Indian "brought up by English nuns, an estranged Indian living in India." (210)

The secondary plot, the role of Gorkha Liberation Front (GNLF) and Gorkha Liberation Army (GLA), is spun out as an Integral part of the main web of the story. Biju, when he comes back from America to India feels, as it were, he has been thrown from fire to the frying pan. India does not give him any solace.

The novelist creates effect by describing the unfamiliar, bizarre and grotesque. The long list of western dishes simply causes irritation. Similarly the tenuous details of the physical posture of Sai (47) and the working of electronic supersonic space-speed machine (81) are simply exasperating.

Besides this, Kiran has the Dickensian habit to create a galaxy of characters which hang like loose threads. What purpose does uncle Potty, Father Booty, Sister Caroline, Chetu and Motu, Mrs. Thondup, Mr. Iype, Jeev Saran, Mr. Lalkaka, Mr. Kakkar serve? They are unnecessary scaffolding created upon the main structure of the tale. Besides this, the tale told is a hackneyed one. The situation has now undergone a radical change. No Indian who now goes to England or United States or any other foreign country loses his moorings with his motherland. He is seldom wounded by the west. On the contrary, he imposes his own civilization and cultural heritage on the foreigners. As a result whereof, thousands and thousands of British and American people come over to India for peace and lesson. But the merits of the novel outweigh its defects. Kiran is still very young. She is full of promise. She may fill the repertory of Indian English fiction with a yet superior work!

NOTES

1. Manoj Sharma, *Sahara Times*, *Panorama*, Oct, 7, 2006, p. 29
2. Vijay Dutt, cited, *Hindustan Times*, Friday, Oct, 13, 2006 (London, Oct. 12).
3. *Ibid.*
4. Pankaj Mishra, Review of *The Inheritance of Loss*, Wounded by the West, Feb. 12, 2006.
5. Kiran Desai, *The Inheritance of Loss* (Penguin, 2006), p. 93.
6. *Hindustan Times*, Patna, Correspondent, Cited, Darjeeling, Nov. 3, 2006.

The Singularity of New Indian Fiction

AUDE FERRAND
University of Marseille

When I was asked to write a review article on the three suggested novels,[1] I had my misgivings. I wondered what they could possibly have in common. True, all three were published around the same time (2006-7), written in English by authors who were born—but not necessarily live—in India. A first attempt at comparison or even at trying to find a point of including the three books in a single review, indeed shows the hasty reader that these novels are very different from one another. If two of them were written by young, prize-winning women writers, one (*Gifted*) is a first novel by an author born in India but raised in Wales, whereas the other is a second novel, written by an author who, according to the Indian Penguin edition, 'continues [. . .] to divide her time between [India, England and the United States], with mixed results.' Additionally, the reader will look for another kind of *inheritance* in Kiran Desai's book: that of literary talent. Finally yet importantly, *The Fourth Monkey*, although another first novel, was written by a retired English literature professor who was born and bred in India, and published in India only.

But the authors' biographies and backgrounds, although of some interest, should not be the basis of a review. If one turns to context, plot, and style, however, the gap between the three still seems to widen. *The Inheritance of Loss* is set on the foothills of the Himalayas in the mid-1980s. One of the central characters is Sai, a teenager who lives with her misanthropic grandfather—Jemubhai—in a decaying house and who falls in love with her Nepali science tutor, Gyan. But the narrative, written in the third person, focuses in turns on a variety of characters from, among others, the old cook, to his son Biju—an illegal migrant in the US—to two elderly anglophile sisters, Lola and Noni. Story and history meet when the Nepali part of the local population rebels and throws the region into a chaos of demonstrations, rampage, and riots.

In a very (post)modern manner, Kiran Desai's writing takes the reader through a series of seemingly independent snap-shots—separated by a line drawn in the middle of the page—into the lives and most intimate thoughts of the characters, thus sweeping through space and time. (His)story and characters are built through a series of layers in which pathos, dramatic irony, and humour are intertwined. I was particularly enthralled by Kiran Desai's attention to detail and the democratic will underlying the whole novel to give voice to the voiceless (a low-caste cook and a young illegal struggling to find his place in the U.S., for instance).[2] It is touching the way descriptive pauses are included in the narrative, rendering the sensory experience of the bored and prone to daydream Sai, thus giving a particular, atemporal omnipresence to the surrounding nature and seasons. The borders between inner consciousness and outer environment are blurred as the extended simile at the very opening of the novel shows:

> All day, the colours had been those of dusk, mist moving like a water creature across the great flanks of mountains possessed of ocean shadows and depths. Briefly visible above the vapour, Kanchenjunga was a far peak whittled out of ice, gathering the last of the light, a plume of snow blown high by the storms at its summit.
>
> Sai, sitting on the veranda, was reading an article about giant squid in an old *National Geographic* (Desai, 1).

The framework of Kiran Desai's novel is complex, its structure anything but linear. It succeeds, to me, in creating a polyphonic, poetic, dramatic, and funny whole—a text of genuine literary quality.

In an openly auto-fictional manner, Sushil Gupta's *The Fourth Monkey*, written in the first person, tells the story of Madan Swaroop. Through a series of analepses embedded in the main narrative, the reader learns about his hopes as a young bachelor and student, moving on to his disappointing marriage with Shelly—who entertains a celestial love-affair with the god Krishna—and a particular turning point: Madan's escape to Bhutan on a teaching programme and the ensuing falling apart of the family. But one should not forget one of the—not to say *the*—main characters of the story: Sunny, namely Madan's penis. Sex is indeed at the centre of the novel, a theme which, if we follow the narrator's point of view, has been ousted from Indian arts and life since about the time of the *Kamasutra!* The tone, purposely ridden with cliché imagery, is set from the beginning:

> We used to gather at the billiard parlour in Connaught Place and then proceed to the nearby coffeehouse to unload our views on every issue. [. . .] In the midst of all the debates, points and counterpoints, no evening ever ended without conversation veering round to sex. Bachelors, in our early twenties, none of us had a girlfriend. [. . .] We suffered from terminal virginity. Our condition was as hopeless as that of the North Indian plains before the arrival of rains. The parched soil of our sex-starved bodies awaited the monsoon of love (Gupta, 4).

Madan talks to Sunny, they 'play cricket' (the metaphor is Madan's)—most often together and, less often, with women.

The reader is given hints as to what they will find in the novel. First, the tongue-in-cheek subtitle: 'a comic, erotic, and 'sophic Tale.' Then, the foreword, which stands as a set of guidelines prior to reading the novel: 'Everything in my novel is true, except the story,' reads the first line (Gupta, vii). Finally, the back cover asks—and answers—the question: 'What's it about?,' mentioning—in order to attract the reluctant reader?— 'The imagery of cricket for sex creates its own humour' and '[Madan] gets involved with two of his students.' My feeling after reading all this, especially the three-page foreword, was that the accumulation of information and hints spoilt the pleasure of starting a new book and was tediously didactic. The author, in a lecture that, to my mind, would be more fit for addressing a roomful of undergraduates, warns us that the text is full of echoes and 'micro-mimicries' (Gupta, vii)—we are even given the keys to the main ones—and to 'watch out for the intra-textual reverberations and the sundry motifs interweaving the narrative' (Gupta, viii). Editorial clumsiness, added to the seemingly lack of confidence of the author in his readers, only succeeded in irritating me. It is in this mood that I finally got to the actual *incipit*. After having enjoyed the elegant prose of Kiran Desai, my first reaction was one of aversion: what kind of literary value could these ramblings on sex and penises have? I was thus tempted, as many other readers certainly will be at first, to see the book as either merely superficial and a provocation to the Indian society or the product of an overly self-involved man.

However, and this is the main point I would like to make regarding *The Fourth Monkey*, once I had forgotten about the paratext and my irritation had faded, I was fully captured by Sushil Gupta's prose which is both rich—in terms of lexicon (after all, it *is* a university professor talking), turns of phrase, humour and self-mockery *à la* Woody Allen—and concise: it may remind the reader of Ernest Hemingway at times with its clipped, asynthetic style and its manly concerns. Even though the figure of the 'fourth monkey'—and therefore sexuality—is central, the novel offers many layers of interpretation and manages to link personal and universal dimensions as well as literature and social comment:

> We developed a taste for avant-garde cinema. [. . .] All our metaphysics, aesthetics, and socio-politics were derived from the images of these master magicians behind the scenes. [. . .] The brooding characters with existential angst in their body language, minimal speech by way of conversation and agonisingly slow movements in performing some trivial act had a hypnotic effect on us. [. . .] We got hold of books on cinema vérité and became avid readers of journals like *Sight and Sound, Cineaste,* and *Cahiers du Cinéma*. An additional lure of the art cinema was its uninhibited depiction of sex. (Gupta, 9)

The last novel plunges the reader into yet another context. Like *The Inheritance of Loss*, it is set in the 1980s—at a time when both authors were growing up into teenagers—but the comparison ends there. *Gifted* is the story of Rumi Vasi, a child and later a teenager who could be like any other—we learn about her everyday life at home with her parents and brother and at school—except that she is nothing like any other child or teenagers. First of all, Rumi's parents are Indian and, having grown up in Britain, she soon comes to feel at odds with their values, even though she cherishes a strong taste for

India and everything Indian. Then Rumi has a very special gift for maths which her father, a scholar himself, encourages with great determination and discipline, and which sets her further apart from the children her own age. Reading *Gifted* may remind one, in some regards—especially the parts about growing up in a deeply dysfunctional family (so dysfunctional it becomes painfully funny) and feeling estranged—of Jeannette Winterson's *Oranges Are Not the Only Fruit* (1985) or of a more recent novel, Kate Atkinson's *Behind the Scenes at the Museum* (1995).

Gifted takes us, through the mediation of a third-person narrator, into the characters' minds—Rumi's, of course, but also the others' (her father Mahesh and her mother Shreene), whose point of view is added to the story, thus creating a polyphony akin to the one present in Kiran Desai's novel. When Nikita Lalwani's prose follows the contours of Rumi's thoughts, it creates a distinctive style:

> She looked at her watch again. Now she was 10 years, 4 months, 13 days, 2 hours, 48 minutes and 4 seconds old. She sang the numbers song in her head. It was almost a lullaby, one she had known since she was a child [. . .]. 1 and 1 are 2. 2 and 2 are 4. 4 and 4 are 8. 8 and 8 are 16—and 16 and 16 are 32. [. . .] They were wholesome, even numbers, created through doubling alone. 32 and 32 are 64 . . . 128 . . . 256 . . . 512. Five hundred and twelve was a lovely number. Really friendly. (Lalwani, 17)

Or:

> The story had four parts, which Rumi referred privately as
> 1. The Arrival (and the biscuits)
> 2. The Palm Reader (and the prediction)
> 3. The Train Journey (and escaping death)
> 4. The Mountain Top (and the wish that came true). (Lalwani, 25)

A rapid glance at the three novels thus reveals great differences. However, reading them one after the other ended up making a surprising whole, weaving links I had not imagined before. These novels first share contemporaneity—they are distinct products of their era and of a globalized context. A typical instance of this is illustrated by a blurb printed on the back cover of *The Inheritance of Loss*: 'Despite being set in the mid-1980s, it seems the best kind of post-9/11 novel,' says *The New York Times*.

But the main common feature is undoubtedly the underlying theme of alienation—feeling alien in one's own family, in one's own country or in a foreign country. This implies a process of distantiation from the part of the characters which is felt all the way through the style—humour and (dramatic) irony are some of the common traits of the novels—as well as a play on language. The underlying alienation also leads to a series of structures embedded within a rigid system—whether it be family or society. Finally, the three novels are tales of growing-up into adulthood. Far from being eventful *bildungsromans* verging on the picaresque, they picture the slow, seamless and sometimes boring or seemingly never-ending process through which a teenager—or a child—becomes an adult.

Alienation and Hybridity

Kiran Desai's novel is built on a distinctive chiasmic structure: it portrays Indians living like Westerners in India (Lola and Noni, who have completely integrated the cultural effects of British colonization) and, on the other hand, 'Non-Resident Indians' or other foreigners from developing countries struggling to make a living in the West. None of the characters can be said to be purely Indian, Nepali, or Western. We follow the track of Sai's grandfather's memories back to his days as a law student in Cambridge, England, as well as the parallel path across the world of Biju, the servant's son, who migrates illegally to the United States, lured by the promises of the American dream. In the U.S., he joins the hierarchy of migrants at the bottom of the social ladder. Working in fancy restaurants or delis, he enters a multicultural microcosm based on exploitation: 'Above, the restaurant was French, but below in the kitchen it was Mexican and Indian [. . .]. Biju at Le Colonial for authentic colonial experience. On top, rich colonial, and down below, poor native. Colombian, Tunisian, Ecuadorian, Gambian' (Desai, 21). There, far from home, he meets people from countries he did not even know existed but he also comes side by side with nationals from India's brother and enemy: Pakistan. '*Desis* against Pakis. Ah, old war, best war—[. . .] Biju felt he was entering a warm amniotic bath. But then it grew cold. This was not, after all, satisfying; it could never go deep enough [. . .] the irritation built on itself and the combatants itched all the more' (Desai, 23). And, in the basement kitchen, Pakistani and Indian 'threw cannonball cabbages at each other' (Desai, 23). As if the bases of all distinction and antagonism were annihilated by globalization—born out of and gone beyond colonization and post-colonization—through which the economy has taken over everything else.

Thus, the age-old struggles for independence (against the British or around the Kashmir issue) and the new ones (between the Nepali rebels and the local Indian population) lead to a standstill and allow no escape. Because, the novel seems to imply, both problem and solution lie elsewhere. From the colonial period to today's globalized world (the world is often said to have become a village—in Kiran Desai's novel, it has become a restaurant kitchen in New York City), individuals have been reduced to roles and slots in the society. In the novel, the characters live in a secluded part of India where the Nepali part of the population demands independence or in a foreign country as illegal aliens. Here the term 'alien,' both noun and adjective, takes all its meaning. Kiran Desai's characters are trapped at the margin of society—their own or their host.

Likewise, Sushil Gupta's Madan Swaroop appears, right from the beginning, to be an outsider—an on-looker—in India. His point of view (the only one in the novel) is that of a man who feels alien in his own country. It is blunt, straightforward and is vented through an even more blunt and straightforward topic—sex, the prism through which Madan's criticism of the Indian society converges. It is clear, however, that this peculiar topic has not been chosen in order to shock but simply to express a reality. Sex is thus a broad-spectrum topic which enables the narrator to broach subjects such as the arts, marriage, history, religion, the relations between East and West. And sex is universal.

Like Kiran Desai's, although in a more frontal way, Sushil Gupta's novel revisits and undermines clichés and stereotypes. Even though the novel presents the point of view of an Indian man living in India, his deep knowledge of Western culture (both high and low) enables him to tackle clichés about India that could well emerge from the mind of a—very ill-informed and naive—Westerner. For instance: Indian culture is ancient and self-reliant, and, except for the period of British colonization, it has been impervious to any kind of outside influence. Or: Eastern and Western cultures have nothing in common. Or: the only Western influence India has ever experienced dates back from the British rule—likewise, the influence of Christianity dates from that period. Or again: Indian culture is still deeply conservative, sex and love-marriages could not possibly be mentioned, even in contemporary arts. The cultural background of *The Fourth Monkey* indeed shows that cultural globalization has been effective for a very long time—it started even before the emergence of the concept of economic globalization—and that it happens naturally (as sex does) in the sense that it falls through the net of colonial influence and liberation discourse.

Madan and his friends, in their youth at the end of the 1960s, play billiards, sit in cafés and chat about films, magazines, their future, girls and their sex-life. Just like many Western young men at the time. We are very far from the picturesque, a-temporal, mystical, and rural India presented to Westerners through, for instance, the documentaries of Arnaud Desjardins: 'We developed a taste for avant-garde cinema. Kurosawa, Godard, Bergman, and Tarkovsky became the new coordinates of our conversation' (Gupta, 8). Or:

> Vivid description of the sex act left little to imagination. Much of my knowledge of sex I owed to no-holds-barred portrayal of human copulation on the screen. Kinsey report, Everything-You-Wanted-to-Know-About-Sex-but-Were-Afraid-to-Ask, Havelock Ellis and some manuals were other sources keenly devoured.
>
> All this was embellished by stray copies of *Playboy*, which Basu's cousin used to bring from his occasional visits to the States. (Gupta, 9)

In Sushil Gupta's novel, culture knows no borders. Madan is a vessel and his own culture is cosmopolitan. References to Western artists are never underlined—they seem completely normal and fall out of any discourse over the hegemony and imperialism of Western culture. Thus, the references are either Indian or Western—whatever the most appropriate for the situation. When Madan watches his beautiful student in candlelight, the sight immediately evokes Western paintings: 'and the candlelight creating a chiaroscùro effect, she looks a Rubens retouched by Rembrandt' (Gupta, 206). I cannot help mentioning here that, to some Western readers, the references to Rembrandt, Godard or Woody Allen may seem universal. There is a definite imbalance however between what Madan and his friends know of Western classics and what the average Western reader knows about Indian ones. Thus, the Western reader may not grasp the full extent of references to Hindu gods, religious texts and art, as well as to Indian classical music. *The Fourth Monkey*, consciously or not, reveals double-standards on the part of the West: what it expects to be universal is merely what it has spawned.

Madan's culture (although he is a born-and-bred Indian and does not seem to have lived or studied in any Western country) is therefore hybrid.[3] This accounts for its richness, but also for the feeling of alienation, that pervades the whole novel. But Madan makes compromises and does not relinquish his Indian heritage altogether. His relation to Indian culture is complex, between criticism and enlightened acceptance: 'I had always ridiculed the institution of arranged marriage and its attendant rituals. After having failed to find a woman on my own, I had to fall back upon this time-honoured mode of getting married' (Gupta, 18). Yet Madan's discourse on India is never provocative. Neither does it use the reference to sex for the mere sake of being labelled as progressive or for the enjoyment of the ensuing, possibly shocked, reaction.

In writing openly about sex, Sushil Gupta merely throws light on what may appear to some—Indian or not—as contradictions inherent to the Indian society. He, like many others, underlines the often-mentioned discrepancy between the romance of Bollywood films and the process of real-life match-making and arranged marriages. The latter seem to him totally devoid of romanticism: 'I was supposed to talk to her over a cup of tea in the presence of others and give my formal consent. I found this asexual prelude to a lifelong bonding utterly unromantic' (Gupta, 12). One of the questions that may arise is whether Madan's criticism of the society he was born in comes from the influence of Western thought—through the acquaintance with its art and pornographic magazines. I think the question is pointless inasmuch as Sushil Gupta's novel is truly postmodern and postcolonial: in introducing the issue of sex as the basis for his novel, the author severs the link between marriage and culture. The main character is driven not by ideology, religion, or tradition, but by a basic physical urge. By re-introducing some nature in the politico-cultural debate, Sushil Gupta avoids the issue of culture and imperialism.

Gifted places otherness at the heart of its diegesis. It is set in Wales—a country itself geographically at the margin— in a family in which the parents feel definitely Indian whereas the children, having been raised in the UK, have a different experience of life and diverging expectations about it. Rumi, the daughter of the family and on whom the story concentrates, further epitomizes the notion of alterity: she is a teenager and, to her classmates, a nerd.

Nikita Lalwani's novel is the only one of the three in which the main characters live in the West. It raises the question of what being Indian in a foreign country means and offers a variety of answers, depending on whether the characters are first or second generation migrants. For instance, racism is never mentioned on Rumi's part, but it has left deep marks in her father's consciousness. The novel opens with a sentence Rumi wrote at school and which upsets Mahesh, her father: 'When we got to her place we stood outside the gate and Sharon said 'I just have to check you can come in Rumi because my mum doesn't like coloured people'[4] (Lalwani, 3). Later on, when Rumi's teacher visits the family to announce Rumi's gift for mathematics and asks the parents: 'Have you heard of a place called Mensa?' Mahesh, himself a scholar, thinks:

> He knew what Mensa was, for goodness' sake. What did she take him for? And why was she so surprised that he and his daughter could string numbers together with reasonable panache? They were hardly shopkeepers.
>
> He was 'peed off,' as they said here: irritated (Lalwani, 7).

The two sides seem to be irreconcilable, forever kept apart by an us *versus* them dichotomy. Mahesh and his (only) friend, the aptly named Whitefoot, can never come to an understanding at the end of their lengthy arguments (which Whitefoot takes less seriously than Mahesh) about the Hindu-Muslim tensions in India or the importance of Gandhi.

The novel's polyphonic structure transcends this by allowing the voice of the different characters to be heard in turns, although that of Rumi dominates. The reader thus does not only have access to the teenager's point of view but to those of her parents. Thanks to that process, the reader comes to grasp the personal difficulties of the parents and gets a view of both sides. Even if we are tempted to take sides with Rumi, who suffers under her parents' disproportioned pressure, we cannot help but sympathize with them: Mahesh feels misunderstood by his born and bred British acquaintances and colleagues, whereas Shreene has bouts of homesickness and fears the influence of British culture on her children:

> The communication gap caused Shreene an almost physical pain when she thought of it. Even after years of working the phone lines, talking to strangers every day, she could not express herself happily to her own daughter. Instead, she came out with platitudes. Awkward generalities.
>
> 'This country has messed everything up,' she would hear herself saying, when they were alone in the kitchen (Lalwani, 45).

The only character who seems to embody true hybridity is Rumi, the teenager—with all the confusion that this may imply. She does not seem to be ostracized by her schoolmates because of her Indian origin, but more so because she is a bespectacled nerd. Even though her parents are particularly strict—but this has nothing to do with their being Indian—Rumi seems to live the life of a typical British teenager—even if, again, she is 'gifted.' But this does not mean she rejects the country of her relatives. However, instead of the politically correct discourse on the positive dimension of having two cultures, *Gifted* shows the almost atavistic, sensory link between Rumi and India. When, for instance, she expresses her malaise through addictive practices like many other teenagers, she does not turn to drugs or alcohol but becomes addicted to cumin seeds, which she chews by the kilo. Likewise, when she falls in love for the first time, it is with her first cousin—a typical Indian theme—and, for the second time, with a Muslim student in Oxford. Like the heroines of the Bollywood films she is so fond of, Rumi seems predestined for forbidden love.

Escape

The Inheritance of Loss—but this could be true of the three novels examined here—with its complex characters whose personality and history resists all reduction, offers an escape in the concept of hybridity and the power of creation. Each character has to be seen in individual terms rather than under the light of colonial or postcolonial taxonomy and ideology. The omniscient narrator never judges and is never above the characters but always on the same level with them. Lola, Noni, Jemubhai, Biju, and his father are never seen in terms of class, caste, relation to the former colonists or current exploiter, but as individuals with their idiosyncrasies and complex (therefore possibly full of contradictions) personal history. Nothing is ever simple and everything resists single-minded ideology: Gyan's blindness to the rebels' real motivation and internal power struggles, as well as their ridiculous methods (kidnapping Jemubhai's dog, for instance) and lack of organisation, clearly show the limits of any purely political interpretation of history.

Kiran Desai's novel shows that the way out of ideology is the power of imagination. Lost in an a-temporal hill station of the Himalayas or in foreign New York, the characters invent their lives in accordance with their personal stories and with History. The thick and complex reality is conveyed through short, intense passages, like flashes of truth in a night of stereotypes, and an innovative language: the use of onomatopoeia, for instance, works to convey a first-hand experience of reality, to show its crude core. At the end of the novel, Sai appears as a converging point where all stories meet:

> She thought of her father and the space program. She thought of all the *National Geographics* and books she had read. Of the judge's journey, of the cook's journey, of Biju's. Of the globe twirling on its axis. And she felt a glimmer of strength. Of resolve. She must leave. (Desai, 323)

She embodies past, present, and future. Taking it all in, she becomes a kaleidoscopic character—like the novel itself, a polyphonic whole—and loses her innocence: 'Never again could she think there was but one narrative and that this narrative belonged only to herself, that she might create her own happiness and live safely within it' (Desai, 323). She realizes that everything and everyone around her is linked, that all borders are porous, that she has been living at the margin and that time has come to plunge into life and mingle.

The end of *The Fourth Monkey*, like that of *The Inheritance of Loss*—where the disillusioned Biju comes back to his village—takes the form of a spiral: its references to the rest of the novel seem to take the reader back to the beginning in a circular fashion, but it is in fact a new beginning, which builds on the past but steers away from it at the same time. It is the same, except that it is totally different. Madan the atheist has had an epiphany during a religious ceremony, although its message is anything but religious. As a whole, the novel portrays, among other things, the impossibility to reconcile worldly and saintly love. To a Western reader, the reference—surprisingly never mentioned in a novel rich in Western references—that comes to mind is Dante. But Madan clearly takes another, less chaste path than the Italian poet's. Once his Beatrice—Shelly—departs earthly life, he embarks on a new life, more in keeping with his taste—and Sunny's. Madan's and Dante's fates do not coincide, yet the outcome is similar, as if to show that creative powers are not hindered by worldly love. Rejuvenated by the idea of a prolonged sex-life, thanks to the advent of Viagra, Madan's sex drive is accompanied by a burst of inspiration: 'A tidal wave of creative urge sweeps over me' (Gupta, 309).

One of the main questions that comes to mind when reading *Gifted* is: how is Rumi going to escape the pressure of her family and grow into a mentally sound adult? A solution actually emerges from the problem itself: because of his constant training of his daughter to become a maths genius, Mahesh only succeeds in having her leave for Oxford at the age of fifteen. There, far from her parents' watch, she experiences freedom but, more importantly, the limitations of her 'gift.' It is in Oxford that Rumi realizes that her true relationship with maths verges more on the literary than it is based on hard sciences. After she has explained to her boyfriend, in the torment of kissing, what amicable numbers are, he answers, spell-bound: 'Maths poetry, eh? You're something else, aren't you? Kind of beautiful crazy' (Lalwani, 226).

Mature and independent, Rumi finally breaks out of the life her parents had planned for her and escapes. Through that last, radical act, Rumi also enables Shreene to assert her independence over Mahesh. When her daughter runs away, Shreene's first reaction is to blame Britain and its culture: 'They thought they knew right from wrong, but how could they?' (Lalwani, 270) But soon, she goes beyond the them *versus* us dichotomy and the stubbornness of her husband to finally follow a simpler truth: her love for her child. Doing so, she reaches a state of liberation. The borders she had established to map her own world vanish: 'Shreene breathed lightly, repeating the oldest mantra in the world, all sounds of the universe together in a single round vowel of calm' (Lalwani, 273).

Conclusion

All three novels are, to me, best characterized by the figure of the spiral. Within this structure, the characters find their own centre by constantly moving off centre. Constancy and change become the two constituents of the same, oxymoronic paradigm. India itself—and the characters' relation to it—seems to embody this paradigm. When arriving at Delhi airport on a trip to attend her father's funeral, Shreene notices: 'But in the cruel beauty of the moment, just standing there, after so many years of exile, she realized that everything was the same' (Lalwani, 42). But the novels do not imply that India and its society are static. On the contrary, the lives and personalities of the characters place change—whether it be striven for or put up with—at the heart of the country. Rather, India becomes the focus of the characters' nostalgia and is crystallized only through their memories, putting the concept of loss at the centre of not only Kiran Desai's novel but of the three works examined here.

India becomes a dreamed entity, a land in a fairy tale: 'India as a word set in the clouds, far, far away' (Lalwani, 52). Several common features crop up from this far away land that is yet so close, the first and foremost being the monsoon. It, of all seasons, epitomizes both change and repetition. It is special and can be distinguished from a mere rainy spell; it is both a relief and inconvenience. Its cyclic arrival announces a change in the people's everyday life and may bring them closer in confinement. In the collective psyche, it also means romance and hidden loves. In *The Fourth Monkey*, it acts as a catalyst between Madan and his unusually chaste wife:

> The loud rap-a-tap-tap of the rain on the sloping tin roof and a waterfall over the cornice all around the house created a strange hypnotic effect on the senses. The mind was lulled. The body clamoured for intimacy. Shelly, unlike her earlier self, clung to me for warmth, both physical and emotional. Night after night, for seven consecutive nights, she abandoned her reserve and gave in to lovemaking. (Gupta, 76-77)

Likewise, when he arrives in Bhutan, the monsoon is like a promise for future intimacy. In Kiran Desai's prose, which verges on the poetic, the monsoon appears to be almost alive, an all-pervading force: 'The caress of the mist through her hair seemed human, and when she held her fingers out, the vapour took them gently into its mouth' (Desai, 2). The sensory experience of the monsoon seems to be engraved in the characters' memories and may emerge again at odd times and places, like the taste of Marcel Proust's *Madeleine*:

> Even though it was not hot, something about the warmth, the rain, and the moon was tugging at Shreene's heart, making an echo of yearning, a feeling she couldn't identify. She tried to locate it. The sense was of warm rain, being outdoors, and children in the street. Then it swamped her. Monsoon. She froze, feeling her body betray her. It was the sudden desolation that often overtook her without warning, come back to ruin her on the way home. (Lalwani, 43)

All three novels answer indirectly the question of Indianness. It is a large-spectrum, complex, contradictory concept, embodied by characters who, for some, do not even live in India and who, for others, feel at odds with it—but this state of mind, in turns, appears to be typically Indian.

Gandhi is another emblematic figure present in those works. He was Indian but spent a substantial period of his life living abroad. He was non-violent but the movement towards and after independence brought its share of violence. He was a Hindu who opposed the Partition and who was assassinated for religious reasons. He was an advocate of chastity who shared his bed with young women. In *Gifted*, Whitefoot debunks the Mahatma by pronouncing his name 'Gandy' and by calling the film by Richard Attenborough propaganda financed by the Indian government (Lalwani, 63). To Mahesh, 'Gandhiji' is a saint and the film a tribute which forbids all criticism.

Gandhi and his representation are yet another embodiment of paradox. Theories and teachings contrast with facts and everyday reality. History and retrospective interpretation shed different lights on the *father of the nation*. Interpretation and gaze are indeed everything. If Madan keeps Gandhi's three monkeys with him, it is more for the fourth monkey—which is present implicitly at their side. But then again, it is not to remind himself of the importance of being chaste—quite the contrary.

India and Indianness are symbols, in the etymological meaning of the term: they remind one of the Greek *sumbolon*, the double-sided coin. This complexity is felt all the way through the language. If India is a country of many languages in which two fellow countrymen may not be able to understand each other, the way the authors deal with language is particularly revealing. In *Gifted*, typically, a Hindi word is replaced by its English nearest equivalent, as Shreene remembers her father drinking 'his evening rose milkshake on the veranda' (Lalwani, 46). The mention of a rose *lassi* would have been perfectly understandable and would have acted as a typical *effet de réel*, but in a novel centred on the concepts of double culture, the English word shows how assimilation creeps in. When Shreene uses Hindi words, struggling to express in English her—rather traditional, to say the least—point of view on love, Rumi, it seems, fails to understand both the words and what they imply:

> 'Only here do they expect to "fall in love," as they call it. And where does that get you? Divorce is where it gets you.'
>
> 'But in the Hindi films . . .'
>
> 'Those are films, *beti*. What are you talking about? [. . .] But [your father] did think something like that. In fact, he went a little *paagal* himself.'
>
> 'How do you mean?' (Lalwani, 79)

Hindi words in italics and English translations coexist in Nikita Lalwani's novel in a way which mirrors her characters' lives. On the other hand, Hindi words seldom crop up in Sushil Gupta's prose. When Tashi says a mock-prayer in Sanskrit, it is translated for the benefit of the reader: '*Guru-lingam sharnam gachchami!*' (I dedicate myself to the service of my teacher's manhood)' (Gupta, 272). The main character being an English literature scholar, his world is unmistakably steeped in the English language. With his students and colleagues in Bhutan—and in Delhi—it is the *lingua franca.* Last but not the least, Madan, feeling like a foreigner in his own country as he does, prefers the language of Shakespeare.

Finally, Kiran Desai, by including whole sentences in Hindi which are marked by italics and are not translated, introduces something foreign, utterly different and irreducible in her text. Through this defamiliarization process, the reader who does not speak Hindi, is put in Biju's shoes, in his basement kitchen in New York City. But one also feels that Kiran Desai is using these precise words at this precise moment because the turn of phrase is the most appropriate to describe what the character feels or wants to say and, above all, for their sonority. Kiran Desai is indeed a poet who re-appropriates language—any language: from her mother tongue to the language of the (neo)colonizer, according to the traditional dichotomy—explores it and creates something new out of it. She plays with sound through the use of onomatopoeias and also uses typography as the painter would his brush: italics, capital letters, and blanks give a striking visual dimension to the text.

If the novels give a large part to the sensory—and even the sensual—Kiran Desai's transcription of Sai's over-acuteness and sensitivity make, to me, *The Inheritance of Loss* the most accomplished of the three. The richness of her poetic prose reminds one of Virginia Woolf at times and the descriptions of the monsoon mist may be seen as an echo of that of the 'little airs' slowly running down the house in the chapter 'Time Passes' in *To the Lighthouse* (Woolf, 172). I was less sensitive to Nikita Lalwani's prose—for instance, her use of the present tense in some chapters does not seem justified to me and does not add anything in terms of contrast to the use of the past tense elsewhere. Likewise, the rhetorical strings in Sushil Gupta's novel appear all too visibly—we sometimes feel too strongly we are reading a book written by a literature specialist, especially in the foreword and at the end, when the narrator brings us back to the beginning in a showing twist.

But these comments should not detract from the inherent quality of the three novels. The world they picture resists all reduction and ideological interpretation. They are rich and tackle reality from a new angle. They embody complexity and paradox. They are truly postmodern in the sense that they revisit things that had been taken for granted on India and Indianness. They are funny and ironical. They are subversive, in a way which shows that writing literature is a political act in itself. Last, they play with language and concepts in a singular way, as only literature can.

Subversion and the exploration of language seem to be a trend in novels published recently by writers of the Indian diaspora. One of them, *Babyji* by Abha Dawesar, tells the story of Anamika, a teen-ager who follows her feelings and her lust and embarks on a series of homosexual relationships which transcend norms, age differences, and castes. Like the three novels analysed here, *Babyji* is a tale of growing up, of finding one's place in one's country—or abroad—and of the dichotomy between education and personal experience. *Babyji* furthermore shares something with *Gifted*: both novels reconcile the worlds of hard science and of poetry—an idea which is very seldom seen in Western novels. The singularity of those works comes to confirm what the winner of the Nobel Prize for literature, Jean-Marie Gustave Le Clézio, declared in his first press conference when a journalist asked him what he recommended to do in a time of political and economic turmoil: 'We must keep reading novels.'

NOTES

1. Kiran Desai, *The Inheritance of Loss*, 2006; Sushil Gupta, *The Fourth Monkey,* 2006; and Nikita Lalwani, *Gifted*, 2007.
2. The novel's epigraph, a poem by Jorge Luis Borges, is in this regard particularly telling. One of its lines reads: 'My humanity is in feeling we are all voices of the same poverty.'
3. One may ask how such hybridity is possible in such a seemingly rigid society. It may be due to Madan's—Sai's—belonging to the middle-class, a Western concept which falls out of the caste system but whose socio-economic reality has come to superimpose on it.
4. This event is just mentioned in passing by Rumi and is part of an essay on a very different topic.

Works Cited

Dawesar, Abha. *Babyji*. New Delhi: Penguin Books India, 2005.

Desai, Kiran, *The Inheritance of Loss*. New Delhi: Penguin Books India, 2006.

Gupta, Sushil, *The Fourth Monkey*. New Delhi: Indialog, 2006.

Lalwani, Nikita, *Gifted*. London: Penguin, 2007.

Woolf, Virginia. *To the Lighthouse*. 1927; rpt. Oxford: Oxford World's Classics, 1

Reprinted from *In-between: Essays & Studies in Literary Criticism*, 15, ii (2006): 139-153, with the permission of the editor.